Get the eBook FREE!
(PDF, ePub, Kindle, and liveBook all included)

We believe that once you buy a book from us, you should be able to read it in any format we have available. To get electronic versions of this book at no additional cost to you, purchase and then register this book at the Manning website.

Go to https://www.manning.com/freebook and follow the instructions to complete your pBook registration.

That's it!
Thanks from Manning!

GitOps and Kubernetes

Continuous Deployment with Argo CD, Jenkins X, and Flux

GitOps and Kubernetes

Continuous Deployment with Argo CD, Jenkins X, and Flux

BILLY YUEN
ALEXANDER MATYUSHENTSEV
TODD EKENSTAM
AND JESSE SUEN

MANNING
SHELTER ISLAND

Manning Publications Co.
20 Baldwin Road
PO Box 761
Shelter Island, NY 11964

Development editor:	Dustin Archibald
Technical development editor:	Al Krinker
Review editor:	Aleks Dragosavljević
Production editor:	Deirdre S. Hiam
Proofreader:	Katie Tennant
Technical proofreader:	Sam Brown
Typesetter and cover designer:	Marija Tudor

ISBN 9781617297977
Printed in the United States of America

contents

preface

As Intuit embarked on the journey from on-premises to cloud-native, the journey itself presented an opportunity to reinvent our build and deployment process. Similar to many large enterprises, our old deployment process was data-center-centric with separate QA, Ops, and Infrastructure teams. Code could take weeks to get deployed, and developers had no access to infrastructure when there were production issues. Infrastructure issues could take a long time to resolve and required many groups' collaboration.

As Marianna Tessel (Intuit CTO) and Jeff Brewer (Intuit SBSEG chief architect) decided to bet big on Kubernetes and Docker, we were fortunate to be the first team to fully migrate one of our production applications with Kubernetes and Docker. Along the way, we got to reinvent our CI/CD pipeline and adopt the GitOps process. Jesse and Alex created Argo CD (CNCF incubator project) to address enterprise needs for GitOps. Todd and his team created world-class cluster management tools so we can scale out to hundreds of clusters with ease.

Having a standard like Kubernetes and Docker enables all engineers to speak a common language in terms of infrastructure and deployment. Engineers can easily contribute to other projects and deploy as soon as the development process is complete. GitOps also allows us to know exactly who and what gets changed in our environments, which is especially important if you are subject to compliance requirements. We cannot imagine going back to the old way we did deployment, and we hope that this book can help accelerate your journey to embrace GitOps!

acknowledgments

This book turned out to be an 18-month journey that required a lot of work and additional research to tell the complete story. We believe that we have delivered what we set out to do, and it is a great book for anyone who wants to adopt GitOps and Kubernetes.

There are quite a few people we'd like to thank for helping us along the way. At Manning, we would like to thank our development editor, Dustin Archibald, project editor, Deirdre Hiam, proofreader, Katie Tennant, and reviewing editor, Aleks Dragosavljevic.

We want to thank Marianna Tessel and Jeff Brewer, who provided us the opportunity and freedom to transform and experiment with GitOps and Kubernetes. We would also like to thank Pratik Wadher, Saradhi Sreegiriaju, Mukulika Kupas, and Edward Lee for their guidance throughout the process. We want to call out Viktor Farcic and Oscar Medina for their insightful contributions to the Jenkins X chapter.

To all the reviewers: Andres Damian Sacco, Angelo Simone Scotto, Björn Neuhaus, Chris Viner, Clifford Thurber, Conor Redmond, Diego Casella, James Liu, Jaume López, Jeremy Bryan, Jerome Meyer, John Guthrie, Marco Massenzio, Matthieu Evrin, Mike Ensor, Mike Jensen, Roman Zhuzha, Samuel Brown, Satej Kumar Sahu, Sean T. Booker, Wendell Beckwith, and Zorodzayi Mukuya, we say thank you. Your suggestions helped make this a better book.

For Jeff Brewer, who inspired us all for this awesome transformation journey!

about this book

Who this book is for

This book is intended for both Kubernetes infrastructure and operation engineers and software developers who want to deploy applications to Kubernetes through a declarative model using the GitOps process. It will benefit anyone looking to improve the stability, reliability, security, and auditability of their Kubernetes clusters while at the same time reducing operational costs through automated continuous software deployments.

Readers are expected to have a working knowledge of Kubernetes (Deployment, Pod, Service, and Ingress resources, for example) as well as an understanding of modern software development practices including continuous integration/continuous deployment (CI/CD), revision control systems (such as Git), and deployment/infra structure automation.

Who this book is not for

Advanced users who have successfully implemented a mature GitOps system may be better off reading a more advanced book on their chosen tool.

This book is not intended to cover all aspects of Kubernetes in depth. While we cover many Kubernetes concepts that are relevant to GitOps, readers looking for a comprehensive guide to Kubernetes should look at the other great books and online resources available on the topic.

How this book is organized: A roadmap

This book describes the benefits of GitOps on Kubernetes, including flexible configuration management, monitoring, robustness, multienvironment support, and security.

You will learn the best practices, techniques, and tools to achieve these benefits, which enable enterprises to use Kubernetes to accelerate application development without compromising on stability, reliability, or security.

You will also gain in-depth understanding of the following topics:

- Multiple-environment management with branching, namespace, and configuration
- Access control with Git, Kubernetes, and pipelines
- Pipeline considerations with CI/CD, promotion, push/pull, and release/rollback
- Observability and drift detection
- Managing Secrets
- Deployment strategy selection among rolling update, blue/green, canary, and progressive delivery

This book takes a hands-on approach with tutorials and exercises to develop the skills you need to embrace GitOps using Kubernetes. After reading this book, you will know how to implement a declarative continuous delivery system for your applications running on Kubernetes. This book contains hands-on tutorials on

- Getting started with managing Kubernetes application deployments
- Configuration and environment management using Kustomize
- Writing your own basic Kubernetes continuous delivery (CD) operator
- Implementing CI/CD using Argo CD,[1] Jenkins X,[2] and Flux[3]

IMPERATIVE VS. DECLARATIVE   There are two basic ways to deploy Kubernetes: imperatively using many `kubectl` commands or declaratively by writing manifests and using `kubectl apply`. The former is useful for learning and interactive experimentation. The latter is best for reproducible deployments and tracking changes.

This book is intended for you to follow along, running the hands-on portion of the tutorials, using your own test Kubernetes cluster. Appendix A describes several options for creating a test cluster.

There are many code listings contained in the book. All code listings and additional supporting material can be found in the publicly accessible GitHub repository for this book:

https://github.com/gitopsbook/resources

We encourage you to clone or fork this repository and use it as you work through the tutorials and exercises in the book.

---

[1] https://argoproj.github.io/argo-cd.
[2] https://jenkins-x.io.
[3] https://github.com/fluxcd/flux.

The following tools and utilities should be installed on your workstation:

- Kubectl (v1.16 or later)
- Minikube (v1.4 or later)
- Bash or the Windows Subsystem for Linux (WSL)

Most tutorials and exercises can be completed using a minikube running on your workstation. If not, we will mention if the cluster running on a cloud provider is needed, and you can refer to appendix A for details on creating the cluster.

> **NOTE** You may incur additional costs for running a test Kubernetes cluster on a cloud provider. While we have attempted to reduce the cost of the recommended test configuration as much as possible, remember you are responsible for these costs. We recommend you delete your test cluster after completing each tutorial or exercise.

This book has 3 parts that cover 11 chapters. Part 1 covers the background and introduces GitOps and Kubernetes:

- Chapter 1 walks you through the journey of software deployment evolution and how GitOps became the latest practice. It also covers the many key concepts and benefits of GitOps.
- Chapter 2 provides key concepts on Kubernetes and why its declarative nature is perfect for GitOps. It also covers the core operator concept and how to implement a simple GitOps operator.

Part 2 goes over the patterns and processes to adopt the GitOps process:

- Chapter 3 discusses the definition of an environment and how Kubernetes Namespaces nicely map as environments. It also covers branching strategy and config management to your environment implementation.
- Chapter 4 goes deep into the GitOps CI/CD pipeline with comprehensive descriptions of all stages necessary for a complete pipeline. It also covers code, image, and environment promotion as well as the rollback mechanism.
- Chapter 5 describes various deployment strategies, including rolling update, blue/green, canary, and progressive delivery. It also covers how to implement each strategy by using native Kubernetes resources and other open source tools.
- Chapter 6 discusses GitOps-driven deployment's attack surfaces and how to mitigate each area. It also reviews Jsonnet, Kustomize, and Helm and how to choose the right configuration management pattern for your use cases.
- Chapter 7 discusses various strategies for managing Secrets for GitOps. It also covers several Secret management tools as well as native Kubernetes Secrets.
- Chapter 8 explains the core concepts of observability and why it is important to GitOps. It also describes various methods to implement observability with GitOps and Kubernetes.

Part 3 goes over several enterprise-grade GitOps tools:

- Chapter 9 discusses the intent and architecture for Argo CD. It also covers configuring application deployment using Argo CD and how to secure Argo CD in production.
- Chapter 10 discusses the intent and architecture for Jenkins X. It also covers configuring application deployment and promotion to various environments.
- Chapter 11 discusses the intent and motivation for Flux. It also covers configuring application deployment using Flux and multitenancy.

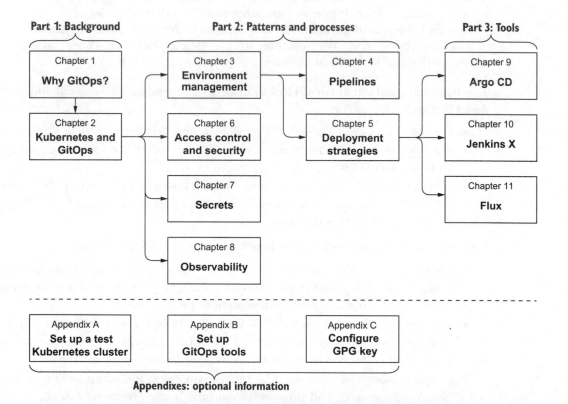

The book was organized to read all the chapters in sequential order. However, if there is a particular area of interest you'd like to jump into, we recommend you read the prerequisite chapters. For example, if you would like to jump right into learning to use Argo CD, we recommend you read chapters 1, 2, 3, and 5 before reading chapter 9.

About the code

This book contains many examples of source code both in numbered listings and inline with normal text. In both cases, source code is formatted in a `fixed-width font` to separate it from ordinary text. Sometimes, code is also in **bold** to highlight code that has changed from previous steps in the chapter, such as when a new feature adds to an existing line of code.

In many cases, the original source code has been reformatted; we've added line breaks and reworked indentation to accommodate the available page space in the book. Additionally, comments in the source code have often been removed from the listings when the code is described in the text. Code annotations accompany many of the listings, highlighting important concepts. Source code for the examples in this book is available for download from https://github.com/gitopsbook /resources.

liveBook discussion forum

Purchase of *GitOps and Kubernetes* includes free access to a private web forum run by Manning Publications where you can make comments about the book, ask technical questions, and receive help from the authors and from other users. To access the forum, go to https://livebook.manning.com/book/GitOps-and-Kubernetes/discussion. You can also learn more about Manning's forums and the rules of conduct at https://livebook.manning.com/#!/discussion.

Manning's commitment to our readers is to provide a venue where a meaningful dialogue between individual readers and between readers and authors can take place. It is not a commitment to any specific amount of participation on the part of the authors, whose contribution to the forum remains voluntary (and unpaid). We suggest you try asking them some challenging questions lest their interest stray! The forum and the archives of previous discussions will be accessible from the publisher's website as long as the book is in print.

about the authors

BILLY YUEN is a principal engineer with Intuit's Platform team, focusing on AWS and Kubernetes adoption, system resiliency, and monitoring. Previously, Billy worked on Netflix's Edge Services team to build the next generation of edge-service infrastructure to support millions of customers (more than 3 billion requests per day) with high scalability, resilience to failure, and rapid innovation. Billy was a speaker at Java One 2016 and Velocity NY 2016 on "Operational Excellence with Netflix Hystrix," "CI/CD at Lightspeed" at KubeCon 2018, and "Automated Canary Release" at Container World 2019.

ALEXANDER MATYUSHENTSEV is a principal engineer on the Intuit Platform team, focusing on building tools that make it easier to use Kubernetes. Alexander is passionate about open source, cloud-native infrastructure, and tools that increase developers' productivity. He is one of the core contributors to the Argo Workflows and Argo CD projects. Alexander was a speaker at KubeCon 2019 on "How Intuit Does Canary and Blue-Green Deployments with a K8s Controller."

TODD EKENSTAM is a principal engineer at Intuit, building a platform for secure, multitenant Kubernetes infrastructure supporting applications serving Intuit's approximately 50 million customers. Todd has worked on a variety of large-scale distributed systems projects during his career of more than 25 years, including hierarchical storage management, peer-to-peer database replication, enterprise storage virtualization, and two-factor authentication SaaS. Todd has presented at academic, government, and industry conferences, most recently as a guest speaker on "Introduction to Open Policy Agent" at KubeCon 2018.

JESSE SUEN is a principal engineer on the Intuit Platform team, developing microservices-based, distributed applications for Kubernetes. He was an early engineer at Applatix (acquired by Intuit), building a platform to help users run containerized workloads in the public cloud. Before that, he was part of the engineering team at Tintri and Data Domain, working on virtualized infrastructure, storage, tooling, and automation. Jesse is one of the core contributors to the open source Argo Workflows and Argo CD projects.

about the cover illustration

The figure on the cover of *GitOps and Kubernetes* is captioned "Habitant de Styrie," or resident of Styria. The illustration is taken from a collection of dress costumes from various countries by Jacques Grasset de Saint-Sauveur (1757-1810), titled *Costumes de Différents Pays,* published in France in 1797. Each illustration is finely drawn and colored by hand. The rich variety of Grasset de Saint-Sauveur's collection reminds us vividly of how culturally apart the world's towns and regions were just 200 years ago. Isolated from each other, people spoke different dialects and languages. In the streets or in the countryside, it was easy to identify where they lived and what their trade or station in life was just by their dress.

The way we dress has changed since then, and the diversity by region, so rich at the time, has faded away. It is now hard to tell apart the inhabitants of different continents, let alone different towns, regions, or countries. Perhaps we have traded cultural diversity for a more varied personal life—certainly for a more varied and fast-paced technological life.

At a time when it is hard to tell one computer book from another, Manning celebrates the inventiveness and initiative of the computer business with book covers based on the rich diversity of regional life of two centuries ago, brought back to life by Grasset de Saint-Sauveur's pictures.

Part 1

Background

This part of the book covers background and gives you an introduction to GitOps and Kubernetes.

Chapter 1 walks you through the journey of software deployment evolution and how GitOps became the latest practice. It also covers the many key concepts and benefits of GitOps.

Chapter 2 provides key concepts of Kubernetes and why its declarative nature is perfect for GitOps. It also covers the core operator concept and how to implement a simple GitOps operator.

After you grasp the core concepts of GitOps and Kubernetes, you will be ready to dive into the patterns and processes required to adopt GitOps in your deployments. Part 2 covers the GitOps CI/CD pipeline along with environment setup and promotion as well as different deployment strategies. It also covers how you can secure your deployment process and reviews several configuration management tools and various techniques to manage Secrets in GitOps. There is also a chapter devoted to observability as it is related to GitOps.

Why GitOps? 1

Kubernetes is a massively popular open source platform that orchestrates and automates operations. Although it improves the management and scaling of infrastructure and applications, Kubernetes frequently has challenges managing the complexity of releasing applications.

Git is the most widely used version-control system in the software industry today. *GitOps* is a set of procedures that uses the power of Git to provide both revision and change control within the Kubernetes platform. A GitOps strategy can play a big part in how quickly and easily teams manage their services' environment creation, promotion, and operation.

Using GitOps with Kubernetes is a natural fit, with the deployment of declarative Kubernetes manifest files being controlled by common Git operations. GitOps brings the core benefits of Infrastructure as Code and immutable infrastructure to the deployment, monitoring, and life-cycle management of Kubernetes applications in an intuitive, accessible way.

1.1 Evolution to GitOps

Two everyday tasks in managing and operating computer systems are infrastructure configuration and software deployment. *Infrastructure configuration* prepares computing resources (such as servers, storage, and load balancers) that enable the software application to operate correctly. *Software deployment* is the process of taking a particular version of a software application and making it ready to run on the computing infrastructure. Managing these two processes is the core of GitOps. Before we dig into how this management is done in GitOps, however, it is useful to understand the challenges that have led the industry toward DevOps and the immutable, declarative infrastructure of GitOps.

1.1.1 Traditional Ops

In a traditional information technology operations model, development teams are responsible for periodically delivering new versions of a software application to a quality-assurance (QA) team that tests the new version and then delivers it to an operations team for deployment. New versions of software may be released once a year, once a quarter, or at shorter intervals. It becomes increasingly difficult for a traditional operations model to support increasingly compressed release cycles.

The operations team is responsible for the infrastructure configuration and deployment of the new software application versions to that infrastructure. The operations team's primary focus is to ensure the reliability, resilience, and security of the system running the software. Without sophisticated management frameworks, infrastructure management can be a difficult task that requires a lot of specialized knowledge.

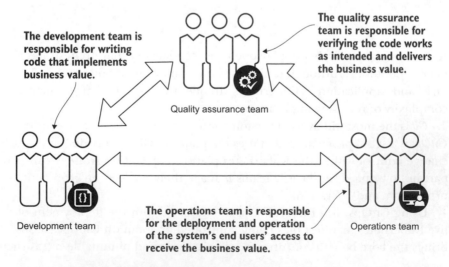

Figure 1.1 Traditional IT teams are typically composed of separate development, QA, and operations teams. Each team specializes in a different aspect of the application development process.

> **IT OPERATIONS**   *IT operations* is the set of all processes and services that are both provisioned by an IT staff to internal or external clients and used by the staff to provide a business's technology needs. Operations work can include responding to tickets generated for maintenance work or customer issues.[1]

Because three teams are involved, often with different management-reporting structures, a detailed handoff process and thorough documentation of the application changes are needed to ensure that the application is adequately tested, appropriate changes are made to infrastructure, and the application is installed correctly. These requirements, however, cause deployments to take a long time and reduce the frequency at which deployments can be made. Also, with each transition between teams, the possibility that essential details will not being communicated increases, possibly leading to gaps in testing or incorrect deployment.

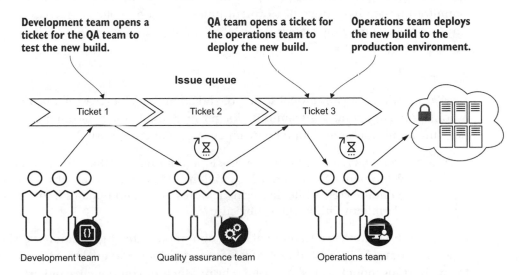

Figure 1.2   In the traditional deployment flow, the development team opens a ticket for the QA team to test a new product version. When the testing is successful, the QA team opens a ticket for the operations team to deploy the latest version to production.

Fortunately, most development teams compile, test, and produce their deployable artifacts by using automated build systems and a process called *continuous integration (CI)*. But the new code's deployment is often a manual process performed by the operations team, involving lengthy manual procedures or partial automation through deployment scripts. In a worst-case scenario, the operations engineer manually copies the executable binary file to the needed location on multiple servers and manually restarts the application to make the new binary version take effect. This process is

---

[1]   https://en.wikipedia.org/wiki/Data_center_management#Operations.

error prone and offers few options for controls such as review, approval, auditability, and rollback.

> **CONTINUOUS INTEGRATION (CI)**   *CI* involves automated building, testing, and packaging of software applications. In a typical development workflow, software engineers make code changes that are checked into the central code repository. These changes must be tested and integrated with the main code branch intended to be deployed to production. A CI system facilitates the review, building, and testing of code to ensure its quality before merging to the main branch.

With the rise of cloud computing infrastructure, the interfaces that manage compute and network resources have become increasingly based on application programming interfaces (APIs), allowing for more automation but requiring more programming skills to implement. This fact, coupled with many organizations' search for ways to optimize operations, reduce deployment times, increase deployment frequency, and improve their computing systems' reliability, stability, and performance, led to a new industry trend: DevOps.

1.1.2   *DevOps*

DevOps is both an organizational structure and a mindset change with an emphasis on automation. An operations team is no longer responsible for deployment and operation; the application's development team takes on these responsibilities.

> **DEVOPS**   *DevOps* is a set of software development practices that combine software development (Dev) and IT operations (Ops) to shorten the system development life cycle while delivering features, fixes, and updates frequently in close alignment with business objectives.[2]

Figure 1.3 shows how, in a traditional operations model, the organization is divided by functional boundaries, with different teams for development, quality, and operations. In the DevOps model, teams are divided by products or components and are interdisciplinary, containing team members who have skill sets across all functions. Although figure 1.3 indicates team members with a specific role, all members of a high-functioning team practicing DevOps contribute across functions; each member is able to code, test, deploy, and operate their product or component.

The benefits of DevOps include

- Better collaboration between development and operations
- Improved product quality
- More frequent releases
- Reduced time to market for new features
- Decreased costs of design, development, and operations

[2]   https://en.wikipedia.org/wiki/DevOps.

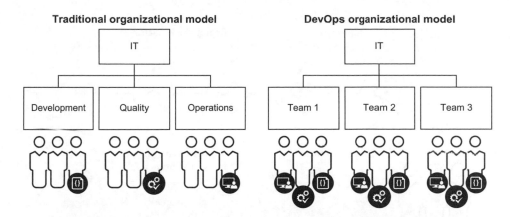

Figure 1.3 The traditional organizational model has separate teams for development, quality, and operations. A DevOps organizational model allows interdisciplinary teams centered on a specific product or component. Each DevOps team is self-sufficient and contains members who have the skills to develop, test, and deploy their application.

Case study: Netflix

Netflix was one of the early adopters of the DevOps process, with every engineer being responsible for coding, testing, deployment, and support of their features. Netflix's culture promotes "Freedom and Responsibility," which means that every engineer can push releases independently but must ensure the proper operation of that release. All deployment processes are fully automated, so engineers can deploy and roll back with the press of a button. All new features are in end users' hands as soon as the functionality is complete.

1.1.3 GitOps

The term *GitOps* was coined in August 2017 in a series of blogs by Alexis Richardson, cofounder and CEO of Weaveworks.[3] Since then, the term has developed significant mindshare in the cloud-native community in general and the Kubernetes community in particular. GitOps is a DevOps process characterized by

- Best practices for deployment, management, and monitoring of containerized applications
- A developer-centric experience for managing applications, with fully automated pipelines/workflows using Git for development and operations
- Use of the Git revision control system to track and approve changes to the infrastructure and run-time environment of applications

---

[3] https://www.weave.works/blog/gitops-operations-by-pull-request.

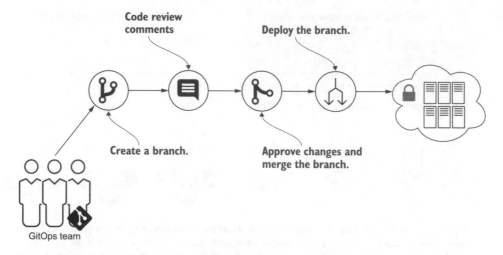

Figure 1.4   The GitOps release workflow starts with creating a branch of the repository containing changes to the definition of the system's desired state.

GitHub (along with GitLab, Bitbucket, and so on) is central to the modern software development life cycle, so it seems natural that it is also used for systems operation and management.

In a GitOps model, the system's desired configuration is stored in a revision control system, such as Git. Instead of making changes directly to the system via a UI or CLI, an engineer makes changes to the configuration files that represent the desired state. A difference between the desired state stored in Git and the system's actual state indicates that not all changes have been deployed. These changes can be reviewed and approved through standard revision control processes such as pull requests, code reviews, and merges to master. When changes have been approved and merged to the main branch, an operator software process is responsible for changing the system's current state to the desired state based on the configuration stored in Git.

In an ideal implementation of GitOps, manual changes to the system are not permitted, and all changes to the configuration must be made to files stored in Git. In an extreme case, permission to change the system is granted only to the operator software process. The infrastructure and operations engineers' role in a GitOps model shifts from performing the infrastructure changes and application deployments to developing and maintaining the GitOps automation and helping teams review and approve changes by using Git.

Git has many features and technical capabilities that make it an ideal choice for use with GitOps:

- Git stores each commit. With proper access control and security configuration (covered in chapter 6), all changes are auditable and tamperproof.
- Each commit in Git represents a complete configuration of the system up to that point in time.

- Each commit object in Git is associated with its parent commit so that as branches are created and merged, the commit history is available when needed.

NOTE   GitOps is important because it enables traceability of changes made to an environment and enables easy rollback, recoverability, and self-healing with Git, a tool with which most developers are already familiar.

Git provides the basis to validate and audit deployments. Although it may be possible to implement GitOps by using a version-control system other than Git, Git's distributed nature, branching and merging strategy, and widespread adoption make it an ideal choice.

GitOps doesn't require a particular set of tools, but the tools must offer this standard functionality:

- Operate on the desired state of the system that is stored in Git
- Detect differences between the desired state and the actual state
- Perform the required operations on the infrastructure to synchronize the actual state with the desired state

Although this book focuses on GitOps in relation to Kubernetes, many of the principles of GitOps could be implemented independently of Kubernetes.

1.2   *Developer benefits of GitOps*

GitOps provides many benefits to developers because it allows them to treat the configuration of infrastructure and deployment of code in much the same way that they manage their software development process, and with a familiar tool: Git.

1.2.1   *Infrastructure as code*

Infrastructure as code (IaC) is a foundational paradigm for GitOps. The configuration of the infrastructure that runs your applications is accomplished by executing an automated process rather than manual steps.[4] In practice, IaC means that infrastructure changes are codified and the source code for the infrastructure is stored in a version-control system. Let's go through the most notable benefits:

- *Repeatability*—Everyone who has experience provisioning infrastructure manually agrees that this process is time consuming and error prone. Don't forget that the same process has to be repeated multiple times, because applications are typically deployed into multiple environments. If a problem is discovered, it is easier to roll back to an earlier working configuration with a repeatable process, allowing quicker recoveries.
- *Reliability*—The automated process significantly reduces the chance of inevitable human errors, thereby reducing the possibility of outages. When the process is codified, infrastructure quality no longer depends on the knowledge and

---

[4]   https://www.hashicorp.com/resources/what-is-infrastructure-as-code.

skill of the particular engineer who is performing the deployment. The automation of the infrastructure configuration can be steadily improved.

- *Efficiency*—IaC increases the productivity of the team. With IaC, engineers are more productive because they use familiar tools, such as APIs, software development kits (SDKs), version-control systems, and text editors. Engineers can use familiar processes and take advantage of code review and automated testing.

- *Savings*—The initial implementation of IaC requires significant investment of effort and time. Despite the initial cost, however, it is more cost effective in the long run. The provisioning of infrastructure for the next environment does not require wasting valuable engineer time for manual configuration. Because provisioning is quick and cheap, there is no need to keep unused environments running. Instead, each environment might be created on demand and destroyed when it is no longer needed.

- *Visibility*—When you define IaC, the code itself documents how the infrastructure should look.

IaC enables developers to produce higher-quality software while saving time and money. It might be easier to configure the infrastructure manually for one environment, but it will become increasingly challenging to maintain that environment, along with dozens of other environments for your application. Using automated infrastructure provisioning and following IaC principles enables repeatable deployments and prevents run-time issues caused by configuration drift or missing dependencies.

1.2.2   Self-service

As mentioned previously, in a traditional operations model, infrastructure management is performed by a dedicated team or even a separate organization within the company.

There is a problem, however: this approach does not scale. The dedicated team will quickly become a bottleneck, no matter how many members it has. Instead of making an infrastructure change themselves, application developers have to file a ticket, send an email, schedule a meeting, and wait. Regardless of the process, a barrier exists, introducing many delays and discouraging the team from proactively proposing infrastructure changes. GitOps aims to break the barrier by automating the process and making it self-service.

Instead of sending a ticket, when using a GitOps model, the developer works on a solution independently and commits a change to the infrastructure's declarative configuration in the repository. The infrastructure change does not require cross-team communication anymore, allowing the application development team to move forward much more quickly and have more freedom to experiment. The ability to make infrastructure changes rapidly and independently encourages developers to take ownership of their application infrastructure. Instead of asking a central operations team for a solution, developers can experiment and develop a design that efficiently solves the business requirements.

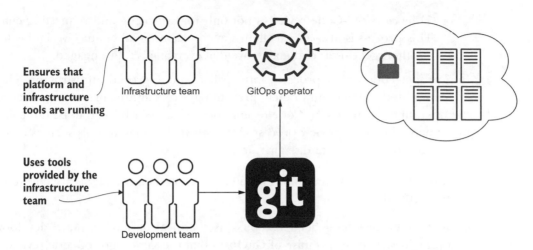

Ensures that platform and infrastructure tools are running

Infrastructure team

GitOps operator

Uses tools provided by the infrastructure team

Development team

Figure 1.5 The development team can change the system's desired state by updating files stored in the Git repository. These changes are code-reviewed by other team members and merged to the main branch upon approval. The main branch is processed by a GitOps operator that deploys the cluster's desired configuration.

Developers don't get full control to do whatever they want, however, possibly compromising security or reliability. Every change requires creating a pull request that can be reviewed by another member of the application development team, as described in the following sections.

The advantage of GitOps is that it allows self-service infrastructure changes and provides the right balance between control and development speed.

1.2.3 Code reviews

Code review is a software development practice in which code changes are proactively examined for errors or omissions by a second pair of eyes, leading to fewer preventable outages. Performing code reviews is a natural process in the software development life cycle with which software engineers doing DevOps/GitOps should be familiar. When the DevOps engineer can treat infrastructure as code, the logical next step is to perform code reviews on the infrastructure changes before deployment. When GitOps is used with Kubernetes, the "code" being reviewed may be primarily Kubernetes YAML manifests or other declarative configuration files, not traditional code written in a programming language.

Besides error prevention, code reviews provide the following benefits:

- *Teaching and sharing knowledge*—While reviewing the changes, the reviewer has a chance not only to give feedback, but also to learn something.
- *Consistency in design and implementation*—During the review, the team can ensure that changes are aligned with the overall code structure and follow the company's code style guidelines.

- *Team cohesion*—Code review is not only for criticizing and requesting changes. This process is also an excellent way for team members to give kudos to one another, get closer, and make sure that everyone is fully engaged.

In a proper code review process, only verified and approved infrastructure changes are committed to the main branch, preventing errors and incorrect modifications to the operating environment. Code review doesn't necessarily need to be done entirely by humans. The code review process also can run automated tools such as code linters,[5] static code analysis, and security tools.

> **NOTE**   Other automated tools for code and vulnerability analysis are covered in chapter 4.

Code reviews have long been accepted as a critical part of software development best practices. The key premise of GitOps is that the same rigor of code reviews used in the application code should be applied to changes in the application operational environment.

1.2.4   *Git pull requests*

The Git version-control system provides a mechanism in which proposed changes can be committed to a branch or fork and then merged with the main branch through a pull request. In 2005, Git introduced a `request-pull` command. This command generates a human-readable summary of all the changes, which can be mailed to the project maintainer manually. The pull request collects all the changes to the repository files and presents the differences for code review and approval.

Pull requests can be used to enforce premerge code reviews. Controls can be put in place to require specific testing or approval before a pull request is merged to the main branch. Like code reviews, pull requests are a familiar process in the software development life cycle that software engineers likely already use.

Figure 1.6 demonstrates the typical pull request life cycle:

1 The developer creates a new branch and starts working on the changes.
2 When changes are ready, the developer sends a pull request for code review.
3 Team members review the pull request and request more changes (if needed).
4 The developer keeps making changes in a branch until the pull request is approved.
5 The project maintainer merges the pull request into the main branch.
6 After the merge, the branch used for the pull request may be deleted.

---

[5]   https://en.wikipedia.org/wiki/Lint_(software).

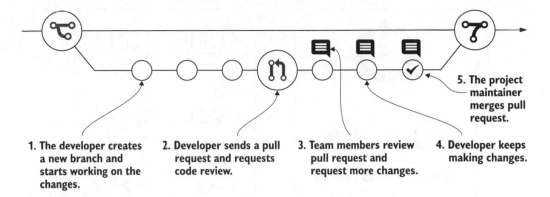

1. **The developer creates a new branch and starts working on the changes.**

2. **Developer sends a pull request and requests code review.**

3. **Team members review pull request and request more changes.**

4. **Developer keeps making changes.**

5. **The project maintainer merges pull request.**

Figure 1.6   The pull request life cycle allows multiple rounds of code review and revisions until the changes are approved. Then the changes may be merged to the main branch and the pull request branch deleted.

The review step is especially interesting when applied to an infrastructure change review. After the pull request is created, the project maintainers receive a notification and review the proposed changes. As a result, reviewers ask questions, receive answers, and possibly request more changes. That information is typically stored and available for future reference, so now the pull request is a live documentation of an infrastructure change. In case of an incident, it is straightforward to find out who made the change and why it was applied.

1.3   *Operational benefits of GitOps*

Combining a GitOps methodology with Kubernetes' declarative configuration and active reconciliation model provides many operational benefits that provide a more predictable and reliable system.

1.3.1   *Declarative*

One of the most prominent paradigms to emerge from the DevOps movement is the model of *declarative systems* and *configuration*. Simply put, with declarative models, you describe *what* you want to achieve as opposed to how to get there. By contrast, in an imperative model, you describe a sequence of instructions for manipulating the system to reach your desired state.

To illustrate this difference, imagine two styles of a television remote control: an *imperative* style and a *declarative* style. Both remotes can control the TV's power, volume, and channel. For the sake of discussion, assume that the TV has only three volume settings (loud, soft, mute) and only three channels (1, 2, 3).

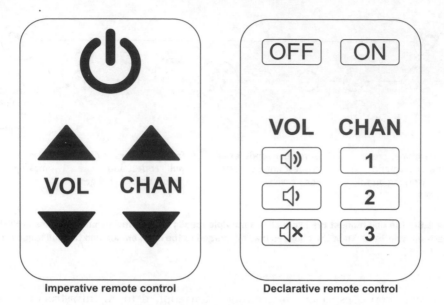

Figure 1.7   This figure illustrates the differences between imperative and declarative remote controls. The imperative remote lets you perform operations such as "Increment the channel by 1" and "Toggle the state of the power." By contrast, the declarative remote lets you perform operations such as "Tune to channel 2" or "Set the state of the power to off."

IMPERATIVE REMOTE EXAMPLE

Suppose that you had the simple task of changing to channel 3 with both remotes. To accomplish this task with the imperative remote, you would use the channel-up button, which signals the TV to increment the current channel by 1. To reach channel 3, you would keep pressing the channel-up button some number of times until the TV reached the desired channel.

DECLARATIVE REMOTE EXAMPLE

By contrast, the declarative remote provides individual buttons that jump directly to the specific numbered channel. In this case, to switch to channel 3, you would press the channel-3 button once, and the TV would be on the correct channel. You are declaring your intended end state (I want the TV to be tuned to channel 3). With the imperative remote, you describe the actions that you need to be performed to achieve your desired state (keep pressing the channel-up button until the TV is tuned to channel 3).

You may have noticed that in the imperative approach to changing channels, the user must consider whether to continue pushing the channel-up button, depending on the channel to which the TV is currently tuned. In the declarative approach, however, you can press the channel-3 button without a second thought because that button on the declarative remote is considered to be idempotent (and the channel-up button on the imperative remote is not).

IDEMPOTENCY *Idempotency* is a property of an operation whereby the operation can be performed any number of times and produce the same result. In other words, an operation is said to be idempotent if you can perform the operation an arbitrary number of times, and the system is in the same state as it would be if you had performed the operation only once. Idempotency is one of the properties that distinguish declarative systems from imperative systems. Declarative systems are idempotent; imperative systems are not.

1.3.2 Observability

Observability is the ability to examine and describe a system's current running state and be alerted when unexpected conditions occur. Deployed environments are expected to be observable. In other words, you should always be able to inspect an environment to see what is currently running and how things are configured. To that end, service and cloud providers provide a fair number of methods to promote observability (including CLIs, APIs, GUIs, dashboards, alerts, and notifications), making it as convenient as possible for users to understand the current state of the environment.

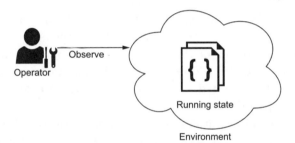

Figure 1.8 Observability is the operator's ability (perhaps human or automated) to determine an environment's running state. The operator can make informed decisions about what changes to the environment are needed only once if the environment's current running state is known. Proper control of an environment requires observability of that environment.

Although these observability mechanisms can help answer the question, "What's currently running in my environment?" they cannot answer the question, "For the resources currently configured and running in my environment, are they *supposed* to be configured and running in that way?" If you have ever held duties as a systems administrator or operator, you're likely to be all too familiar with this problem. At one point or another—typically, when troubleshooting an environment—you come across a suspicious configuration setting and think that it doesn't seem right. Did someone (possibly you) accidentally or mistakenly change this setting, or is the setting intentional?

In all likelihood, you may already be practicing a fundamental principle of GitOps: storing a copy of your application configuration in source control and using it as a source of truth for the desired state of your application. You may not be storing this configuration in Git to drive continuous deployment—only to have a copy duplicated *somewhere* so that the environment can be reproduced, such as in a disaster recovery scenario. This copy can be thought of as the desired application state, and aside from the disaster recovery use case, it serves another useful purpose: it enables operators to

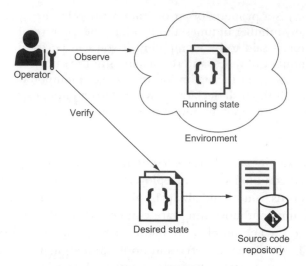

Figure 1.9   If the environment's running state can be observed, and the desired state of the environment is defined in Git, the environment can be verified by comparing the two states.

compare the actual running state with the desired state held in source control at any point in time to verify that the states match.

The ability to verify your environment is a core tenet of GitOps that has been formalized as a practice. By storing your desired state in one system (such as Git) and regularly comparing that desired state with the running state, you unlock a new dimension of observability. Not only do you have the standard observability mechanisms provided by your provider, but also, you are able to detect divergence from the desired state.

Divergence from your desired state, also called *configuration drift*, can happen for any number of reasons. Common examples include mistakes made by operators, unintended side effects due to automation, and error scenarios. Configuration drift could even be expected, such as a temporary state caused by a transition period (maintenance mode, for example).

But the most significant reason for a divergence in configuration could be malicious. In the worst case, a bad actor could have compromised the environment and reconfigured the system to run a malicious image. For this reason, observability and verification are crucial for the security of the system. Unless you have a source of truth of your desired state in place, and without a mechanism to verify convergence to that source of truth, it is impossible to know that your environment is truly secure.

1.3.3   *Auditability and compliance*

Allowing for compliance and auditability is a must for organizations that do business in countries whose laws and regulations affect information management and frameworks for assessing compliance—which is most countries in this day and age. Some industries are more regulated than others, but almost all companies need to comply with basic privacy and data security laws. Many organizations have to invest substantially in their processes and systems to be compliant and auditable. With GitOps and Kubernetes, most of the compliance and auditability requirements can be satisfied with minimal effort.

Compliance refers to verifying that an organization's information system meets a particular set of industry standards, typically focused on customer data security and adherence to the organization's documented policies on the people and systems that have access to that customer data. Chapter 6 covers access control in depth, and chapter 4 covers pipelines to define and enforce your deployment process for compliance.

Auditability is a system's capability to be verified as being compliant with a set of standards. If a system can't be shown to an internal or external auditor to be compliant, no statement about the system's compliance can be made. Chapter 8 covers observability, including using the Git commit history and Kubernetes events for auditability.

Case study: Facebook and Cambridge Analytica

Cambridge Analytica, a political data firm hired by President Trump's 2016 election campaign, gained improper access to the private information of more than 50 million Facebook users. The data was used to generate a personality score for each user and match that user with US voter records. Cambridge Analytica used this information for its voter profiling and targeted advertising services. Facebook was found not to have implemented the proper controls required to enforce data privacy and was eventually fined $5 billion by the Federal Trade Commission due to the breach.[a]

---

[a] https://www.ftc.gov/news-events/press-releases/2019/07/ftc-imposes-5-billion-penalty-sweeping-new-privacy-restrictions

---

Auditability also refers to an auditor's ability to achieve a comprehensive examination of an organization's internal controls. In a typical audit, the auditor requests evidence to ensure that rules and policies are enforced accordingly. Evidence could include the process of restricting access to user data, the handling of personally identifiable information (PII), and the integrity of the software release process.

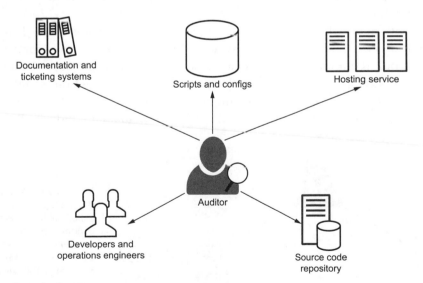

Figure 1.10 In a traditional audit process, it is often difficult to determine the system's desired state. Auditors may need to look at various sources of this information, including documentation, change requests, and deployment scripts.

Case study: Payment Card Industry Data Security Standard

The Payment Card Industry Data Security Standard (PCI DSS) is an information security standard for organizations that handle branded credit cards from the major card networks. Violation of the PCI DSS could result in steep fines and, in the worst case, suspension from credit card processing. PCI DSS dictates that "access control systems are configured to enforce privileges assigned to individuals based on job classification and function." During an audit, organizations need to provide evidence that access control systems are in place for PCI compliance.[a]

[a] https://en.wikipedia.org/wiki/Payment_Card_Industry_Data_Security_Standard

What does all that have to do with GitOps?

Git is version-control software that helps organizations manage changes and access control to their code. Git keeps track of every modification to the code in a special kind of database designed to preserve the managed source code's integrity. The files' content and the true relationships among files and directories, versions, tags, and commits in the Git repository are secured with the Secure Hash Algorithm (SHA) checksum hashing algorithm. This algorithm protects the code and the change history from both accidental and malicious change and ensures that the history is fully traceable.

Git's history tracking also includes the author, date, and written notes on each change's purpose. With well-written commit comments, you know *why* a particular commit was made. Git can also integrate with project management and bug-tracking software, allowing full traceability of all changes and enabling root-cause analysis and other forensics.

As mentioned earlier, Git supports the pull request mechanism, which prevents any single person from altering the system without approval by a second person. When the pull request is approved, changes are recorded in the secured Git change history. Git's strength in change control, traceability, and change history authenticity, along with Kubernetes' declarative configuration, naturally satisfy the security, availability, and processing integrity principles needed for auditability and compliance.

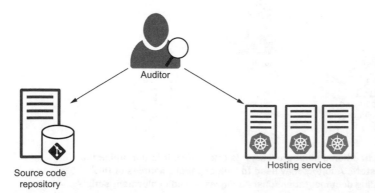

Auditor

Source code repository

Hosting service

Figure 1.11 With GitOps, the audit process can be simplified because the auditor can determine the system's desired state by examining the source code repository. The current state of the system can be determined by reviewing the hosting service and Kubernetes objects.

1.3.4 *Disaster recovery*

Disasters happen for many reasons and take many forms. A disaster may be naturally occurring (an earthquake hitting a data center), caused by an equipment failure (loss of hard drives in a storage array), accidental (a software bug corrupting a critical database table), or even malicious (a cyberattack causing data loss).

GitOps helps in the recovery of infrastructure environments by storing declarative specifications of the environment under source control as a source of truth. Having a complete definition of what the environment should be facilitates the re-creation of the environment in the event of a disaster. Disaster recovery becomes a simple exercise of (re)applying all the configuration stored in the Git repository. You might observe that there is not much difference between the procedures followed during a disaster versus those used in routine day-to-day upgrades and deployments. With GitOps, you are in effect practicing disaster recovery procedures on a regular basis, making you well prepared if a real disaster strikes.

> **IMPORTANCE OF DATA BACKUPS** Although GitOps helps simplify disaster recovery for computing and networking infrastructure, recovery of persistent and stateful applications needs to be handled differently. There is no substitute for traditional disaster recovery solutions for storage-related infrastructure: backups, snapshotting, and replication.

Summary

- GitOps is a DevOps deployment process that uses Git as the system of record to manage deployment in complex systems.
- Traditional Ops requires a separate team for deployment, and a new version can take days (if not weeks) to be deployed.
- DevOps enables engineers to deploy a new version as soon as the code is complete without waiting for a centralized operations team.
- GitOps provides full traceability and release control.
- Declarative models describe what you want to achieve instead of the steps necessary to achieve it.
- Idempotency is a property of an operation whereby the operation can be performed any number of times and produce the same result.
- Additional GitOps benefits include
  - Pull requests for code quality and release control
  - Observable running state and desired state
  - Simplified compliance and auditability process with historical authenticity and traceability
  - Straightforward disaster recovery and rollback procedures that are consistent with the familiar deployment experience

Kubernetes and GitOps

In chapter 1, you learned about Kubernetes and why its declarative model makes it an excellent match to be managed using GitOps. This chapter will briefly introduce Kubernetes architecture and objects and the differences between declarative and imperative object management. By the end of this chapter, you will implement a basic GitOps Kubernetes deployment operator.

2.1 *Kubernetes introduction*

Before diving into why Kubernetes and GitOps work so well together, let's talk about Kubernetes itself. This section provides a high-level overview of Kubernetes, how it compares to other container orchestration systems, and its architecture. We will also have an exercise that demonstrates how to run Kubernetes locally, which will be used for the other exercises in this book. This section is only a brief introduction and refresher on Kubernetes. For a fun but informative overview of Kubernetes, check out "The Illustrated Children's Guide to Kubernetes" and "Phippy Goes to the Zoo" by the Cloud Native Computing Foundation.[1] If you are completely new to Kubernetes, we recommend reading *Kubernetes in Action, Second Edition*, by Marko Lukša (Manning, 2020) and then returning to this book. If you are already familiar with Kubernetes and running minikube, you may skip to the exercise at the end of section 2.1.

2.1.1 What is Kubernetes?

Kubernetes is an open source container orchestration system released in 2014. OK, but what are containers, and why do you need to orchestrate them?

Containers provide a standard way to package your application's code, configuration, and dependencies into a single resource. This enables developers to ensure that the application will run properly on any other machine regardless of any customized settings that machine may have that could differ from the machine used for writing and testing the code. Docker simplified and popularized containerization, which is now recognized as a fundamental technology used to build distributed systems.

> **CHROOT** An operation available in UNIX operating systems, which changes the apparent root directory for the current running process and its children. Chroot provides a way to isolate a process and its children from the rest of the system. It was a precursor to containerization and Docker.[2]

While Docker solved the packaging and isolation problem of individual applications, there were still many questions about how to orchestrate the operation of multiple applications into a working distributed system:

- How do containers communicate?
- How is traffic routed between containers?
- How are containers scaled up to handle additional application load?
- How is the underlying infrastructure of the cluster scaled up to run the required containers?

All these operations are the responsibility of a container orchestration system and are provided by Kubernetes. Kubernetes helps to automate the deployment, scaling, and management of applications using containers.

> **NOTE** Borg is Google's internal container cluster management system used to power online services like Google search, Gmail, and YouTube. Kubernetes leverages Borg's innovations and lessons learned, explaining why it is more stable and moves so much more quickly than its competitors.[3]

---

[1] https://www.cncf.io/phippy.
[2] https://en.wikipedia.org/wiki/Chroot.
[3] https://kubernetes.io/blog/2015/04/borg-predecessor-to-kubernetes.

Kubernetes was initially developed and open-sourced by Google based on a decade of experience with container orchestration using Borg, Google's proprietary cluster management system. Because of this, Kubernetes is relatively stable and mature for a system so complex. Because of its open API and extendable architecture, Kubernetes has developed an extensive community around it, which has further fueled its success. It is one of the top GitHub projects (as measured by stars), provides excellent documentation, and has a significant Slack and Stack Overflow community. An endless number of blogs and presentations from community members share their knowledge of using Kubernetes. Despite being started by Google, Kubernetes is not influenced by a single vendor. This makes the community open, collaborative, and innovative.

2.1.2 *Other container orchestrators*

Since late 2016, Kubernetes has become recognized as the dominant de facto industry-standard container orchestration system in much the same way that Docker has become the standard for containers. However, several Kubernetes alternatives address the same container orchestration problem as Kubernetes. Docker Swarm is Docker's native container orchestration engine that was released in 2015. It is tightly integrated with the Docker API and uses a YAML-based deployment model called Docker Compose. Apache Mesos was officially released in 2016 (although it has a history well before then) and supports large clusters, scaling to thousands of nodes.

  While it may be possible to apply a GitOps approach to deploying applications using other container orchestration systems, this book focuses on Kubernetes.

2.1.3 *Kubernetes architecture*

By the end of this chapter, you will complete an exercise that implements a basic GitOps continuous deployment operator for Kubernetes. But to understand how a GitOps operator functions, it is essential that you first understand a few Kubernetes core concepts and learn how it is organized at a high level.

  Kubernetes is an extensive and robust system with many different types of resources and operations that can be performed on those resources. Kubernetes provides a layer of abstraction over the infrastructure and introduces the following set of basic objects that represent the desired cluster state:

- *Pod*—A group of containers deployed together on the same host. The Pod is the smallest deployable unit on a node and provides a way to mount storage, set environment variables, and provide other container configuration information. When all the containers of a Pod exit, the Pod dies also.
- *Service*—An abstraction that defines a logical set of Pods and a policy to access them.
- *Volume*—A directory accessible to containers running in a Pod.

Kubernetes architecture uses primary resources as a foundational layer for a set of higher-level resources. The higher-level resources implement features needed for real

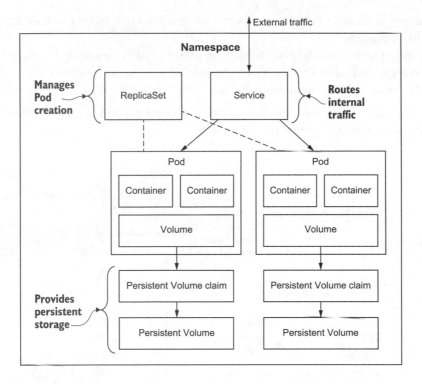

Figure 2.1 This diagram illustrates a typical Kubernetes environment deployed in a Namespace. A ReplicaSet is an example of a higher-level resource that manages the life cycle of Pods, which are lower-level, primary resources.

production use cases that leverage/extend the primary resources' functionality. In figure 2.1, you see that the ReplicaSet resource controls the creation of one or more Pod resources. Some other examples of high-level resources include

- *ReplicaSet*—Defines that a desired number of identically configured Pods are running. If a Pod in the ReplicaSet terminates, a new Pod will be started to bring the number of running Pods back to the desired number.
- *Deployment*—Enables declarative updates for Pods and ReplicaSets.
- *Job*—Creates one or more Pods that run to completion.
- *CronJob*—Creates Jobs on a time-based schedule.

Another important Kubernetes resource is the Namespace. Most kinds of Kubernetes resources belong to one (and only one) Namespace. A Namespace defines a naming scope where resources within a particular Namespace must be uniquely named. Namespaces also provide a way to isolate users and applications from each other through role-based access controls (RBACs), network policies, and resource quotas. These controls allow creating a multitenant Kubernetes cluster where multiple users share the same cluster and avoid impacting each other (for example, the "noisy neighbor" problem).

As we will see in chapter 3, Namespaces are also essential in GitOps for defining application environments.

Kubernetes objects are stored in a control plane,[4] which monitors the cluster state, makes changes, schedules work, and responds to events. To perform these duties, each Kubernetes control plane runs the following three processes:

- `kube-apiserver`—An entry point to the cluster providing a REST API to evaluate and update the desired cluster state

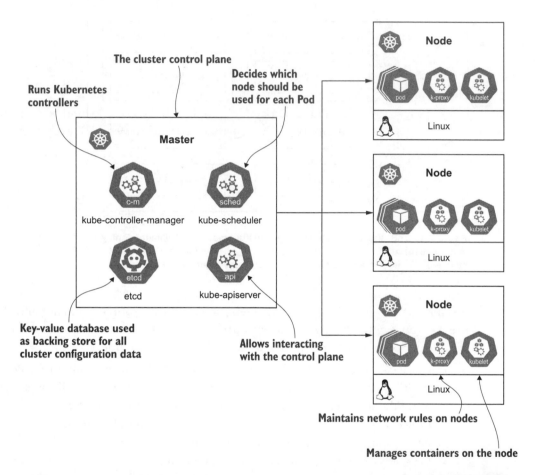

Figure 2.2   A Kubernetes cluster consists of several Services that run on the master nodes of the control plane and several other Services that run on the cluster's worker nodes. Together, these Services provide the essential Services that make up a Kubernetes cluster.

---

[4]   https://kubernetes.io/docs/concepts/overview/components/#control-plane-components.

- `kube-controller-manager`—Daemon continuously monitoring the shared state of the cluster through the API server to make changes attempting to move the current state toward the desired state
- `kube-scheduler`—A component that is responsible for scheduling the workloads across the available nodes in the cluster
- `etcd`—A highly available key-value database typically used as Kubernetes' backing store for all cluster configuration data

The actual cluster workloads run using the compute resources of Kubernetes nodes. A node is a worker machine (either a VM or physical machine) that runs the necessary software to allow it to be managed by the cluster. Similar to the masters, each node runs a predefined set of processes:

- `kubelet`—The primary "node agent" that manages the actual containers on the node
- `kube-proxy`—A network proxy that reflects Services as defined in the Kubernetes API on each node and can do simple TCP, UDP, and SCTP stream forwarding

2.1.4 *Deploying to Kubernetes*

In this exercise, you will deploy a website using NGINX on Kubernetes. You will review some basic Kubernetes operations and become familiar with minikube, the single-node Kubernetes environment you will use for most exercises in this book.

> **KUBERNETES TEST ENVIRONMENT: MINIKUBE** Refer to appendix A to set up a Kubernetes test environment using minikube to complete this exercise.

CREATING A POD

As was mentioned earlier in the chapter, a Pod is the smallest object in Kubernetes and represents a particular application workload. A Pod represents a group of related containers running on the same host and having the same operating requirements. All containers of a single Pod share the same network address, port space, and (optionally) file system using Kubernetes Volumes.

> **NGINX** NGINX is an open source software web server used by many organizations and enterprises to host their websites because of its performance and stability.

In this exercise, you will create a Pod that hosts a website using NGINX. In Kubernetes, objects can be defined by a YAML text file "manifest" that provides all the information needed for Kubernetes to create and manage the object. Here is the listing for our NGINX Pod manifest.

Listing 2.1   NGINX Pod manifest (http://mng.bz/e5JJ)

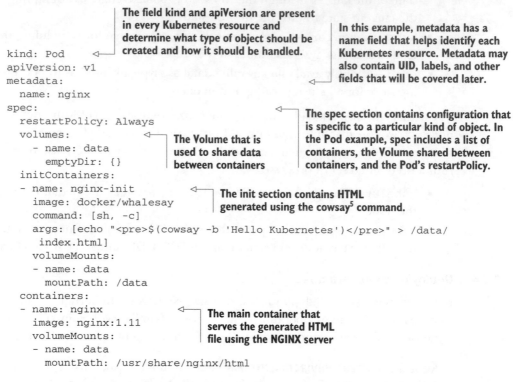

The field kind and apiVersion are present in every Kubernetes resource and determine what type of object should be created and how it should be handled.

In this example, metadata has a name field that helps identify each Kubernetes resource. Metadata may also contain UID, labels, and other fields that will be covered later.

The spec section contains configuration that is specific to a particular kind of object. In the Pod example, spec includes a list of containers, the Volume shared between containers, and the Pod's restartPolicy.

The Volume that is used to share data between containers

The init section contains HTML generated using the cowsay[5] command.

The main container that serves the generated HTML file using the NGINX server

```
kind: Pod
apiVersion: v1
metadata:
  name: nginx
spec:
  restartPolicy: Always
  volumes:
    - name: data
      emptyDir: {}
  initContainers:
  - name: nginx-init
    image: docker/whalesay
    command: [sh, -c]
    args: [echo "<pre>$(cowsay -b 'Hello Kubernetes')</pre>" > /data/
    index.html]
    volumeMounts:
    - name: data
      mountPath: /data
  containers:
  - name: nginx
    image: nginx:1.11
    volumeMounts:
    - name: data
      mountPath: /usr/share/nginx/html
```

You are welcome to type in this listing and save it with a filename of nginx-Pod.yaml. However, since this book's object isn't to improve your typing skills, we recommend cloning our public Git repository mentioned in chapter 1 that contains all the listings in this book and using those files directly:

https://github.com/gitopsbook/resources

Let's go ahead and start a minikube cluster and create the NGINX Pod using the following commands:

```
$ minikube start
(minikube/default)
😊   minikube v1.1.1 on darwin (amd64)
🐳   Creating virtualbox VM (CPUs=2, Memory=2048MB, Disk=20000MB) ...
🐳   Configuring environment for Kubernetes v1.14.3 on Docker 18.09.6
🐳   Pulling images ...
🚀   Launching Kubernetes ...
⌛   Verifying: apiserver proxy etcd scheduler controller dns
🏄   Done! kubectl is now configured to use "minikube"
$ kubectl create -f nginx-Pod.yaml
Pod/nginx created
```

---

[5] https://en.wikipedia.org/wiki/Cowsay.

Figure 2.3 shows what the Pod looks like running inside the minikube.

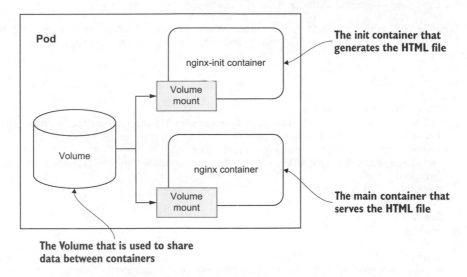

Figure 2.3   The nginx-init container writes the desired index.html file to the mounted Volume. The main NGINX container also mounts the Volume and displays the generated index.html when receiving HTTP requests.

GETTING POD STATUS

As soon as the Pod is created, Kubernetes inspects the spec field and attempts to run the configured set of containers on an appropriate node in the cluster. The information about progress is available in the Pod manifest in the status field. The kubectl utility provides several commands to access it. Let's try to get the Pod status using the kubectl get Pods command:

```
$ kubectl get Pods
NAME    READY    STATUS    RESTARTS    AGE
nginx   1/1      Running   0           36s
```

The get Pods command provides a list of all the Pods running in a particular Namespace. In this case, we didn't specify a Namespace, so it gives the list of Pods running in the default Namespace. Assuming all goes well, the NGINX Pod should be in the Running state.

To learn even more about a Pod's status or debug why the Pod is not in the Running state, the kubectl describe Pod command outputs detailed information, including related Kubernetes events:

```
$ kubectl describe Pod nginx
Name:        nginx
Namespace:   default
Priority:    0
Node:        minikube/192.168.90.101
```

```
Start Time:    Sat, 26 Oct 2019 21:58:43 -0700
Labels:        <none>
Annotations:   kubectl.kubernetes.io/last-applied-configuration:

{"apiVersion":"v1","kind":"Pod","metadata":{"annotations":{},"name":"nginx",
    "Namespace":"default"},"spec":{"containers":[{"image":"nginx:1...
Status:        Running
IP:            172.17.0.4
Init Containers:
  nginx-init:
    Container ID:  docker://
      128c98e40bd6b840313f05435c7590df0eacfc6ce989ec15cb7b484dc60d9bca
    Image:          docker/whalesay
    Image ID:       docker-pullable://docker/
      whalesay@sha256:178598e51a26abbc958b8a2e48825c90bc22e641de3d31e18aaf55f325
      8ba93b
    Port:           <none>
    Host Port:      <none>
    Command:
      sh
      -c
    Args:
      echo "<pre>$(cowsay -b 'Hello Kubernetes')</pre>" > /data/index.html
    State:          Terminated
      Reason:       Completed
      Exit Code:    0
      Started:      Sat, 26 Oct 2019 21:58:45 -0700
      Finished:     Sat, 26 Oct 2019 21:58:45 -0700
    Ready:          True
    Restart Count:  0
    Environment:    <none>
    Mounts:
      /data from data (rw)
      /var/run/secrets/kubernetes.io/serviceaccount from default-token-vbhsd
      (ro)
Containers:
  nginx:
    Container ID:  docker://
      071dd946709580003b728cef12a5d185660d929ebfeb84816dd060167853e245
    Image:          nginx:1.11
    Image ID:       docker-pullable://
      nginx@sha256:e6693c20186f837fc393390135d8a598a96a833917917789d63766cab6c59
      582
    Port:           <none>
    Host Port:      <none>
    State:          Running
      Started:      Sat, 26 Oct 2019 21:58:46 -0700
    Ready:          True
    Restart Count:  0
    Environment:    <none>
    Mounts:
      /usr/share/nginx/html from data (rw)
      /var/run/secrets/kubernetes.io/serviceaccount from default-token-vbhsd (ro)
Conditions:
  Type          Status
  Initialized   True
```

```
    Ready              True
    ContainersReady    True
    PodScheduled       True
Volumes:
  data:
    Type:        EmptyDir (a temporary directory that shares a Pod's lifetime)
    Medium:
    SizeLimit:   <unset>
  default-token-vbhsd:
    Type:        Secret (a volume populated by a Secret)
    SecretName:  default-token-vbhsd
    Optional:    false
QoS Class:       BestEffort
Node-Selectors:  <none>
Tolerations:     node.kubernetes.io/not-ready:NoExecute for 300s
                 node.kubernetes.io/unreachable:NoExecute for 300s
Events:
  Type     Reason      Age    From              Message
  ----     ------      ----   ----              -------
  Normal   Scheduled   37m    default-scheduler Successfully assigned default/
     nginx to minikube
  Normal   Pulling     37m    kubelet, minikube Pulling image "docker/whalesay"
  Normal   Pulled      37m    kubelet, minikube Successfully pulled image
     "docker/whalesay"
  Normal   Created     37m    kubelet, minikube Created container nginx-init
  Normal   Started     37m    kubelet, minikube Started container nginx-init
  Normal   Pulled      37m    kubelet, minikube Container image "nginx:1.11"
     already present on machine
  Normal   Created     37m    kubelet, minikube Created container nginx
  Normal   Started     37m    kubelet, minikube Started container nginx
```

Typically, the events section will contain clues as to why a Pod is not in the `Running` state.

The most exhaustive information is available via `kubectl get Pod nginx -o=yaml`, which outputs the full internal representation of the object in YAML format. The raw YAML output is difficult to read, and it is typically meant for programmatic access by resource controllers. Kubernetes resource controllers will be covered in more detail later in this chapter.

ACCESSING THE POD

A Pod in the `Running` state means that all containers successfully started and the NGINX Pod is ready to serve requests. If the NGINX Pod in our cluster is running, we can try accessing it and prove that it is working.

Pods are not accessible from outside the cluster by default. There are multiple ways to configure external access, which include Kubernetes Services, Ingress, and more. For the sake of simplicity, we are going to use the command `kubectl port-forward` that forwards connections from a local port to a port on a Pod:

```
$ kubectl port-forward nginx 8080:80
Forwarding from 127.0.0.1:8080 -> 80
Forwarding from [::1]:8080 -> 80
```

Keep the `kubectl port-forward` command running, and try opening http://localhost:8080/ in your browser. You should see the generated HTML file!

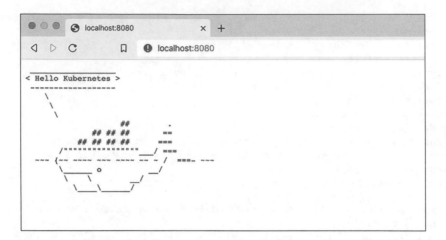

Figure 2.4   The generated HTML file content from the docker/whalesay image is an ASCII rendering of a cute whale with a speech bubble of greeting passed as a command argument. The `port-forward` command allows port 80 of the Pod (HTML) to be accessed on port 8080 of the local host.

Exercise 2.1

Now that your NGINX Pod is running, use the `kubectl exec` command to get a shell on the running container.

> **HINT** The command would be something like `kubectl exec -it <POD_NAME> -- /bin/bash`. Poke around in the shell. Run `ls`, `df`, and `ps -ef` as well as other Linux commands. What happens if you terminate the NGINX process?

As the final step in this exercise, let's delete the Pod to free up cluster resources. The Pod can be deleted using the following command:

```
$ kubectl delete Pod nginx
Pod "nginx" deleted
```

2.2   *Declarative vs. imperative object management*

The Kubernetes `kubectl` command-line tool is used to create, update, and manage Kubernetes objects and supports imperative commands, imperative object configuration, and declarative object configuration.[6] Let's go through a real-world example that demonstrates the difference between an imperative/procedural configuration and a

---

6   http://mng.bz/pVdP.

declarative configuration in Kubernetes. First, let's look at how kubectl can be used imperatively.

> **DECLARATIVE VS. IMPERATIVE** Please refer to section 1.3.1 for a detailed explanation of declarative versus imperative.

In the following example, let's create a script that will deploy an NGINX service with three replicas and some annotations on the deployment.

Listing 2.2 Imperative kubectl commands (imperative-deployment.sh)

Creates a new deployment object called nginx-imperative

Scales the nginx-imperative deployment to have three replicas of the Pod

```
#!/bin/sh
kubectl create deployment nginx-imperative --image=nginx:latest
kubectl scale deployment/nginx-imperative --replicas 3
kubectl annotate deployment/nginx-imperative environment=prod
kubectl annotate deployment/nginx-imperative organization=sales
```

Adds an annotation with the key environment and value prod to the nginx-imperative deployment

Adds an annotation with the key organization and value sales to the nginx-imperative deployment

---

Try running the script against your minikube cluster, and check that the deployment was created successfully:

```
$ imperative-deployment.sh
deployment.apps/nginx-imperative created
deployment.apps/nginx-imperative scaled
deployment.apps/nginx-imperative annotated
deployment.apps/nginx-imperative annotated
$ kubectl get deployments
NAME              READY   UP-TO-DATE   AVAILABLE   AGE
nginx-imperative  3/3     3            3           27s
```

Great! The deployment was created as expected. But now let's edit our `deployment.sh` script to change the value of the `organization` annotation from `sales` to `marketing` and then rerun the script:

```
$ imperative-deployment-new.sh
Error from server (AlreadyExists): deployments.apps "nginx-imperative"
    already exists
deployment.apps/nginx-imperative scaled
error: --overwrite is false but found the following declared annotation(s):
    'environment' already has a value (prod)
error: --overwrite is false but found the following declared annotation(s):
    'organization' already has a value (sales)
```

As you can see, the new script failed because the deployment and annotations already exist. To make it work, we would need to enhance our script with additional commands and logic to handle the update case in addition to the creation case. Sure, this can be done, but it turns out we don't have to do all that work because kubectl can itself examine the current state of the system and do the right thing using declarative object configuration.

The following manifest defines a deployment identical to the one created by our script (except that the deployment's name is `nginx-declarative`).

Listing 2.3   Declarative (http://mng.bz/OEpP)

```
apiVersion: apps/v1
kind: Deployment
metadata:
  name: nginx-declarative
  annotations:
    environment: prod
    organization: sales
spec:
  replicas: 3
  selector:
    matchLabels:
      app: nginx
  template:
    metadata:
      labels:
        app: nginx
    spec:
      containers:
      - name: nginx
        image: nginx:latest
```

We can use the semi-magical `kubectl apply` command to create the `nginx-declarative` deployment:

```
$ kubectl apply -f declarative-deployment.yaml
deployment.apps/nginx-declarative created
$ kubectl get deployments
NAME                  READY   UP-TO-DATE   AVAILABLE   AGE
nginx-declarative     3/3     3            3           5m29s
nginx-imperative      3/3     3            3           24m
```

After running the `apply`, we see the `nginx-declarative` deployment resource created. But what happens when we run `kubectl apply` again?

```
$ kubectl apply -f declarative-deployment.yaml
deployment.apps/nginx-declarative unchanged
```

Notice the change in the output message. The second time `kubectl apply` was run, the program detected that no changes needed to be made and subsequently reported that the deployment was unchanged. This is a subtle but critical difference between a `kubectl create` versus a `kubectl apply`. A `kubectl create` will fail if the resource already exists. The `kubectl apply` command first detects whether the resource exists and performs a create operation if the object doesn't exist or an update if it already exists.

As with the imperative example, what if we want to change the value of the organization annotation from sales to marketing? Let's edit the declarative-deployment.yaml file and change the `metadata.annotations.organization` field from `sales` to `marketing`. But before we run `kubectl apply` again, let's run `kubectl diff`:

```
$ kubectl diff -f declarative-deployment.yaml
:
-    organization: sales                          The value of the organization label was
+    organization: marketing                      changed from sales to marketing.
     creationTimestamp: "2019-10-15T00:57:44Z"
-  generation: 1                                  The generation of this resource
+  generation: 2                                  was changed by the system
   name: nginx-declarative                        when doing kubectl apply.
   Namespace: default
   resourceVersion: "347771"

$ kubectl apply -f declarative-deployment.yaml
deployment.apps/nginx-declarative configured
```

As you can see, `kubectl diff` correctly identified that the organization was changed from `sales` to `marketing`. We also see that `kubectl apply` successfully applied the new changes.

In this exercise, both the imperative and declarative examples result in a deployment resource configured in precisely the same way. And at first glance, the imperative approach may appear to be much simpler. It contains only a few code lines compared to the declarative deployment spec's verbosity that is five times the script's size. However, it contains problems that make it a poor choice to use in practice:

- The code is not idempotent and may have different results if executed more than once. If run a second time, an error will be thrown complaining that the deployment NGINX already exists. In contrast, the deployment spec is idempotent, meaning it can be applied as many times as needed, handling the case where the deployment already exists.

- It is more difficult to manage changes to the resource over time, especially when the difference is subtractive. Suppose you no longer wanted organization to be annotated on the deployment. Simply removing the `kubectl annotate` command from the scripted code would not help since it would do nothing to remove the existing deployment's annotation. A separate operation would be needed to remove it. On the other hand, with the declarative approach, you only need to remove the annotation line from the spec, and Kubernetes would take care of removing the annotation to reflect your desired state.

- It is more difficult to *understand* changes. If a team member sent a pull request modifying the script to do something differently, it would be like any other source code review. The reviewer would need to mentally walk through the script's logic to verify the algorithm achieves the desired outcome. There can even be bugs in the script. On the other hand, a pull request that changes a declarative deployment specification clearly shows the change to the system's desired state. It is simpler to review, as there is no logic to check, only a configuration change.

- The code is not atomic, meaning that if one of the four commands in the script failed, the system's state would be partially changed and wouldn't be in the original state, nor would it be in the desired state. With the declarative approach, the entire spec is received as a single request, and the system attempts to fulfill all aspects of the desired state as a whole.

As you can imagine, what started as a simple shell script would need to become more and more complicated to achieve idempotency. There are dozens of options available in the Kubernetes deployment spec. With the scripted approach, if/else checks would need to be littered throughout the script to understand the existing state and conditionally modify the deployment.

2.2.1   How declarative configuration works

As we saw in the previous exercise, declarative configuration management is powered by the `kubectl apply` command. In contrast with imperative kubectl commands, like `scale` and `annotate`, the `kubectl apply` command has one parameter, the path to the file containing the resource manifest:

```
kubectl apply -f ./resource.yaml
```

The command is responsible for figuring out which changes should be applied to the matching resource in the Kubernetes cluster and update the resource using the Kubernetes API. It is a critical feature that makes Kubernetes a perfect fit for GitOps. Let's learn more about the logic behind `kubectl apply` and understand what it can and cannot do. To understand which problems `kubectl apply` is solving, let's go through different scenarios using the Deployment resource we created earlier.

The simplest scenario is when the matching resource does not exist in the Kubernetes cluster. In this case, kubectl creates a new resource using the manifest stored in the specified file.

If the matching resource exists, why doesn't kubectl replace it? The answer is obvious if you look at the complete manifest resource using the `kubectl get` command. Following is a partial listing of the Deployment resource that was created in the example. Some parts of the manifest have been omitted for clarity (indicated with ellipses):

```
$ kubectl get deployment nginx-declarative -o=yaml
apiVersion: apps/v1
kind: Deployment
metadata:
  annotations:
    deployment.kubernetes.io/revision: "1"
    environment: prod
    kubectl.kubernetes.io/last-applied-configuration: |
      { ... }
    organization: marketing
```

```
    creationTimestamp: "2019-10-15T00:57:44Z"
    generation: 2
    name: nginx-declarative
    Namespace: default
    resourceVersion: "349411"
    selfLink: /apis/apps/v1/Namespaces/default/deployments/nginx-declarative
    uid: d41cf3dc-a3e8-40dd-bc81-76afd4a032b1
  spec:
    progressDeadlineSeconds: 600
    replicas: 3
    revisionHistoryLimit: 10
    selector:
      matchLabels:
        app: nginx-declarative
    strategy:
      rollingUpdate:
        maxSurge: 25%
        maxUnavailable: 25%
      type: RollingUpdate
    template:
      ...
  status:
    ...
```

As you may have noticed, a live resource manifest includes all the fields specified in the file plus dozens of new fields such as additional metadata, the `status` field, and other fields in the resource spec. All these additional fields are populated by the Deployment controller and contain important information about the resource's running state. The controller populates information about resource state in the `status` field and applies default values of all unspecified optional fields, such as `revisionHistoryLimit` and `strategy`. To preserve this information, `kubectl apply` merges the manifest from the specified file and the live resource manifest. As a result, the command updates only fields specified in the file, keeping everything else untouched. So if we decide to scale down the deployment and change the `replicas` field to 1, then kubectl changes only that field in the live resource and saves it back to Kubernetes using an update API.

In real life, we don't want to control all possible fields that influence resource behavior in a declarative way. It makes sense to leave some room for imperativeness and skip fields that should be changed dynamically. The `replicas` field of the Deployment resource is a perfect example. Instead of hardcoding the number of replicas you want to use, the Horizontal Pod Autoscaler can be used to dynamically scale up or scale down your application based on load.

HORIZONTAL POD AUTOSCALER The Horizontal Pod Autoscaler automatically scales the number of Pods in a replication controller, deployment, or replica set based on observed CPU utilization (or, with custom metrics support, on some other application-provided metric).

Let's go ahead and remove the `replicas` field from the Deployment manifest. After applying this change, the `replicas` field is reset to the default value of one replica. But wait! The `kubectl apply` command updates only those fields that are specified in the file and ignores the rest. How does it know that the `replicas` field was deleted? The additional information that allows kubectl to handle the delete use case is hidden in an annotation of the live resource. Every time the `kubectl apply` command updates a resource, it saves the input manifest in the `kubectl.kubernetes.io/last-applied-configuration` annotation. So when the command is executed the next time, it retrieves the most recently applied manifest from the annotation, representing the common ancestor of the new desired manifest and live resource manifest. This allows kubectl to execute a three-way diff/merge and properly handle the case where some fields are removed from the resource manifest.

> **THREE-WAY MERGE**   A *three-way merge* is a merge algorithm that automatically analyzes differences between two files while also considering the origin or the common ancestor of both files.

Finally, let's discuss the situations where `kubectl apply` might not work as expected and should be used carefully.

First off, you typically should not mix imperative commands, such as `kubectl edit` or `kubectl scale`, with declarative resource management. This will make the current state not match the `last-applied-configuration` annotation and will defeat the merge algorithm kubectl uses to determine deleted fields. The typical scenario is when you experiment with the resource using `kubectl edit` and want to roll back changes by applying the original manifests stored in files. Unfortunately, it might not work since changes made by the `kubectl edit` command are not stored anywhere. For example, if you temporarily add the resource `limits` field to the deployment, the `kubectl apply` won't remove it since the `limits` field is not mentioned in the `last-applied-configuration` annotation or the manifest from the file. The `kubectl replace` command similarly ignores the `last-applied-configuration` annotation and removes that annotation altogether after applying the changes. So if you make any changes imperatively, you should be ready to undo the changes using imperative commands before continuing with declarative configuration.

You should also be careful when you want to stop managing fields declaratively. A typical example of this problem is adding the Horizontal Pod Autoscaler to manage scaling the number of replicas for an existing deployment. Typically, before introducing the Horizontal Pod Autoscaler, the number of deployment replicas is managed declaratively. To pass control of the `replicas` field over to the Horizontal Pod Autoscaler, the `replicas` field must first be deleted from the file that contains the Deployment manifest. This is so the next `kubectl apply` does not override the `replicas` value set by the Horizontal Pod Autoscaler. However, don't forget that the `replicas` field might also be stored in the `last-applied-configuration` annotation. If that is the case, the missing `replicas` field in the manifest file will be treated as a field deletion, so whenever `kubectl apply` is run, the `replicas` value set imperatively by the Horizontal Pod Autoscaler will be removed from the live Deployment. The Deployment will scale down to the default of one replica.

In this section, we covered the different mechanisms for managing Kubernetes objects: imperative and declarative. You also learned a little about the internals of kubectl and how it identifies changes to apply to live objects. But at this point, you may be wondering what all this has to do with GitOps. The answer is simple: everything! Understanding how kubectl and Kubernetes manages changes to live objects is critical for understanding how the GitOps tools discussed in later chapters identify if the Git repository holding the Kubernetes configuration is in sync with the live state and how it tracks and applies changes.

2.3 Controller architecture

So far, we've learned about Kubernetes' declarative nature and the benefits it provides. Let's talk about what is behind each Kubernetes resource: the controller architecture. Understanding how controllers work will help us use Kubernetes more efficiently and understand how it can be extended.

Controllers are brains that understand what a particular kind of resource manifest means and execute the necessary work to make the system's actual state match the desired state as described by the manifest. Each controller is typically responsible for only one resource type. Through listening to the API server events related to the resource type being managed, the controller continuously watches for changes to the resource's configuration and performs the necessary work to move the current state toward the desired state. An essential feature of Kubernetes controllers is the ability to delegate work to other controllers. This layered architecture is powerful and allows you to reuse functionality provided by different resource types effectively. Let's consider a concrete example to understand the delegation concept better.

2.3.1 Controller delegation

The Deployment, ReplicaSet, and Pod resources perfectly demonstrate how delegation empowers Kubernetes. The Pod provides the ability to run one or more containers that have requested resources on a node in the cluster. This allows the Pod controller to focus simply on running an instance of an application and abstract the logic related to infrastructure provisioning, scaling up and down, networking, and other complicated details, leaving those to other controllers. Although the Pod resource provides many features, it is still not enough to run an application in production. We need to run multiple instances of the same application (for resiliency and performance), which means we need multiple Pods. The ReplicaSet controller solves this problem. Instead of directly managing multiple containers, it orchestrates multiple Pods and delegates the container orchestration to the Pod resource. Similarly, the

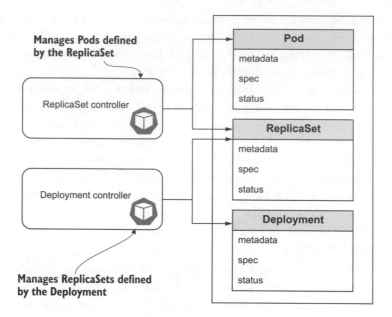

Figure 2.5   Kubernetes allows for a resource hierarchy. Higher-level resources providing additional functionality, such as ReplicaSets and Deployments, can manage other higher-level resources or primary resources, such as Pods. This is implemented through a series of controllers, each managing events related to the resources it controls.

Deployment controller leverages functionality provided by ReplicaSets to implement various deployment strategies such as rolling updates.

> **CONTROLLER DELEGATION BENEFIT**   With controller delegation, Kubernetes functionality can be easily extended to support new capabilities. For example, services that are not backward-compatible can only be deployed with a blue/ green strategy (not rolling updates). Controller delegation allows a new controller to be rewritten to support blue/green deployment and still leverage the Deployment controller functionality through delegation without reimplementing the Deployment controller's core functionality.

So as you can see from this example, controller delegation allows Kubernetes to build progressively more complex resources from simple ones.

2.3.2   *Controller pattern*

Although all controllers have different responsibilities, the implementation of each controller follows the same simple pattern. Each controller runs an infinite loop, and every iteration reconciles the desired and the actual state of the cluster resources it is responsible for. During reconciliation, the controller is looking for differences between the actual and desired states and making the changes necessary to move the current state towards the desired state.

The desired state is represented by the spec field of the resource manifest. The question is, how does the controller know about the actual state? This information is available in the status field. After every successful reconciliation, the controller updates the status field. The status field provides information about cluster state to end users and enables the work of higher-level controllers. Figure 2.6 demonstrates the reconciliation loop.

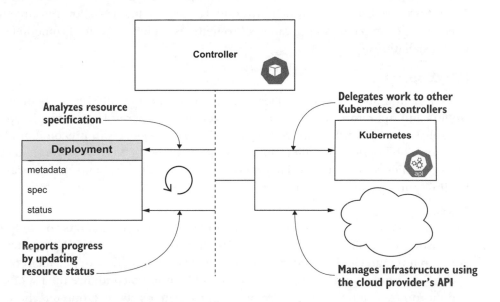

Figure 2.6 A controller operates in a continuous reconciliation loop where it attempts to converge the desired state as defined in the spec with the current state. Changes and updates to the resource are reported by updating the resource status. The controller may delegate work to other Kubernetes controllers or perform other operations, such as managing external resources using the cloud provider's API.

CONTROLLERS VS. OPERATORS

Two terms that are often confused are *operator* and *controller*. In this book, the term *GitOps operator* is used to describe continuous delivery tools instead of *GitOps controller*. The reason for this is we are representing a specific type of controller that is application and domain-specific.

KUBERNETES OPERATORS A *Kubernetes operator* is an application-specific controller that extends the Kubernetes API to create, configure, and manage instances of complex stateful applications on behalf of a Kubernetes user. It builds upon the primary Kubernetes resource and controller concepts and includes domain or application-specific knowledge to automate everyday tasks.

The terms *operator* and *controller* are often confused since they are sometimes used interchangeably, and the line between the two is often blurred. However, another way to think about it is that the term *operator* is used to describe application-specific controllers. All operators use the controller pattern, but not all controllers are operators. Generally speaking, controllers tend to manage lower-level, reusable building-block resources, whereas operators operate at a higher level and are application-specific. Some examples of controllers are all of the built-in controllers that manage Kubernetes native types (Deployments, Jobs, Ingresses, and so on), as well as third-party controllers such as cert-manager (which provisions and manages TLS certificates) and the Argo Workflow Controller, which introduces a new job-like workflow resource in the cluster. An example of an operator is Prometheus, which manages Prometheus database installations.

2.3.3   *NGINX operator*

After learning about the controller fundamentals and the differences between controllers and operators, we are ready to implement an operator! The sample operator will solve a real-life task: managing a suite of NGINX servers with preconfigured static content. The operator will allow the user to specify a list of NGINX servers and configure static files mounted on each server. The task is not trivial and demonstrates the flexibility and power of Kubernetes.

DESIGN

As mentioned earlier in this chapter, Kubernetes' architecture allows you to leverage an existing controller's functionality through delegation. Our NGINX controller is going to leverage Deployment resources to delegate the NGINX deployment task.

The next question is which resource should be used to configure the list of servers and customized static content. The most appropriate existing resource is the Config-Map. According to the official Kubernetes documentation, the ConfigMap is "an API object used to store non-confidential data in key-value pairs."[7] The ConfigMap can be consumed as environment variables, command-line arguments, or config files in a Volume. The controller will create a Deployment for each ConfigMap and mount the ConfigMap data into the default NGINX static website directory.

IMPLEMENTATION

Once we've decided on the design of the main building blocks, it is time to write some code. Most Kubernetes-related projects, including Kubernetes itself, are implemented using Go. However, Kubernetes controllers can be implemented using any language, including Java, C++, or even JavaScript. For the sake of simplicity, we are going to use a language that is most likely familiar to you: the Bash scripting language.

In section 2.3.2 we mentioned that each controller maintains an infinite loop and continuously reconciles the desired and actual state. In our example, the desired state is represented by the list of ConfigMaps. The most efficient way to loop through every

---

[7]   http://mng.bz/Yq67.

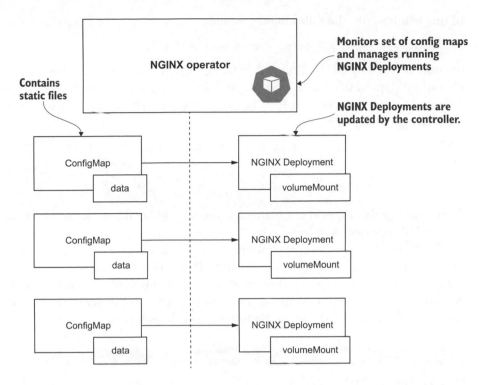

Figure 2.7   In the NGINX operator design, a ConfigMap is created containing the data to be served by NGINX. The NGINX operator creates a Deployment for each ConfigMap. Additional NGINX Deployments can be created simply by creating a ConfigMap with the web page data.

ConfigMap change is using the Kubernetes watch API. The watch feature is provided by the Kubernetes API for most resource types and allows the caller to be notified when a resource is created, modified, or deleted. The   kubectl utility allows watching for resource changes using the get command with the --watch flag. The --output-watch-events command instructs kubectl to output the change type, which takes one of the following values: ADDED, MODIFIED, or DELETED.

> **KUBECTL VERSION**   Ensure that you are using the latest version of kubectl for this tutorial (version 1.16 or later). The --output-watch-events option was added relatively recently.

Listing 2.4   Sample ConfigMap (http://mng.bz/GxRN)

```
apiVersion: v1
kind: ConfigMap
metadata:
  name: sample
data:
  index.html: hello world
```

In one window, run the following command:

```
$ kubectl get --watch --output-watch-events configmap
```

In another terminal window, run `kubectl apply -f sample.yaml` to create the sample ConfigMap. Notice the new output in the window running the `kubectl --watch` command. Now run `kubectl delete -f sample.yaml`. You should now see a DELETED event appear:

```
$ kubectl get --watch --output-watch-events configmap
EVENT       NAME      DATA    AGE
ADDED       sample    1       3m30s
DELETED     sample    1       3m40s
```

After running this experiment manually, you should be able to see how we can write our NGINX operator as a Bash script.

The `kubectl get --watch` command outputs a new line every time a ConfigMap resource is created, changed, or deleted. The script will consume the output of `kubectl get --watch` and either create a new Deployment or delete a Deployment depending on the output ConfigMap event type. Without further delay, the full operator implementation is shown in the following code listing.

Listing 2.5   NGINX controller (http://mng.bz/zxmZ)

```
#!/usr/bin/env bash

kubectl get --watch --output-watch-events configmap \      ◁─── This kubectl command
-o=custom-columns=type:type,name:object.metadata.name \         outputs all the events that
--no-headers | \                                                occur for configmap objects.
while read next; do                       ◁──── The output from kubectl is
                                                processed by this infinite loop.
    NAME=$(echo $next | cut -d' ' -f2)
    EVENT=$(echo $next | cut -d' ' -f1)      ◁──── The name of the configmap
                                                   and the event type are parsed
                                                   from the kubectl output.
    case $EVENT in
        ADDED|MODIFIED)               ◁──── If the configmap has been
            kubectl apply -f - << EOF        ADDED or MODIFIED, apply the
apiVersion: apps/v1                          NGINX deployment manifest
kind: Deployment                             (everything between the two
metadata: { name: $NAME }                    EOF tags) for that configmap.
spec:
  selector:
    matchLabels: { app: $NAME }
  template:
    metadata:
      labels: { app: $NAME }
      annotations: { kubectl.kubernetes.io/restartedAt: $(date) }
    spec:
      containers:
      - image: nginx:1.7.9
        name: $NAME
        ports:
        - containerPort: 80
```

```
        volumeMounts:
        - { name: data, mountPath: /usr/share/nginx/html }
      volumes:
      - name: data
        configMap:
          name: $NAME
EOF
          ;;
        DELETED)
            kubectl delete deploy $NAME
            ;;
    esac
done
```

> **If the configmap has been DELETED, delete the NGINX deployment for that configmap.**

TESTING

Now that the implementation is done, we are ready to test our controller. In real life, the controller is packaged into a Docker image and runs inside the cluster. It is OK to run the controller outside of the cluster for testing purposes, which is precisely what we are going to do. Using instructions from appendix A, start a minikube cluster, save the controller code into a file called controller.sh, and start it using this Bash command:

```
$ bash controller.sh
```

> **NOTE** This example requires kubectl version 1.16 or later.

The controller is running and waiting for the ConfigMap. Let's create one. Refer to listing 2.4 for the manifest of the ConfigMap.

We create the ConfigMap using the kubectl apply command:

```
$ kubectl apply -f sample.yaml
configmap/sample created
```

The controller notices the change and creates an instance of Deployment using the kubectl apply command:

```
$ bash controller.sh
deployment.apps/sample created
```

Exercise 2.2

Try accessing the NGINX controller by forwarding port 80 locally to make sure the controller works as expected. Try to delete or modify the ConfigMap and see how the controller reacts accordingly.

Exercise 2.3

Create additional ConfigMaps to launch an NGINX server for each member of your family that displays Hello <name>!. Also, don't forget to call/text/Snapchat them IRL.

Exercise 2.4

Write a Dockerfile to package the NGINX controller. Deploy it to your test Kubernetes cluster. Hint: You will need to create RBAC resources for the operator.

2.4   *Kubernetes + GitOps*

GitOps assumes that every piece of infrastructure is represented as a file stored in a revision control system, and there is an automated process that seamlessly applies changes to the application runtime environment. Without a system like Kubernetes, this is, unfortunately, easier said than done. There are too many things to worry about and many different technologies that do not work well together. These two assumptions often become an unsolvable obstacle that prevents the implementation of an efficient infrastructure-as-code process.

Kubernetes has dramatically improved the situation. As Kubernetes gained more and more adoption, the idea of infrastructure as code (IaC) has evolved, which resulted in the creation of new tooling that implements GitOps. So what is so special about Kubernetes, and how and why did it lead to the rise of GitOps?

Kubernetes enables GitOps by fully embracing declarative APIs as its primary mode of operation and providing the controller patterns and backend framework necessary to implement those APIs. The system was designed with the principles of declarative specifications and eventual consistency and convergence from its inception.

> **EVENTUAL CONSISTENCY**   *Eventual consistency* is a consistency model used in distributed computing to achieve high availability that informally guarantees that, if no new updates are made to a given data item, eventually all accesses to that item will return the last updated value.

This decision is what led to the prominence of GitOps in Kubernetes. Unlike traditional systems, in Kubernetes there are almost no APIs that can modify only a subset of some existing resources. For example, there is no API (and never will be) that changes only the container image of a Pod. Instead, the Kubernetes API server expects all API requests to provide a complete manifest of the resource to the API server. It was an intentional decision not to give any convenience APIs to users. As a result, Kubernetes users are essentially forced into a declarative mode of operation, which leads these same users to the need to store these declarative specifications somewhere. Git became the natural medium to store these specifications, and GitOps then became the natural delivery tool to deploy these manifests from Git.

2.5   *Getting started with CI/CD*

Now that you've learned the basic architecture and principles of a Kubernetes controller and how Kubernetes is a good fit for GitOps, it's time to implement your own GitOps operator. In this tutorial, we will first be creating a rudimentary GitOps operator to drive continuous delivery. This is followed by an example of how you would integrate continuous integration (CI) with a GitOps-based continuous delivery (CD) solution.

2.5.1 Basic GitOps operator

To implement your own GitOps operator, a continuously running control loop needs to be implemented that performs the three steps illustrated in figure 2.8.

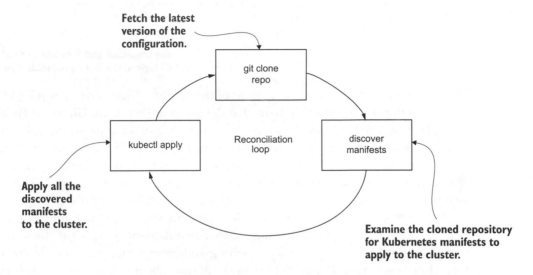

Figure 2.8 The GitOps reconciliation loop begins by cloning the repository to fetch the configuration repository's latest version into local storage. Next, the manifest discovery step walks the cloned repository's filesystem, looking for any Kubernetes manifests to apply to the cluster. Last, the `kubectl apply` step performs the actual deployment by applying all of the discovered manifests to the cluster.

While this control loop could be implemented in any number of ways, most simply, it could be implemented as a Kubernetes CronJob.

Listing 2.6 CronJob GitOps operator (http://mng.bz/Omyz)

```
apiVersion: batch/v1beta1
kind: CronJob
metadata:
  name: gitops-cron
  Namespace: gitops
spec:
  schedule: "*/5 * * * *"          ⊲── Executes the GitOps
  concurrencyPolicy: Forbid            reconciliation loop
  jobTemplate:                         every five minutes
    spec:                                         Prevents concurrent
      backoffLimit: 0                              executions of the job
      template:                ⊲── Doesn't retry failed jobs since this is a
        spec:                      recurring CronJob; retries happen naturally
          restartPolicy: Never              Doesn't restart the container
                                     ⊲──    when it completes
```

A Kubernetes Service account that has sufficient privileges to create and modify objects into the cluster

The Docker image that has the git, find, and kubectl binaries preloaded into it

```
serviceAccountName: gitops-serviceaccount
containers:
- name: gitops-operator
  image: gitopsbook/example-operator:v1.0
  command: [sh, -e, -c]
  args:
  - git clone https://github.com/gitopsbook/sample-app-
deployment.git /tmp/example &&
        find /tmp/example -name '*.yaml' -exec kubectl apply -f {} \;
```

The command and args fields contain the actual logic of the GitOps reconciliation loop.

The job template spec contains the meat of the operator logic. The CronJob `gitops-cron` contains the control loop logic that deploys manifests from Git to the cluster on a regularly scheduled basis. The `schedule` field is a `cron` expression, which in this example will result in the job being executed every five minutes. Setting the `concurrencyPolicy` to `Forbid` prevents concurrent executions of the job, allowing the current execution to complete before attempting to start a second. Note that this will only happen if a single execution takes longer than five minutes.

The `jobTemplate` is a Kubernetes Job template spec. The Job template spec contains a Pod template spec (jobTemplate.spec.template.spec), which is the same spec that you may be familiar with from writing Kubernetes manifests for Deployments, Pods, Jobs, and so on. The `backoffLimit` specifies the number of retries before considering a Job as failed. A value of zero means that it will not retry. Since this is a recurring CronJob, retries happen naturally, so there is no need to retry immediately. A `restartPolicy` of `Never` is required to prevent the Job from restarting the container when it completes, which is a container's normal behavior. The `service-AccountName` field references a Kubernetes Service account with sufficient privileges to create and modify objects in the cluster. Since this operator could potentially deploy any type of resource, the gitops-operator Service account should be bound to an admin-level ClusterRole.

The `command` and `args` fields contain the actual logic of the GitOps reconciliation loop. It consists of only two commands:

- `git clone`—Clones the latest repository to local storage
- `find`—Discovers YAML files in the repo, and for each YAML file located, executes the `kubectl apply` command

To use this, simply apply the CronJob to the cluster. Note that you would first need to apply the following supporting resources.

Listing 2.7   CronJob GitOps resources (http://mng.bz/KMln)

```
apiVersion: v1
kind: Namespace
```

Namespace gitops is where the CronJob and ServiceAccount will live.

```
metadata:
  name: gitops


---
apiVersion: v1
kind: ServiceAccount
metadata:
  name: gitops-serviceaccount
  Namespace: gitops


---
apiVersion: rbac.authorization.k8s.io/v1
kind: ClusterRoleBinding
metadata:
  name: gitops-operator
roleRef:
  apiGroup: rbac.authorization.k8s.io
  kind: ClusterRole
  name: admin
subjects:
- kind: ServiceAccount
  name: gitops-serviceaccount
  Namespace: gitops
```

ServiceAccount gitops-serviceaccount is the Kubernetes Service account that will have privileges to deploy to the cluster.

ClusterRoleBinding gitops-operator binds/ grants cluster admin-level privileges to the ServiceAccount, gitops-serviceaccount.

MULTIRESOURCE YAML FILES Management of multiple resources can be simplified by grouping them in the same file (separated by --- in YAML). Listing 2.7 is an example of a single YAML file defining multiple related resources.

This example is primitive, meant to illustrate the fundamental concepts of a GitOps continuous delivery operator. It is not meant for any real production use since it lacks many features needed in a real-world production environment. For example, it cannot prune any resources that are no longer defined in Git. Another limitation is that it does not deal with any credentials required to connect to the Git repository.

Exercise 2.5
Modify the CronJob to point to your own GitHub repository. Apply the new CronJob, and add YAML files to your repository. Verify that the corresponding Kubernetes resources are created.

2.5.2 *Continuous integration pipeline*

In the previous section, we implemented a basic GitOps CD mechanism that continuously delivers manifests in a Git repository to the cluster. The next step is to integrate this process with a CI pipeline, which publishes new container images and updates the Kubernetes manifests with the new image. GitOps integrates well with any CI system, as the process is more or less the same as a typical build pipeline. The main difference is that instead of the CI pipeline communicating directly to the Kubernetes API server, it commits the desired change into Git and trusts that sometime later, the new changes will be detected by the GitOps operator and applied.

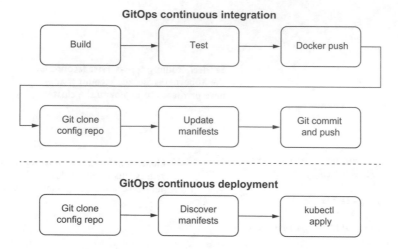

Figure 2.9   A GitOps CI pipeline is similar to a typical CI pipeline. The code is built and tested, and then the artifact (a tagged Docker image) is pushed to the image registry. The additional step is the GitOps CI pipeline also updates the manifests in the configuration repo with the latest image tag. This update may trigger a GitOps CD job to apply the updated manifests to the cluster.

The goal of a GitOps CI pipeline is to

- Build your application and run unit testing as necessary
- Publish a new container image to a container registry
- Update the Kubernetes manifests in Git to reflect the new image

The following example is a typical series of commands that would be executed in a CI pipeline to achieve this.

Listing 2.8   Example GitOps CI (http://mng.bz/9M18)

Uses the first seven characters of the current commit-SHA as the version to uniquely identify the artifacts from this build

Builds the container image, pushes it to a container registry, and incorporates the unique version as part of the container image tag

Builds and tests your application's binaries as you usually would

Clones the Git deployment repo containing the Kubernetes manifests

Updates the manifests with the new image

```
export VERSION=$(git rev-parse HEAD | cut -c1-7)
make build
make test

export NEW_IMAGE="gitopsbook/sample-app:${VERSION}"
docker build -t ${NEW_IMAGE} .
docker push ${NEW_IMAGE}

git clone http://github.com/gitopsbook/sample-app-deployment.git
cd sample-app-deployment

kubectl patch \
```

```
  --local \
  -o yaml \
  -f deployment.yaml \
  -p "spec:
      template:
        spec:
          containers:
          - name: sample-app
            image: ${NEW_IMAGE}" \
  > /tmp/newdeployment.yaml
mv /tmp/newdeployment.yaml deployment.yaml

git commit deployment.yaml -m "Update sample-app image to ${NEW_IMAGE}"
git push
```

Commits and pushes the manifest changes to the deployment configuration repo

This example pipeline is one way that a GitOps CI pipeline may look. There are some important points to highlight regarding the different choices you might make that would better suit your needs.

IMAGE TAGS AND THE TRAP OF THE LATEST TAG

Notice in the first two steps of the example pipeline, the current Git commit-SHA of the application's Git repository is used as a version variable, which is then incorporated as part of the container's image tag. A resulting container image in the example pipeline might look like `gitopsbook/sample-app:cc52a36`, where `cc52a36` is the commit-SHA at the time of the build.

It is important to use a unique version string (like a commit-SHA) that is different in each build since the version is incorporated as part of the container image tag. A common mistake that people make is to use `latest` as their image tag (such as `gitopsbook/sample-app:latest`) or reuse the same image tag from build to build. A naive pipeline might make the following mistake:

```
make build
docker build -t gitopsbook/sample-app:latest .
docker push gitopsbook/sample-app:latest
```

Reusing image tags from build to build is a terrible practice for several reasons.

The first reason why container tags should not be reused is that when container image tags are reused, Kubernetes will not deploy the new version to the cluster. This is because the second time the manifests are attempted to be applied, Kubernetes will not detect any change in the manifests, and the second `kubectl apply` will have zero effect. For example, say build #1 publishes the image `gitopsbook/sample-app:latest` and deploys it to the cluster. The Deployment manifest for this might look something like this.

> **Listing 2.9 Sample app deployment (http://mng.bz/j4m9)**

```
apiVersion: apps/v1
kind: Deployment
metadata:
```

```
    name: sample-app
spec:
  replicas: 1
  revisionHistoryLimit: 3
  selector:
    matchLabels:
      app: sample-app
  template:
    metadata:
      labels:
        app: sample-app
    spec:
      containers:
      - image: gitopsbook/sample-app:latest
        name: sample-app
        command:
          - /app/sample-app
        ports:
        - containerPort: 8080
```

When build #2 runs, even though a new container image for `gitopsbook/sample-app:latest` has been pushed to the container registry, the Kubernetes Deployment YAML for the application is the same as it was in build #1. The Deployment specs are the same from the perspective of Kubernetes; there is no difference between what is being applied in build #1 versus build #2. Kubernetes treats the second apply as a no-op (no operation) and does nothing. For Kubernetes to redeploy, something needs to be different in the Deployment spec from the first build to the second. Using unique container image tags ensures there is a difference.

Another reason for incorporating a unique version into the image tag is that it enables traceability. By incorporating something like the application's Git commit-SHA into the tag, there is never any question about what version of the software is currently running in the cluster. For example, you could run the following kubectl command, which outputs the images of all deployments in the Namespace:

```
$ kubectl get deploy -o wide | awk '{print $1,$7}' | column -t
NAME         IMAGES
sample-app  gitopsbook/sample-app:508d3df
```

By using the convention of tying container image tags to Git commit-SHAs of your application repository, you can trace the currently running version of the `sample-app` to commit `508d3df`. From there, you have full knowledge of exactly what version of your application is running in the cluster.

The third and possibly most important reason for not reusing image tags such as `latest` is that rollback to the older version becomes impossible. When you reuse image tags, you are overriding or rewriting the meaning of that overwritten image. Imagine the following sequence of events:

1   Build #1 publishes the container image `gitopsbook/sample-app:latest` and deploys it to the cluster.

2 Build #2 republishes the container image `gitopsbook/sample-app:latest`, overwriting the image tag deployed in build #1. It redeploys this image to the cluster.

3 Sometime after build #2 is deployed, it is discovered that a severe bug exists in the latest version of the code, and immediate rollback is necessary to the version created in build #1.

There is no easy way to redeploy the version of the `sample-app` created during build #1 because there is no image tag representing that version of the software. The second build overwrote the `latest` image tag, effectively making the original image unreachable (at least not without extreme measures).

For these reasons, it is not recommended to reuse image tags, such as `latest`, at least in production environments. With that said, in dev and test environments, continuously creating new and unique image tags (which likely never get cleaned up) could cause an excessive amount of disk usage in your container registry or become unmanageable just by the sheer number of image tags. In these scenarios, reusing image tags may be appropriate, understanding Kubernetes' behavior of not doing anything when the same specification is applied twice.

KUBECTL ROLLOUT RESTART Kubectl has a convenience command, `kubectl rollout restart`, which causes all the Pods of a deployment to restart (even if the image tag is the same). It is useful in dev and test scenarios where the image tag has been overwritten and redeploy is desired. It works by injecting an arbitrary timestamp into the Pod template metadata annotations. This causes the Pod spec to be different from what it was before, which causes a regular, rolling update of the Pods.

One thing to note is that our CI example uses a Git commit-SHA as the unique image tag. But instead of a Git commit-SHA, the image tag could incorporate any other unique identifier, such as a semantic version, a build number, a date/time string, or even a combination of these pieces of information.

SEMANTIC VERSION A *semantic version* is a versioning methodology that uses a three-digit convention (MAJOR.MINOR.PATCH) to convey the meaning of a version (such as v2.0.1). MAJOR is incremented when there are incompatible API changes. MINOR is incremented when functionality is added in a backward-compatible manner. PATCH is incremented when there are backward-compatible bug fixes.

Summary

- Kubernetes is a container orchestration system for deployment, scaling, and management of containers.
- Basic Kubernetes objects are Pod, Service, and Volume.
- The Kubernetes control plane consists of `kube-apiserver`, `kube-controller-manager`, and `kube-scheduler`.

- Each Kubernetes worker node runs `kubelet` and `kube-proxy`.
- A `Running` Service in a Pod is accessible from your computer using `kubectl port-forward`.
- Pods can be deployed by using imperative or declarative syntax. Imperative deployment is not idempotent, and declarative deployment is idempotent. For GitOps, declarative is the preferred method.
- Controllers are the brains in Kubernetes to bring the `Running` state into the desired state.
- A Kubernetes operator can be implemented simply as a shell script by monitoring ConfigMap changes and updating deployment.
- Kubernetes configuration is declarative.
- GitOps complements Kubernetes due to its declarative nature.
- GitOps operators trigger deployments to your Kubernetes cluster based on changes to revision-controlled configuration files stored in Git.
- A simple GitOps operator can be implemented as a script by regularly checking the manifest Git repo for changes.
- CI pipeline can be implemented as a script with steps to build the Docker image and update the manifest with the new image tag.

Part 2

Patterns and processes

Now that you have a good understanding of GitOps and Kubernetes, you are ready to go over the patterns and processes required to adopt GitOps.

Chapter 3 discusses the definition of an environment and how Kubernetes Namespaces nicely map an environment. It also covers branching strategy and config management to support your environment implementation.

Chapter 4 goes deep into the GitOps CI/CD pipeline with comprehensive descriptions of all stages necessary for a complete pipeline. It also covers code, image, and environment promotion as well as the rollback mechanism.

Chapter 5 describes various deployment strategies, including rolling update, blue-green, canary, and progressive delivery. It also covers how to implement each strategy by using native Kubernetes resources and other open source tools.

Chapter 6 discusses GitOps-driven deployment's attack surfaces and how to mitigate each area. It also reviews Jsonnet, Kustomize, and Helm and how to choose the right configuration management pattern for your use cases.

Chapter 7 discusses various strategies for managing secrets for GitOps. It also covers several secret management tools as well as native Kubernetes Secrets.

Chapter 8 explains the core concepts of observability and why it is important to GitOps. It also describes various methods to implement observability with GitOps and Kubernetes.

With a deeper understanding of GitOps patterns and processes, you are ready to transform your deployment process. You are also equipped with the knowledge to choose the GitOps tool that fits your situation best.

In part 3, we will cover several open source GitOps tools (Argo CD, Jenkins X, and Flux) that can simplify and automate your GitOps process. We will discuss the motivation and design of our tools and provide tutorials to get you started.

Environment management

In chapter 2, you learned how GitOps can deploy applications to a run-time environment. This chapter teaches us more about those different run-time environments and how Kubernetes Namespaces can define environment boundaries. We'll also learn about several configuration management tools (Helm, Kustomize, and Jsonnet) and how they can help manage an application's configuration consistently in multiple environments.

We recommend you read chapters 1 and 2 before reading this chapter.

3.1   *Introduction to environment management*

In software deployment, an *environment* is where code is deployed and executed. Different environments serve different purposes in the life cycle of software development. For example, a local development environment (aka laptop) is where engineers can create, test, and debug new code versions. After engineers complete the code development, the next step is to commit the changes to Git and kick off a deployment to different environments for integration testing and eventual production release. This process is known as *continuous integration/continuous deployment* (CI/CD) and typically consists of the following environments: *QA, E2E, Stage, and Prod.*

The QA environment is where the new code will be tested against hardware, data, and other production-like dependencies to ensure your service's correctness. If all tests pass in QA, the new code will be promoted to the E2E environment as a stable environment for other prerelease services to test/integrate with. QA and E2E environments are also known as preproduction (preprod) environments because they do not host production traffic or use production data.

When a new version of code is ready for production release, the code will typically deploy first in the Stage environment (which has access to actual production dependencies) to ensure all production dependencies are in place before the code goes live in the Prod environment. For example, new code may require a new DB schema update, and the Stage environment can be used to verify the new schema is in place. Configuration is done to only direct test traffic to the Stage environment so that any problems introduced by the new code would not impact actual customers. However, the Stage environment is typically configured to use the "real" production database operations. Tests performed on the Stage environment must be carefully reviewed to ensure they are safe to perform in production. Once all tests pass in Stage, the new code will finally be deployed in Prod for live production traffic. Since Stage and Prod both have access to production data, they are both considered production environments.

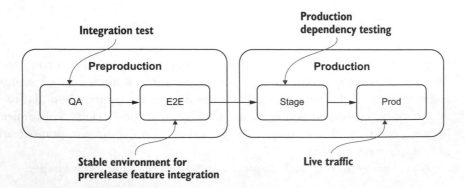

Figure 3.1   Preproduction has a QA environment for integration testing and an E2E environment for prerelease feature integration. Production environments may have a Staging environment for production dependency testing and the actual production environment for live traffic.

3.1.1 *Components of an environment*

An environment is composed of three equally important components:

- Code
- Run-time prerequisites
- Configuration

Code is the machine instructions of the application to execute specific tasks. To execute the code, run-time dependencies may also be required. For example, Node.js code will require the Node.js binary and other npm packages in order to execute successfully. In the case of Kubernetes, all run-time dependencies and code are packaged as a deployable unit (aka Docker image) and orchestrated through the Docker daemon. The application's Docker image can be confidently run in any environment, from the developer's laptop to the production cluster running in the cloud, because the image encapsulates the code and all the dependencies, eliminating potential incompatibilities between environments.

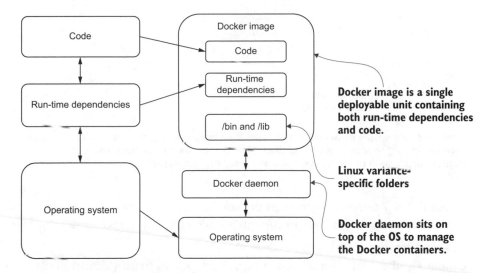

Figure 3.2 **The left side represents a non-container-based deployment that requires operating systems and run-time dependencies before the code can be deployed. The right side represents a container-based deployment that contains both code and run-time dependencies.**

Configuration of environment-specific application properties is typically deployed along with code and run-time dependencies, so the application instance can behave and connect to the correct dependencies per environment. Each environment could contain DB storage, distributed cache, or messaging (such as data) for isolation. Environments also have their own networking policy for ingress and egress for traffic isolation and custom access control. For example, ingress and egress can be configured to block traffic between preprod and prod environments for security. Access control can

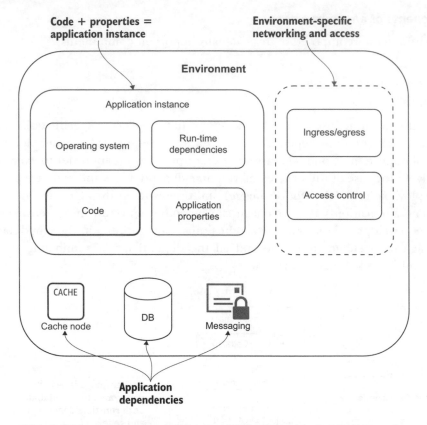

Figure 3.3   An environment consists of application instances, ingress/egress for networking, and access control to protect its resources. An environment also includes application dependencies such as cache, DB, or messaging.

be configured to restrict access to the production environment to only a small set of engineers, while preprod environments are accessible by the entire development team.

PICKING THE RIGHT GRANULARITY

Ultimately, the goal is for all new code to be deployed to production so that customers and end users can begin using it as soon as it passes quality testing. Delays in deploying code to production result in the postponement of realizing the new code's business value produced by the development team. Picking the right environment granularity is critical for code to be deployed without delay. Factors to be considered are

- *Release independence*—If the code needs to be bundled with code from other teams to be deployed, one team's deployment cycle is subject to the readiness of the code produced by the other teams. The right granularity should enable your code to be deployed without dependencies on other teams/code.
- *Test boundary*—Like release independence, testing of the new code should be independent of other code releases. If new code testing depends on other teams/code, the release cycle will be subject to the readiness of the others.

- *Access control*—In addition to separate access control for preprod and prod, each environment can limit access control to only the team actively working on the codebase.
- *Isolation*—Each environment is a logical work unit and should be isolated from other environments to avoid the "noisy neighbor" problem and limit access from different environments for security reasons.

3.1.2 Namespace management

Namespaces are a natural construct in Kubernetes to support environments. They allow dividing cluster resources among multiple teams or projects. Namespaces provide a scope for unique resource naming, resource quotas, RBAC, hardware isolation, and network configuration:

Kubernetes Namespace ~= Environment

In each Namespace, the application instance (aka Pod) is one or more Docker containers injected with environment-specific application properties during deployment. These application properties define how the environment should run (such as feature flags) and what external dependencies should be used (such as database connection strings).

In addition to the application Pods, the Namespace may also contain other Pods that provide additional functionality required by the environment.

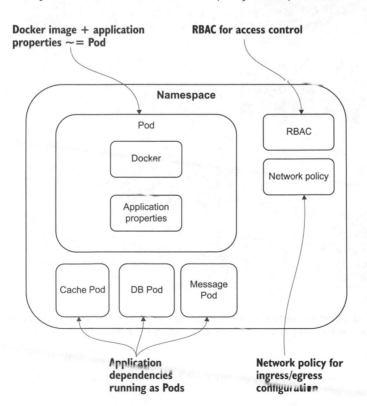

Figure 3.4 A Namespace is the equivalent of an environment in Kubernetes. Namespaces may consist of Pods (application instance), network policies (ingress/egress), and RBAC (access control), as well as application dependencies running in separate Pods.

RBAC is a method of regulating access to computer or network resources based on the roles of individual users within an enterprise. In Kubernetes, a role contains rules that represent a set of permissions. Permissions are purely additive (there are no deny rules). A role can be defined within a Namespace with a role or clusterwide with a ClusterRole.

Namespaces can also have dedicated hardware and networking policies to optimize their configuration based on application requirements. For example, a CPU-intensive application can deploy in a Namespace with dedicated multicore hardware. Another service requiring heavy disk I/O can be deployed in a separate Namespace with high-speed SSD. Each Namespace can also define its networking policy (ingress/egress) to limit cross-Namespace traffic or accessing other Namespaces within the cluster using unqualified DNS names.

DEPLOY AN APP IN TWO DIFFERENT ENVIRONMENTS

In this section, you will learn how to deploy the same app in two different environments (a test environment called guestbook-qa and a preprod end-to-end environment called guestbook-e2e) with different configurations using Namespaces. The application we will use for this exercise is the Guestbook Kubernetes example application.[1]

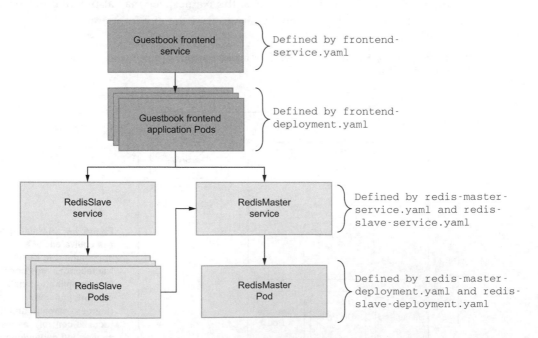

Figure 3.5   Guestbook front\end architecture will have a service to expose the guestbook web frontend to live traffic. The backend architecture consists of Redis Master and Redis Slave for the data.

---

[1]   https://kubernetes.io/docs/tutorials/stateless-application/guestbook.

Exercise overview

1 Create environment Namespaces (guestbook-qa and guestbook-e2e).
2 Deploy the guestbook application to the guestbook-qa environment.
3 Test the guestbook-qa environment.
4 Promote the guestbook application to the guestbook-e2e environment.
5 Test the guestbook-e2e environment.

VERIFY KUBERNETES CLUSTER CONNECTION   Before you begin, verify that you have correctly configured your KUBECONFIG environment variable to point to the desired Kubernetes cluster. Please refer to appendix A for more information.

First, create the guestbook-qa and guestbook-e2e Namespaces for each of your guestbook environments:

```
$ kubectl create namespace guestbook-qa
namespace/guestbook-qa created
$ kubectl create namespace guestbook-e2e
namespace/guestbook-e2e created
$ kubectl get namespaces
NAME              STATUS    AGE
default           Active    2m27s
guestbook-e2e     Active    9s
guestbook-qa      Active    19s
kube-node-lease   Active    2m30s
kube-public       Active    2m30s
kube-system       Active    2m30s
```

Now you can deploy the guestbook application to the guestbook-qa environment using the following commands:

```
$ export K8S_GUESTBOOK_URL=https://k8s.io/examples/application/guestbook
$ kubectl apply -n guestbook-qa -f ${K8S_GUESTBOOK_URL}/redis-master-
    deployment.yaml
deployment.apps/redis-master created
$ kubectl apply -n guestbook-qa -f ${K8S_GUESTBOOK_URL}/redis-master-
    service.yaml
service/redis-master created
$ kubectl apply -n guestbook-qa -f ${K8S_GUESTBOOK_URL}/redis-slave-
    deployment.yaml
deployment.apps/redis-slave created
$ kubectl apply -n guestbook-qa -f ${K8S_GUESTBOOK_URL}/redis-slave-service.yaml
service/redis-slave created
$ kubectl apply -n guestbook-qa -f ${K8S_GUESTBOOK_URL}/frontend-deployment.yaml
deployment.apps/frontend created
$ kubectl apply -n guestbook-qa -f ${K8S_GUESTBOOK_URL}/frontend-service.yaml
service/frontend created
```

Before we proceed, let's test that the guestbook-qa environment is working as expected. Use the following minikube command to find the URL to the guestbook-qa service, and then open the URL in your web browser:

```
$ minikube -n guestbook-qa service frontend --url
http://192.168.99.100:31671
$ open http://192.168.99.100:31671
```

In the Messages text edit of the guestbook application, type something like `This is the guestbook-qa environment` and press the Submit button. Your screen should look something like figure 3.6.

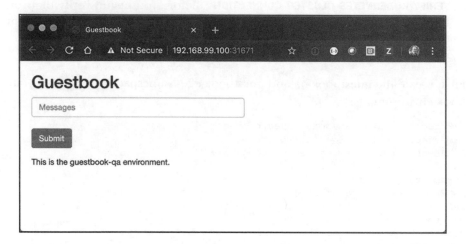

Figure 3.6   When you have your guestbook app deployed to QA, you can open the browser and submit a test message to verify your deployment.

Now that we have the Guestbook application running in the guestbook-qa environment and have tested that it is working correctly, let's promote guestbook-qa to the guestbook-e2e environment. In this case, we are going to use exactly the same YAML as was used in the guestbook-qa environment. This is similar to how your automated CD pipeline would work:

```
$ export K8S_GUESTBOOK_URL=https://k8s.io/examples/application/guestbook
$ kubectl apply -n guestbook-e2e -f ${K8S_GUESTBOOK_URL}/redis-master-
    deployment.yaml
deployment.apps/redis-master created
$ kubectl apply -n guestbook-e2e -f ${K8S_GUESTBOOK_URL}/redis-master-
    service.yaml
service/redis-master created
$ kubectl apply -n guestbook-e2e -f ${K8S_GUESTBOOK_URL}/redis-slave-
    deployment.yaml
deployment.apps/redis-slave created
$ kubectl apply -n guestbook-e2e -f ${K8S_GUESTBOOK_URL}/redis-slave-
    service.yaml
service/redis-slave created
$ kubectl apply -n guestbook-e2e -f ${K8S_GUESTBOOK_URL}/frontend-
    deployment.yaml
deployment.apps/frontend created
```

```
$ kubectl apply -n guestbook-e2e -f ${K8S_GUESTBOOK_URL}/frontend-
    service.yaml
service/frontend created
```

Great! The Guestbook app has now been deployed to the guestbook-e2e environment. Now let's test that the guestbook-e2e environment is working correctly:

```
$ minikube -n guestbook-e2e service frontend --url
http://192.168.99.100:31090
$ open http://192.168.99.100:31090
```

Similar to what you did in the guestbook-qa environment, type something like This is the guestbook-e2e environment, NOT the guestbook-qa environment! in the Messages text edit and press the Submit button. Your screen should look something like figure 3.7.

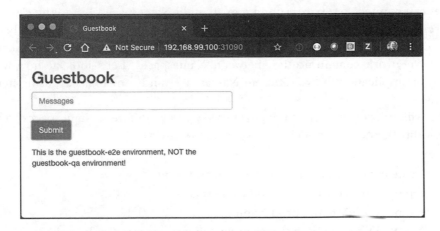

Figure 3.7   When you have your guestbook app deployed to QA, you can open the browser and submit a test message to verify your deployment.

The important thing here is to realize that you have identical applications running in two different environments defined by Kubernetes Namespaces. Notice that each application is maintaining an independent copy of its data. If you enter a message in the QA Guestbook, it doesn't show up in the E2E Guestbook. These are two different environments.

Exercise 3.1

Now that you have created two preprod environments, guestbook-qa and guestbook-e2e, create two additional production environments, guestbook-stage and guestbook-prod, in a new production cluster.

> **HINT** You can create a new minikube cluster with the command minikube start -p production and switch between them using kubectl config use-context <name>.

Case study: Intuit environment management

At Intuit, we organize our Namespaces per service and per environment in each AWS region with the separation of preprod and prod clusters. A typical service will have six Namespaces: QA, E2E, Stage/Prod West, and Stage/Prod East. QA and E2E Namespaces will be in the preprod cluster with open access to the corresponding team. Stage/Prod West and Stage/Prod East will be in the production cluster with restricted access.[a]

---
[a] https://www.cncf.io/case-study/intuit.

3.1.3   *Network isolation*

A critical aspect of defining environments for deploying your application is to ensure only the intended clients can access the specific environment. By default, all Namespaces can connect to services running in all other Namespaces. But in the case of two different environments, such as QA and Prod, you would not want cross-talk between those environments. Luckily, it is possible to apply a Namespace network policy that restricts network communication between Namespaces. Let's look at how we can deploy an application to two different Namespaces and control access using network policies.

We will go over the steps to deploy services in two different Namespaces. You will also modify the network policies and observe the effects.

Overview

1 Create environment Namespaces (qa and prod).
2 Deploy curl to the qa and prod Namespaces.
3 Deploy NGINX to the prod Namespace.
4 Curl NGINX from both the qa and prod Namespaces (both work).
5 Block incoming traffic to the prod Namespace from the qa Namespace.
6 Curl NGINX from the qa Namespace (blocked).

EGRESS   *Egress* traffic is network traffic that begins inside a network and proceeds through its routers to a destination somewhere outside the network.

INGRESS   *Ingress* traffic is composed of all the data communications and network traffic originating from external networks.

VERIFY KUBERNETES CLUSTER CONNECTION Before you begin, verify that you have correctly configured your KUBECONFIG environment variable to point to the desired Kubernetes cluster. Please refer to appendix A for more information.

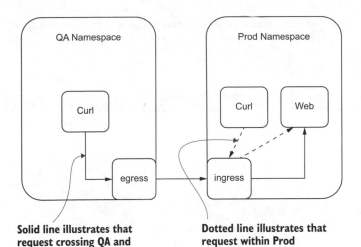

Figure 3.8 For the Curl Pod in QA to reach the Web Pod in Prod, the Curl Pod will need to go through the QA egress to reach the Prod ingress. Then the Prod ingress will route the traffic to the Web Pod in Prod.

Solid line illustrates that request crossing QA and Prod will be intercepted by QA egress and Prod ingress.

Dotted line illustrates that request within Prod will only be intercepted by Prod ingress.

First, create the Namespaces for each of your environments:

```
$ kubectl create namespace qa
namespace/qa created
$ kubectl create namespace prod
namespace/prod created
$ kubectl get namespaces
NAME             STATUS    AGE
qa               Active    2m27s
prod             Active    9s
```

Now we will create a Pod in both Namespaces from where we can run the Linux command `curl`:

```
$ kubectl -n qa apply -f curlpod.yaml
$ kubectl -n prod apply -f curlpod.yaml
```

Listing 3.1   curlpod.yaml

```
apiVersion: v1
kind: Pod
metadata:
  name: curl-pod
spec:
  containers:
  - name: curlpod
    image: radial/busyboxplus:curl
    command:
    - sh
    - -c
    - while true; do sleep 1; done
```

In the prod Namespace, we will run an NGINX server that will receive the `curl` HTTP request:

```
$ kubectl -n prod apply -f web.yaml
```

Listing 3.2   web.yaml

```
apiVersion: v1
kind: Pod
metadata:
  name: web
spec:
  containers:
  - image: nginx
    imagePullPolicy: Always
    name: nginx
    ports:
    - containerPort: 80
      protocol: TCP
```

By default, Pods running in a Namespace can send network traffic to other Pods running in different Namespaces. Let's prove this by executing a `curl` command from the Pod in the qa Namespace to the NGINX Pod in the prod Namespace:

```
$ kubectl describe pod web -n prod | grep IP        ⮜──┘ Gets the web Pod
                                                          IP address
$ kubectl -n qa   exec curl-pod -- curl -I http://<web pod ip>   ⮜── Gets back
                                                                     HTTP 200
$ kubectl -n prod exec curl-pod -- curl -I http://<web pod ip>   ⮜── Gets back
                                                                     HTTP 200
```

Typically, you never want your qa and prod environments to have dependencies between each other. It may be that if both instances of the application were properly configured, there would not be dependencies between qa and prod, but what if there was a bug in the configuration of qa where it was accidentally sending traffic to prod? You could potentially be corrupting production data. Or even within production, what if one environment was hosting your marketing site and another environment was hosting an HR application with sensitive data? In these cases, it may be appropriate to block network traffic between Namespaces or only allow network traffic between particular Namespaces. This can be accomplished by adding a `Network-Policy` to a Namespace.

Let's add a `NetworkPolicy` to our Pods in each Namespace:

```
$ kubectl apply -f block-other-namespace.yaml
```

> **CONTAINER NETWORK INTERFACE**   Network policy is supported only if Container Network Interface (CNI)[2] is configured (neither minikube nor Docker

---

[2]   http://mng.bz/8N1g.

desktop). Please refer to appendix A for more information to test the configuration of network policies.

Listing 3.3   Network policy (http://mng.bz/WdAX)

```
apiVersion: networking.k8s.io/v1
kind: NetworkPolicy
metadata:                              Applies to
  namespace: prod          ◁─┘         Namespace prod
  name: block-other-namespace
spec:                                  Selects all Pods
  podSelector: {}          ◁─┘         in Namespace prod
  ingress:
  - from:                      Specifies ingress to allow requests coming from prod Namespace
    - podSelector: {}  ◁─┘     only. Requests from other Namespaces will be blocked.
```

This `NetworkPolicy` is applied to the prod Namespace and allows only ingress (incoming network traffic) from the prod Namespace. Correctly using `Network-Policy` constraints is a critical aspect of defining environment boundaries.

With the `NetworkPolicy` applied, we can rerun our `curl` commands to verify that each Namespace is now isolated from the others:

```
$ kubectl -n qa exec curl-pod -- curl -I http://<web pod ip>    ◁─┘  Curl from namespace
                                                                     qa is blocked!
$ kubectl -n prod exec curl-pod -- curl -I http://<web pod ip>  ◁─┐
                                                                  │  Gets back
                                                                  │  Http 200
```

3.1.4 Preprod and prod clusters

Now that you know how to create multiple environments using Namespaces, it might seem like a trivial thing to use one cluster and create all the environments you need on that single cluster. For example, you may need QA, E2E, Stage, and Prod environments for your application. However, depending on your specific use case, this may not be the best approach. Our recommendation is to have two clusters to host your environments, one preprod cluster for preproduction environments and one prod cluster for production environments.

The primary reason for having two separate clusters to host your environments is to protect your production environment from accidental outages or other impacts related to work being done with the preproduction environments.

> **CLUSTER ISOLATION IN AMAZON WEB SERVICES (AWS)**   In AWS, a separate VPC can be created for preprod and prod as a logical boundary to isolate the traffic and data. For even stronger isolation and more control on production credentials and access, the separate production virtual private cloud should be hosted in a different production AWS account.

Someone might ask why we should have so many environments and separation of preprod and prod clusters. The simple answer is that a preprod cluster is needed to test the code before release into the production cluster. At Intuit, we use our QA environment for integration testing and E2E environment as a stable environment for other services to test prerelease features. If you are doing multibranch concurrent development, you can also configure additional preprod test environments for each of the branches.

A key advantage of configuration management with Kubernetes is that since it uses Docker Containers, which are immutable portable images, the only differences with the deployments between environments is the Namespace configuration, environment-specific properties, and application dependencies such as caching or database. Preprod testing can verify your service code's correctness, while the stage environment in the production cluster can be used to verify your application dependencies' correctness.

Preprod and prod clusters should follow the same security best practices and operational rigor. Security issues can be detected early in the development cycle, and developer productivity is not interrupted if preprod clusters are operated with the same standards as production.

3.2   *Git strategies*

Using a separate Git repository to hold your Kubernetes manifests (aka config), keeping the config separate from your application source code, is highly recommended for the following reasons:

- It provides a clean separation of application code and application config. There will be times when you wish to modify the manifests without triggering an entire CI build. For example, you likely do not want to trigger a build if you simply want to bump the number of replicas in a Deployment spec.

> **APPLICATION CONFIG VS. SECRETS**   In GitOps, application configuration generally excludes secrets since using Git to store secrets is a bad practice. There are several approaches for handling sensitive information (passwords, certificates, and so on), discussed in detail in chapter 7.

- Audit log is cleaner. For auditing purposes, a repo that only holds configuration will have a much cleaner Git history of what changes were made without the noise coming from check-ins due to regular development activity.
- Your application may comprise services built from multiple Git repositories but deployed as a single unit. Frequently, microservices applications are composed of services with different versioning schemes and release cycles (such as ELK, Kafka, and Zookeeper). It may not make sense to store the manifests in one of the source code repositories of a single component.
- Access is separated. The developers who are developing the application may not necessarily be the same people who can/should push to production environments, either intentionally or unintentionally. Having separate repositories allows commit access to be given to the source code repo and not the application config repo, which can be reserved for a more select group of team members.

- If you are automating your CI pipeline, pushing manifest changes to the same Git repository can trigger an infinite loop of build jobs and Git commit triggers. Having a separate repo to push config changes to prevents this from happening.

For your code repositories, you can use whatever branching strategy you like (such as GitFlow) since it is only used for your CI. For your config repositories (which will be used for your CD), you need to consider the following strategies based on your organization size and tooling.

3.2.1 Single branch (multiple directories)

With the single-branch strategy, the main branch will always contain the exact config used in each environment. There will be a default config for all environments with an environment-specific overlay defined in separate environment-specific directories. The single-branch strategy can be easily supported by tools such as Kustomize (section 3.3).

Figure 3.9   The single-branch strategy will have one master branch and a subdirectory for each environment. Each subdirectory will contain the environment-specific overlay.

In our CI/CD example, we will have environment-specific override directories for qa, e2e, stage, and prod. Each directory will contain environment-specific settings such as replica count, CPU, and memory request/limit.

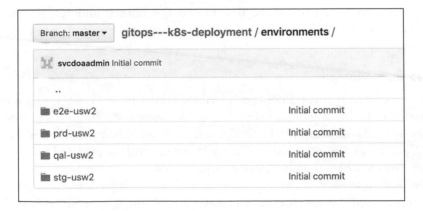

Figure 3.10   Example with qal, e2e, stage, and production subdirectories. Each subdirectory will contain overlays such as replica count, CPU, and memory request/limit

3.2.2   *Multiple branches*

With the multiple-branches strategy, each branch is equivalent to an environment. The advantage here is that each branch will have the exact manifest for the environment without using any tool such as Kustomize. Each branch will also have a separate commit history for audit trail and rollback if needed. The disadvantage is that there will be no sharing of the common config among environments since tooling such as Kustomize does not work with Git branches.

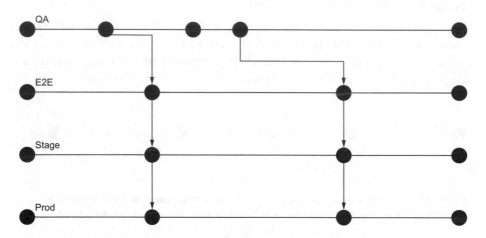

Figure 3.11   In the multiple-branches strategy, each branch is equivalent to an environment. Each branch will contain the exact manifest instead of an overlay.

It may be possible to merge common infrastructure changes between multiple branches. Suppose that a new resource needs to be added to all environments. In that case, that resource could be added first to the QA branch and tested, and then merged (cherry-picked) into each successive branch after the appropriate testing was completed.

3.2.3   *Multirepo vs. monorepo*

If you are in a startup environment with a single scrum team, you may not want (or need) the complexity of multiple repositories. All your code could be in one code repository with all your deployment configuration in one deployment repository.

However, if you are in an enterprise environment with dozens (or hundreds) of developers, you will likely want to have multiple repos so that teams can be decoupled from each other and each run at their own speed. For example, different teams within the organization will have a different cadence and release process for their code. If a mono config repo is used, some features may be completed for weeks but need to wait for the scheduled release. This could mean delaying getting features into the hands of end users and discovering potential code issues. Rollback is also problematic since one code defect will require rolling back all changes from every team.

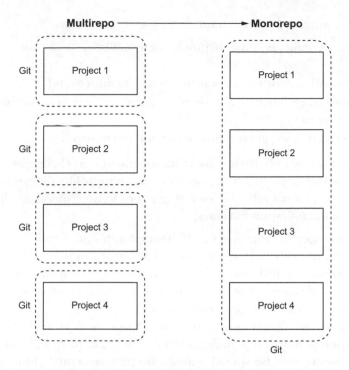

Figure 3.12   Monorepo is a single Git repo with multiple projects. In multirepo, each project will have a dedicated Git repo.

Another consideration for using multiple repos is to organize applications based on capabilities. If the repos are focused on discrete deployable capabilities, it will be easier to move the responsibility of those capabilities among teams (such as after a reorg).

3.3   *Configuration management*

As we saw in the tutorial and exercises in section 3.1, environment configuration management can be as simple as having a directory for each environment that contains the YAML manifests of all resources that should be deployed. All the values in these YAML manifests can be hardcoded to the particular values desired for that environment. To deploy, you run `kubectl apply -f <directory>`.

However, the reality is that managing multiple configurations in that way becomes unwieldy and error prone quickly. What if you need to add a new resource? You need to make sure you add that resource to the YAML in each of your environments. What if that resource needs specific properties (like replicas) to have different values for different environments? You need to carefully make all the correct customizations in all the right files.

Several tools have been developed that address this need for configuration management. We will review each of the more popular configuration management tools later in this section. But first, let's discuss what the factors are that you should consider when choosing which particular tool to use.

Good Kubernetes configuration tools have the following properties:

- *Declarative*—The config is unambiguous, deterministic, and not system-dependent.
- *Readable*—The config is written in a way that is easy to understand.
- *Flexible*—The tool helps facilitate and does not get in the way of accomplishing what you are trying to do.
- *Maintainable*—The tool should promote reuse and composability.

There are several reasons why Kubernetes config management is so challenging: what sounds like a simple act of deploying an application can have wildly different, even opposing, requirements, and it's difficult for a single tool to accommodate all such requirements. Imagine the following use cases:

- A cluster operator deploys third-party, off-the-shelf applications such as Word-Press to their cluster with little to no customization of those apps. The most important criterion for this use case is to easily receive updates from an upstream source and upgrade their application as quickly and seamlessly as possible (new versions, security patches, and so on).
- A software-as-a-service (SaaS) application developer deploys their bespoke application to one or more environments (Dev, Staging, Prod-West, Prod-East). These environments may be spread across different accounts, clusters, and Namespaces with subtle differences between them, so configuration reuse is paramount. For this use case, it is important to go from a Git commit in their codebase to deploy to each of their environments in a fully automated way and manage their environments in a straightforward and maintainable way. These developers have zero interest in semantic versioning of their releases since they might be deploying multiple times a day. The notion of major, minor, and patch versions ultimately has no meaning for their application.

As you can see, these are entirely different use cases, and more often than not, a tool that excels at one doesn't handle the other well.

3.3.1 Helm

Love it or hate it, Helm, being the first config tool on the scene, is an integral part of the Kubernetes ecosystem, and chances are that you've installed something at one point or another by running `helm install`.

The important thing to note about Helm is that it is a self-described package manager for Kubernetes and doesn't claim to be a configuration management tool. However, since many people use Helm templating for precisely this purpose, it belongs in this discussion. These users invariably end up maintaining several values.yaml, one for each environment (such as values-base.yaml, values-prod.yaml, and values-dev.yaml) and then parameterize their chart in such a way that environment-specific values can be used in the chart. This method more or less works, but it makes the templates unwieldy since Go templating is flat and needs to support every conceivable parameter for each environment, which ultimately litters the entire template with `{{-if / else}}` switches.

The good:

- *There's a chart for that.* Undoubtedly, Helm's biggest strength is its excellent chart repository. Just recently, we needed to run a highly available Redis, without a persistent volume, to be used as a throwaway cache. There is something to be said for just being able to throw the `redis-ha` chart into your namespace, set `persistentVolume.enabled: false`, and point your service at it, and someone else has already done the hard work of figuring out how to run Redis reliably on a Kubernetes cluster.

The bad:

- *Go templating*—"Look at that beautiful and elegant Helm template!" said no one ever. It is well known that Helm templates suffer from a readability problem. We don't doubt that this will be addressed with Helm 3's support for Lua, but until then, well, we hope you like curly braces.
- *Complicated SaaS CD pipelines*—For SaaS CI/CD pipelines, assuming you are using Helm the way it is intended (i.e., by running `helm install/upgrade`), an automated deploy in your pipeline might go several ways. In the best case, deploying from your pipeline will be as simple as

```
$ docker push mycompany/guestbook:v2
$ helm upgrade guestbook --set guestbook.image.tag=v2
```

But in the worst case, where existing chart parameters cannot support your desired manifest changes, you go through a whole song and dance of bundling a new Helm chart, bumping its semantic version, publishing it to a chart repository, and redeploying with a Helm upgrade. In the Linux world, this is analogous to building a new RPM, publishing the RPM to a Yum repository, and then running `yum install`, all so you can get your shiny new CLI into /usr/bin. While this model works great for packaging and distribution, it's an unnecessarily complicated and roundabout way to deploy your applications in the case of bespoke SaaS applications. For this reason, many people choose to run `helm template` and pipe the output to `kubectl apply`, but at that point, you are better off using some other tool that is specifically designed for this purpose.

- *Nondeclarative by default*—If you ever added `--set param=value` to any one of your Helm deploys, I'm sorry to tell you that your deployment process is not declarative. These values are only recorded in the Helm ConfigMap netherworld (and maybe your Bash history), so hopefully you wrote those down somewhere. This is far from ideal if you ever need to re-create your cluster from scratch. A slightly better way would be to record all parameters in a new custom values.yaml that you can store in Git and deploy using `-f my-values.yaml`. However, this is annoying when you're deploying an OTS chart from the Helm stable, and you don't have an obvious place to store that values.yaml side-by-side to the relevant chart. The best solution that I've come up with is composing a new dummy chart with the upstream chart as a dependency. Still, we have yet to find a canonical way of updating a parameter in a values.yaml in a pipeline using a one-liner, short of running `sed`.

CONFIGURING MANIFESTS FOR PREPROD VS. PROD USING HELM

In this exercise, we will take the guestbook app we deployed earlier in the chapter and use Helm to manage its configuration for different environments.

Helm uses the following directory structure to structure its charts.

Listing 3.4   Helm chart directory structure

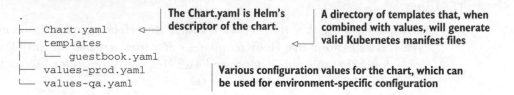

```
.
├── Chart.yaml          ◁─────┐   The Chart.yaml is Helm's          A directory of templates that, when
├── templates                     descriptor of the chart.         combined with values, will generate
│   └── guestbook.yaml                                        ◁──  valid Kubernetes manifest files
├── values-prod.yaml
└── values-qa.yaml           Various configuration values for the chart, which can
                             be used for environment-specific configuration
```

A Helm template file uses a text templating language to generate Kubernetes YAML. Helm template files look like Kubernetes YAML, but with template variables sprinkled throughout the file. As a result, even a basic Helm template file ends up looking like this.

Listing 3.5   Sample app Helm template

```
apiVersion: apps/v1
kind: Deployment
metadata:
  name: {{ include "sample-app.fullname" . }}
  labels:
    {{- include "sample-app.labels" . | nindent 4 }}
spec:
  selector:
    matchLabels:
      {{- include "sample-app.selectorLabels" . | nindent 6 }}
  template:
    metadata:
    {{- with .Values.podAnnotations }}
      annotations:
        {{- toYaml . | nindent 8 }}
    {{- end }}
      labels:
        {{- include "sample-app.selectorLabels" . | nindent 8 }}
    spec:
      containers:
        - name: {{ .Chart.Name }}
          image: "{{ .Values.image.repository }}:{{ .Values.image.tag |
    default .Chart.AppVersion }}"
          {{- with .Values.environmentVars }}
          env:
            {{- toYaml . | nindent 12 }}
          {{- end }}
```

As you can see, Helm templates are not very readable. But they are incredibly flexible since the final resulting YAML can be customized in any way the user desires.

Finally, when customizing a specific environment using Helm charts, an environment-specific values file is created containing the values to use for that environment. For example, for the production version of this application, the values file may look like this.

Listing 3.6   Sample app Helm values

```
# Default values for sample-app.
# This is a YAML-formatted file.
# Declare variables to be passed into your templates.

image:
  repository: gitopsbook/sample-app
  tag: "v0.2"                        ←—— Overrides the image tag whose
                                          default is the chart appVersion
nameOverride: "sample-app"
fullnameOverride: "sample-app"

podAnnotations: {}

environmentVars: [       ←—— Sets the DEBUG environment
  {                           variable to true
    name: "DEBUG",
    value: "true"
  }
]
```

The final qa manifest can be installed to minikube in the qa-heml namespace with the following commands:

```
$ kubectl create namespace qa-helm
$ helm template . --values values.yaml | kubectl apply -n qa-helm -f -
deployment.apps/sample-app created
$ kubectl get all -n qa-helm
NAME                          READY    STATUS      RESTARTS    AGE
pod/sample-app-7595985689-46fbj  1/1   Running     0           11s

NAME                          READY    UP-TO-DATE  AVAILABLE   AGE
deployment.apps/sample-app    1/1      1           1           11s

NAME                                    DESIRED  CURRENT   READY   AGE
replicaset.apps/sample-app-7595985689   1        1         1       11s
```

Exercise 3.2

In the preceding tutorial, we parameterized the guestbook image tag for QA and Prod environments using Helm. Add additional parameterization for the number of replicas desired for each guestbook deployment. Set the number of replicas to 1 for QA and 3 for Prod.

3.3.2 *Kustomize*

Kustomize was created around the design principles described in Brian Grant's excellent dissertation regarding declarative application management.[3] Kustomize has seen a meteoric rise in popularity, and, in the eight months since it started, it has already been merged into kubectl. Whether or not you agree with how it was merged, it goes without saying that Kustomize applications will now be a permanent mainstay in the Kubernetes ecosystem and will be the default choice that users will gravitate toward for config management. Yes, it helps to be part of kubectl!

The good:

- *No parameters and templates*—Kustomize apps are extremely easy to reason about, and really, a pleasure to look at. It's about as close as you can get to Kubernetes YAML since the overlays you compose to perform customizations are simply subsets of Kubernetes YAML.

The bad:

- *No parameters and templates*—The same property that makes Kustomize applications so readable can also make it limiting. For example, I was recently trying to get the Kustomize CLI to set an image tag for a custom resource instead of a Deployment but was unable to. Kustomize does have a concept of vars, which look a lot like parameters but somehow aren't, and can only be used in Kustomize's sanctioned whitelist of field paths. We feel like this is one of those times when the solution, despite making the hard things easy, ends up making the easy things hard.

CONFIGURE MANIFESTS FOR PREPROD VS. PROD USING KUSTOMIZE

In this exercise, we will use a sample application that we will use later in part 3 and use Kustomize to deploy it.

We will organize our configuration files into the following directory structure.

Listing 3.7   Kustomize directory structure

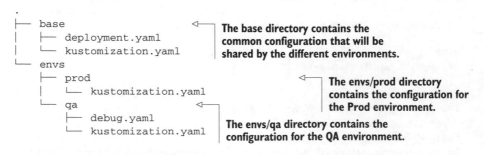

---

[3] https://github.com/kubernetes/community/blob/master/contributors/design-proposals/architecture/declarative-application-management.md.

The manifests in the base directory contain all the resources that are common to all environments. In this simple example, we have a single Deployment resource.

Listing 3.8 Base deployment

```
apiVersion: apps/v1
kind: Deployment
metadata:
  name: sample-app
spec:
  replicas: 1
  revisionHistoryLimit: 3
  selector:
    matchLabels:
      app: sample-app
  template:
    metadata:
      labels:
        app: sample-app
    spec:
      containers:
      - command:
        - /app/sample-app
        image: gitopsbook/sample-app:REPLACEME  ◁──┐
        name: sample-app
        ports:
        - containerPort: 8080
```

> **The image defined in the base config is irrelevant. This version of the image will never be deployed since the child overlay environments in this example will override this value.**

To use the base directory as a base to other environments, a kustomization.yaml must be present in the directory. The following is the simplest kustomization.yaml possible. It merely lists the guestbook.yaml as the single resource comprising the application.

Listing 3.9 Base Kustomization

```
apiVersion: kustomize.config.k8s.io/v1beta1
kind: Kustomization

resources:
- deployment.yaml
```

Now that we've established the kustomize base directory, we can start customizing our environments. To customize and modify resources for a specific environment, we define an overlay directory that contains all the patches and customizations we want to be applied on top of the base resources. Our first overlay is the envs/qa directory. Inside this directory is another kustomization.yaml that specifies the patches that should be applied on top of the base. The following two listings provide an example of a qa overlay that

- Sets a different guestbook image to be deployed to a new tag (v0.2)
- Adds an environment variable, DEBUG=true, to the guestbook container

Listing 3.10   QA environment Kustomization

```
apiVersion: kustomize.config.k8s.io/v1beta1
kind: Kustomization

bases:
- ../../base

patchesStrategicMerge:
- debug.yaml

images:
- name: gitopsbook/sample-app
  newTag: v0.2
```

bases references the "base" directory that contains the shared configuration.

debug.yaml is a reference to a Kustomize patch that will modify the sample-app Deployment object and set the DEBUG environment variable.

images overrides any container images defined in the base, with different tags or image repositories. This example overrides the image tag REPLACEME, with v0.2.

Notice that Kustomize patches look very similar to actual Kubernetes resources. This is because they are in fact incomplete versions of them.

Listing 3.11   QA environment debug patch

```
apiVersion: apps/v1
kind: Deployment
metadata:
  name: sample-app
spec:
  template:
    spec:
      containers:
      - name: sample-app
        env:
        - name: DEBUG
          value: "true"
```

The apiVersion group (apps), the kind (Deployment), and name (sample-app) are key pieces of information that inform Kustomize about which resource in the base this patch should be applied to.

The name field is used to identify which container will have the new environment variables.

Finally, the new DEBUG environment variable we want in the QA environment is defined.

After all that is said and done, we run `kustomize build envs/qa`. This produces the final, rendered manifests for the QA environment.

Listing 3.12   Kustomize build envs/qa

```
$ kustomize build envs/qa
apiVersion: apps/v1
kind: Deployment
metadata:
  name: sample-app
spec:
  replicas: 1
  revisionHistoryLimit: 3
  selector:
    matchLabels:
      app: sample-app
  template:
    metadata:
      labels:
        app: sample-app
```

```
    spec:
      containers:
      - command:
        - /app/sample-app
        env:                          ┌ The DEBUG environment
        - name: DEBUG        ◄──────┘ variable is added.
          value: "true"                    ┌ The image tag
        image: gitopsbook/sample-app:v0.2  ◄──┘ is set to v0.2.
        name: sample-app
        ports:
        - containerPort: 8080
```

The final qa manifest can be installed to minikube in the qa namespace with the following commands:

```
$ kubectl create namespace qa
$ kustomize build envs/qa | kubectl apply -n qa -f -
# kubectl get all -n qa
NAME                                 READY    STATUS     RESTARTS    AGE
pod/sample-app-7595985689-46fbj      1/1      Running    0           11s

NAME                           READY    UP-TO-DATE    AVAILABLE    AGE
deployment.apps/sample-app     1/1      1             1            11s

NAME                                      DESIRED    CURRENT    READY    AGE
replicaset.apps/sample-app-7595985689     1          1          1        11s
```

Exercise 3.3
In the previous tutorial, we parameterized the guestbook image tag for QA and Prod environments using Kustomize.

> **HINT** Create a replica_count.yaml patch file.

Add additional parameterization for the number of replicas desired for each sample-app deployment. Set the number of replicas to 1 for QA and 3 for Prod. Deploy the QA environment to the qa namespace and the Prod environment to the prod namespace.

Exercise 3.4
Currently, the Prod environment runs version v0.1 of the sample app, and QA runs version v0.2. Let's assume we have completed the testing in QA. Update the customization.yaml file to promote version v0.2 to run in Prod. Update the Prod environment in the prod namespace.

3.3.3 Jsonnet

Jsonnet is a language and not really a tool. Furthermore, its use is not specific to Kubernetes (although it's been popularized by Kubernetes). The best way to think of Jsonnet is as a super-powered JSON combined with a sane way to do templating. Jsonnet combines all the things you wish you could do with JSON (comments, text blocks, parameters, variables, conditionals, file imports) without any of the things that you hate about go/Jinja2 templating, and adds features that you didn't even know you needed or wanted (functions, object orientation, mixins). It does all of this in a declarative and hermetic (code as data) way.

When we look at a basic Jsonnet file, it looks very similar to JSON, which makes sense because Jsonnet is a superset of JSON. All JSON is valid Jsonnet. But notice in our example, we can also have comments in the document. If you have been managing configuration in JSON for long enough, you will immediately understand how useful this is!

Listing 3.13   Basic Jsonnet

```
{
    // Look! It's JSON with comments!
    "apiVersion": "apps/v1",
    "kind": "Deployment",
    "metadata": {
        "name": "nginx"
    },
    "spec": {
        "selector": {
            "matchLabels": {
                "app": "nginx"
            }
        },
        "replicas": 2,
        "template": {
            "metadata": {
                "labels": {
                    "app": "nginx"
                }
            },
            "spec": {
                "containers": [
                    {
                        "name": "nginx",
                        "image": "nginx:1.14.2",
                        "ports": [
                            {
                                "containerPort": 80
                            }
                        ]
                    }
                ]
            }
        }
    }
}
```

Continuing with the example, let's see how we can start leveraging simple Jsonnet features. One of the simplest ways to reduce repetition, and better organize your code/configuration, is to use variables. In our next example, we declare a few variables at the top of the Jsonnet file (name, version, and replicas) and reference those variables throughout the document. This allows us to make changes at a single, visible place, without resorting to scanning the entire document for all other areas that need that same change, which would be error prone, especially in large documents.

Listing 3.14   Variables

```jsonnet
local name = "nginx";
local version = "1.14.2";
local replicas = 2;
{
    "apiVersion": "apps/v1",
    "kind": "Deployment",
    "metadata": {
        "name": name
    },
    "spec": {
        "selector": {
            "matchLabels": {
                "app": name
            }
        },
        "replicas": replicas,
        "template": {
            "metadata": {
                "labels": {
                    "app": name
                }
            },
            "spec": {
                "containers": [
                    {
                        "name": name,
                        "image": "nginx:" + version,
                        "ports": [
                            {
                                "containerPort": 80
                            }
                        ]
                    }
                ]
            }
        }
    }
}
```

Finally, with our advanced example, we start leveraging a few of the unique and powerful features of Jsonnet: functions, arguments, references, and conditionals. The next example starts to demonstrate the power of Jsonnet.

Listing 3.15   Advanced Jsonnet

```jsonnet
function(prod=false) {
    "apiVersion": "apps/v1",
    "kind": "Deployment",
```

Unlike previous examples, the configuration is defined as a Jsonnet function instead of a normal Jsonnet object. This allows the configuration to declare inputs and accept arguments from the command line. prod is a Boolean argument to the function, with a default value of false.

```
        "metadata": {
            "name": "nginx"
        },
        "spec": {
            "selector": {
                "matchLabels": {
                    "app": $.metadata.name
                }
            },
            "replicas": if prod then 10 else 1,
            "template": {
                "metadata": {
                    "labels": {
                        "app": $.metadata.name
                    }
                },
                "spec": {
                    "containers": [
                        {
                            "name": $.metadata.name,
                            "image": "nginx:1.14.2",
                            "ports": [
                                {
                                    "containerPort": 80
                                }
                            ]
                        }
                    ]
                }
            }
        }
    }
}
```

We can self-reference other parts of the document without using variables.

The number of replicas is set based on a condition.

Exercise 3.5

In listing 3.15, try running the following two commands and compare the output:

```
$ jsonnet advanced.jsonnet
```

```
$ jsonnet --tla-code prod=true advanced.jsonnet
```

There are many more language features in Jsonnet, and we haven't even scratched the surface of its capabilities. Jsonnet is not widely adopted in the Kubernetes community, which is unfortunate because, of all the tools described here, Jsonnet is hands down the most powerful configuration tool available and is why several offshoot tools are built on top of it. Explaining what's possible with Jsonnet is a chapter in and of itself, which is why we encourage you to read how Databricks uses Jsonnet with Kubernetes, and Jsonnet's excellent tutorial.[4]

The good:

- *Extremely powerful*—It's rare to hit a situation that couldn't be expressed in some concise and elegant snippet of Jsonnet. With Jsonnet, you are continually finding new ways to maximize reuse and avoid repeating yourself.

[4] http://mng.bz/NYmX.

The bad:

- *It's not YAML*—This might be an issue with unfamiliarity, but most people will experience some level of cognitive load when they're staring at a nontrivial Jsonnet file. In the same way you would need to run a Helm template to verify your Helm chart is producing what you expect, you will similarly need to run `jsonnet --yaml-stream guestbook.jsonnet` to verify your Jsonnet is correct. The good news is that, unlike with Go templating, which can produce syntactically incorrect YAML due to some misplaced whitespace, these types of errors are caught with Jsonnet during the build, and the resulting output is guaranteed to be valid JSON/YAML.

KSONNET Not to be confused with Jsonnet, *ksonnet* is a defunct tool for creating application manifests that can be deployed to a Kubernetes cluster. However, ksonnet is no longer maintained, and other tools should be considered instead.

3.3.4 Configuration management summary

As with everything, there are trade-offs to using each tool. Table 3.1 shows a summary of how these specific tools compare in terms of the four qualities we value in configuration management.

Table 3.1 Features comparison

	Helm	Kustomize	Jsonnet
Declarative	Fair	Excellent	Excellent
Readability	Poor	Excellent	Fair
Flexibility	Excellent	Poor	Excellent
Maintainability	Fair	Excellent	Excellent

Note that the tools discussed in this chapter are just the ones that happen to be the most popular in the Kubernetes community at the time of writing. This is a continually evolving space, and there are many other configuration management tools to consider.

3.4 Durable vs. ephemeral environments

Durable environments are environments that will always be available. For example, the production environment always needs to be available so that services do not get interrupted. In a durable environment, resources (memory, CPU, storage) will be committed permanently to achieve always-on availability. Often, E2E is a durable environment for internal integration, and Prod is a durable environment for production traffic.

Ephemeral environments are temporary environments that are not relied on by other services. Ephemeral environments also do not require resources to be permanently committed. For example, Stage is used for testing production readiness for the new code and does not need to be around after testing is complete. Another use case is for previewing a pull request for correctness to guarantee that only good code is merged into master. In this case, a temporary environment will be created with the pull request changes so it can be tested. Once all testing is complete, the PR environment will be deleted, and the PR changes will only be allowed to be merged back to master if all tests pass.

Given durable environments will be used by others, defects in a durable environment could interrupt others and might require rollback to restore the correct functionality. With GitOps and Kubernetes, rollback is simply to reapply the previous config through Git. Kubernetes will detect the changes in the manifest and restore the environment to the previous state.

Kubernetes makes rollback in environments consistent and straightforward, but what about other resources like databases? Since user data is stored in a database, we cannot simply roll back the database to a previous snapshot, resulting in the loss of user data. As with the rolling updates deployment in Kubernetes, new and old versions of the code need to be compatible with rolling updates. In the case of the database, the DB schema needs to be backward compatible to avoid disruption during rollback and loss of user data. In practice, it means columns can only be added (not removed), and column definitions cannot be altered. Schema changes should be controlled with other change management frameworks, such as Flyway,[5] so DB changes can also follow the GitOps process.

Summary

- Environments are where code is deployed and executed for a specific purpose.
- Each environment will have its own access control, networking, configuration, and dependencies.
- Factors for picking environment granularity are release independence, test boundary, access control, and isolation.
- The Kubernetes Namespace is a natural construct to implement an environment.
- Since a namespace is equivalent to an environment, deploying to a specific environment is merely specifying the targeted namespace.
- Inter-environment traffic can be controlled by network policy.
- Preprod and prod should follow the same security best practices and operation vigor.
- Separation of the Git repo for Kubernetes manifest and the Git repo for code is highly recommended to allow environment changes independent from code changes.
- A single branch works well with tooling like Kustomize for overlay.

---

[5] https://flywaydb.org/.

- Monorepo for config works well for startups; multirepo works well for large enterprises.
- Helm is a package manager.
- Kustomize is a built-in config management tool, part of kubectl.
- Jsonnet is a language that is for JSON templating.
- Choosing the right config management tools should be based on the following criteria: declarative, readability, flexibility, and maintainability.
- Durable environments are always on for others to use, and ephemeral environments are for short-lived testing and previewing.

This chapter covers

- Stages in a GitOps CI/CD pipeline
- Promoting code, image, and environment
- Rollback
- Compliance pipeline

This chapter builds on the concepts learned in chapter 3 and discusses how pipelines are created to build and test application code and then deploy it to different environments. You will also learn about different promotion strategies and how to revert, reset, or roll back application changes.

We recommend you read chapters 1, 2, and 3 before reading this chapter.

4.1 Stages in CI/CD pipelines

Continuous integration (CI) is a software development practice in which all developers merge code changes in a central repository (Git). With CI, each code change (commit) triggers an automated build-and-test stage for the given repo and provides feedback to the developer(s) who made the change. The main difference between GitOps compared to traditional CI is that with GitOps, the CI pipeline also updates the application manifest with the new image version after the build and test stages have been completed successfully.

Continuous delivery (CD) is the practice of automating the entire software release process. CD includes infrastructure provisioning in addition to deployment. What makes GitOps CD different from traditional CD is using a GitOps operator to monitor the manifest changes and orchestrate the deployment. As long as the CI build is complete and the manifest is updated, the GitOps operator takes care of the eventual deployment.

NOTE Please refer to section 2.5 for GitOps CI/CD and operator basics.

This chapter takes an in-depth look at a comprehensive CI/CD pipeline and why it is important for software development. A CI/CD pipeline is a collection of stages, and each stage performs a specific task to achieve the following objectives:

- *Productivity*—Provide valuable feedback for the developers early in the development cycle in terms of design, coding style, and quality without context switching. Code review, unit test, code coverage, code analysis, integration test, and run-time vulnerability are essential stages for design, quality, and security feedback to the developers.
- *Security*—Detect code and component vulnerabilities that are attack surfaces for potential exploitation. A vulnerability scan can detect security issues with third-party libraries. A run-time vulnerability scan can detect run-time security issues with code.
- *Defect escape*—Reduce failure of customer interactions and costly rollback. A new release is typically providing new features or enhancing existing ones. If the features do not provide the correct functionality, the consequence will be customer dissatisfaction and potential revenue loss. Unit tests verify correctness at the module level, and functional tests verify correctness across two or more modules.
- *Scalability*—Discover scalability issues before the production release. Unit tests and functional tests can verify the features' correctness, but these stages cannot detect problems such as memory leaks, thread leaks, or resource contention issues. Canary release is a way to deploy the new version to detect scalability issues using production traffic and dependencies.
- *Time to market*—Deliver features to customers quicker. With a fully automated CI/CD pipeline, there is no time-intensive manual work to deploy the software. The code can be released as soon as it passes all stages in the pipeline.
- *Reporting*—Insight for continuous improvement and metrics for auditability. CI/CD pipeline execution time in minutes versus hours can affect developers' behavior and productivity. Continuously monitoring and improving the pipeline execution time can dramatically improve team productivity. Collecting and storing build metrics is also required for many regulatory audits. Please refer to the CI and CD metrics publishing stages for detail.

4.1.1   *GitOps continuous integration*

Figure 4.1 illustrates a comprehensive CI pipeline building on the GitOps CI/CD (figure 2.9) in chapter 2. The boxes in gray are new stages for a complete CI solution. This section will help you plan and design stages relevant to your business based on your complexity, maturity, and compliance requirements.

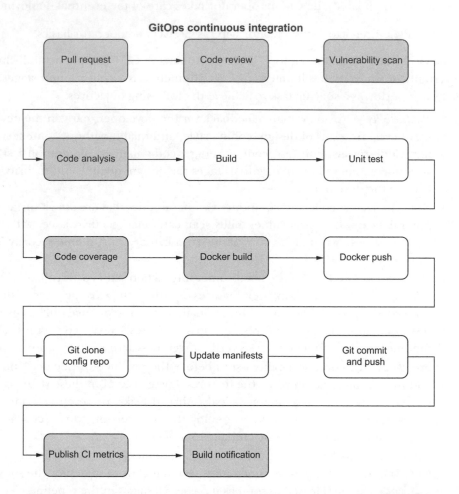

Figure 4.1   These are the stages in a GitOps CI pipeline. White boxes are from the GitOps CI pipeline from figure 2.9, and gray boxes are the additional stages for building a complete CI pipeline.

PREBUILD STAGES

The following stages are also known as *static analysis* stages. They are a combination of manual and automated scanning of the code before the code is built and packaged into a Docker image.

Pull request/code review

All CI/CD pipelines should always start with a pull request, which allows code review to ensure consistency between design and implementation and catch other potential errors. As discussed in chapter 1, code review also helps share best practices, coding standards, and team cohesion.

Vulnerability scan

Open source libraries can provide many functionalities without custom development, but those libraries can also come with vulnerabilities, defects, and licensing issues. Integrating an open source library scanning tool like Nexus Vulnerability Scanner can detect known vulnerabilities and licensing issues early in the development cycle and remediate the problems by either upgrading the libraries or using alternative libraries.

> **NOTE** The old saying "If it ain't broke, don't fix it" doesn't work anymore in the rapidly changing software industry. Vulnerabilities are discovered every day with open source libraries, and it is prudent to upgrade as soon as possible to avoid being exposed to exploits. At Intuit, we leverage open source software heavily to accelerate our development. Instead of doing an annual security audit, we now have a vulnerability scan step in our CI pipelines to detect and address security issues regularly during the development cycle.

Code analysis

While manual code review is excellent for design and implementation consistency, coding standards, duplicate code, and code complexity issues (aka code smells)[1] are better suited to an automated linting or code analysis tool such as SonarQube. These tools are not a replacement for code review, but they can catch the mundane issues more effectively.

> **NOTE** It is unrealistic to expect every minor issue to be fixed before the new code can be deployed. With tools such as SonarQube, the trend data is also reported so the team can see how their code smell is getting better or worse over time so the team can address these issues before they have gone too far.

Exercise 4.1

To prevent known security issues with your open source library, what stage(s) do you need to plan in your CI/CD pipeline?

To ensure implementation matching the design, what stage(s) do you need to plan in your CI/CD pipeline?

BUILD STAGES

After static analysis, it is time to build the code. In addition to building and creating the deployable artifact (aka Docker image), unit (module) testing and the effectiveness of the unit tests (code coverage) are integral parts of the build process.

---

[1] https://en.wikipedia.org/wiki/Code_smell.

Build

The build stage typically starts with downloading the dependency libraries before the project source code's actual compilation. (Scripting languages such as Python and Node.js do not require compilation.) For compiled languages like Java, Ruby, and Go, the code is compiled into bytecode/machine binary using the respective compiler. Additionally, the generated binary and its dependency libraries need to be packaged into a deployable unit (such as jar or war in Java) for deployment.

> **NOTE** In our experience, the most time-consuming portion of the build is downloading the dependencies. It is highly recommended to cache your dependencies in your build system to reduce the build time.

Unit test

A unit test is for verifying a small piece of code doing what it is supposed to do. Unit tests should have no dependencies on code outside the unit tested. Unit testing mainly focuses on testing the functionality of individual units only and does not uncover the issues that arise when different modules are interacting with each other. During unit testing, external calls are typically "mocked" to eliminate dependencies issues and reduce the test execution time.

> **NOTE** In a unit test, mock objects can simulate the behavior of complex, real objects and are therefore useful when a real object is impractical or impossible to incorporate into a unit test.[2] In our experience, mocking is a required investment and will save the team time (faster test execution) and effort (troubleshooting flaky tests).

Code coverage

Code coverage measures the percentage of code that is covered by automated unit tests. Code coverage measurement simply determines which statements in a body of code have been executed through a test run and which statements have not. In general, a code coverage system instruments the source code and gathers the run-time information to generate a report on the test suite's code coverage.

Code coverage is a critical part of a feedback loop in the development process. As tests are developed, code coverage highlights aspects of the code that may not be adequately tested and require additional testing. This loop continues until coverage meets some specified target. Coverage should follow an 80-20 rule as increasing coverage values becomes difficult and return diminishes. Coverage measurement is not a replacement for thorough code review and programming best practices.

> **NOTE** Driving code coverage percentages higher alone can lead to wrong behavior and may actually lower quality. Code coverage measures the percentage of lines being executed but does not measure the correctness of the code. 100-percent code coverage with partial assertions will *not* achieve the quality goal of unit testing. Our recommendation is to focus on increasing the

---

[2] https://en.wikipedia.org/wiki/Mock_object.

number of unit tests and code coverage over time instead of focusing on an absolute code coverage number.

Docker build

A Docker image is the deployable unit for Kubernetes. Once code has been built, you can create the Docker image with a unique image id for your build artifacts by creating a Dockerfile and executing the `docker build` command. A Docker image should have its unique naming convention, and each version should be tagged with a unique version number. Additionally, you can also run a Docker image scanning tool at this stage to detect potential vulnerability issues with your base images and dependencies.

> **DOCKER TAG AND GIT HASH** Since Git creates a unique hash for each commit, it is recommended to use the Git hash to tag the Docker image instead of creating an arbitrary version number. In addition to uniqueness, each Docker image can easily trace back to the Git repo history using the Git hash to determine the exact code in the Docker image. Please refer to section 2.5.2 for additional information.

Docker push

The newly built Docker image needs to be published to a Docker registry[3] for Kubernetes to orchestrate the eventual deployment. A Docker registry is a stateless, highly scalable server-side application that stores and lets you distribute Docker images. For in-house development, the best practice is to host a private registry to have tight control over where the images are stored. Please refer to chapter 6 for how best to host a secured private Docker registry.

Exercise 4.2

Plan the build stage(s) required so code coverage metrics can be measured.

If the image is tagged with the latest tag, can you tell what was packaged in the Docker image?

GitOps CI stages

With traditional CI, the pipeline will end after the build stages. With GitOps, additional GitOps specific stages are required to update the manifest for the eventual deployment. Please refer to figure 4.1.

Git clone config repo

Assuming your Kubernetes config is stored in a separate repo, this stage performs a Git clone to clone the Kubernetes config to the build environment for the subsequent stage to update your manifest.

Update manifests

Once you have the manifests in your build environment, you can update the manifests with the newly created image id using a configuration management tool like Kustomize. Depending on your deployment strategy, one or more environment-specific

---

[3] https://docs.docker.com/registry/.

manifests are updated with the new image id. Please refer to chapter 3 for additional information on Kustomize.

Git commit and push

Once the manifests are updated with a new image id, the last step is to commit the manifests back to the Git repo. The CI pipeline is complete at this point. Your GitOps operator detects the change in your manifests and deploys the change to the Kubernetes cluster. The following is an example of implementing the three stages with the Git command.

POSTBUILD STAGES

After everything is complete for the GitOps CI, additional stages are needed to gather metrics for continuous improvement and audit reporting and to notify the team of the build status.

Publish CI metrics

CI metrics should be stored in a separate data store for

- *Build issues*—Development teams need relevant data to triage issues with build failure or unit test failure.
- *CI*—Long build time can affect engineering teams' behavior and productivity. Reduction in code coverage can potentially result in more production defects. Having historical build time and code coverage metrics enables teams to monitor trending, decrease build time, and increase code coverage.
- *Compliance requirements*—For SOC2 or PCI requirements, build information such as test results, who did the release, and what was released are required to be maintained anywhere from 14 months up to 7 years.

NOTE   It is costly to maintain build history for greater than one year for most build systems. One alternative is to export the build metrics to external storage, such as S3, to fulfill the compliance and reporting requirements.

Build notification

For CI/CD deployment, most teams would prefer the "No news is good news" model, which means that if all stages are successful, they don't need to be bothered with the build status. In the case of build issues, teams should be informed right away so they can get feedback and rectify the problem. This stage is typically implemented using team messaging or an email system, so teams can be notified as soon as the CI/CD pipeline is complete.

Exercise 4.3

What are the steps for the development team to determine build status if there is no build notification?

 Is 80% code coverage good or bad?

HINT   Trending.

If the CI/CD pipeline typically takes an hour to run, what other tasks can developers do during that time? What if the CI/CD pipeline takes 10 minutes instead?

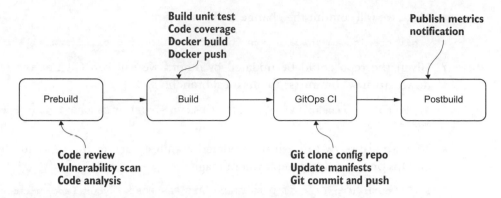

Figure 4.2 Prebuild will involve code review and static analysis. After build completion, GitOps CI will update the manifest (subsequently deployed by GitOps operator).

Exercise 4.4

There are two challenges with the GitOps stages, and this exercise will provide the steps to address these issues.

1 Which Git user should you use to track the manifest update and commit?
2 How do you handle concurrent CI builds which can update the repo simultaneously?

Before you start, please fork the repo https://github.com/gitopsbook/resources.git. This exercise will assume that your local computer is the build system.

3 Clone the repo from Git. We will assume that guestbook.yaml in the folder chapter-04/exercise4.4 is your application manifest:

```
$ git clone https://github.com/<your repo>/resources.git
```

4 Use git config to specify the committer user email and name. Depending on your requirement, you can use a service account or the actual committer account:

```
$ git config --global user.email <committerEmail>
$ git config --global user.name <commmitterName>
```

NOTE Please refer to section 4.2.1 for creating strong identity guarantees. The specified-user also needs to exist in your remote Git repo.

5 Let's assume that the new Docker image has the Git hashtag zzzzzz. We will update the manifest with tag zzzzzz:

```
$ sed -i .bak 's+acme.co.3m/guestbook:.*$*+acme.com/guestbook:zzzzzz+' chapter-04/exercise4.4/guestbook.yaml
```

NOTE To keep it simple, we will use cd to update the manifest in this exercise. Typically, you should be using config tools like Kustomize to update the image id.

6 Next, we will commit the change to the manifest:

```
$ git commit -am "update container for QAL during build zzzzzz"
```

7 Given the repo could be updated by others, we will run Git `rebase` to pull down any new commit(s) to our local branch:

```
$ git pull --rebase https://<GIT_USERNAME>:<GIT_PASSWORD>@<your repo>
master
```

8 Now we are ready to push the updated manifest back to the repo and let the GitOps operator do its deployment magic:

```
$ git push https://<GIT_USERNAME>:<GIT_PASSWORD>@<your repo> master
Enumerating objects: 9, done.
Counting objects: 100% (9/9), done.
Delta compression using up to 16 threads
Compressing objects: 100% (7/7), done.
Writing objects: 100% (7/7), 796 bytes | 796.00 KiB/s, done.
Total 7 (delta 4), reused 0 (delta 0)
remote: Resolving deltas: 100% (4/4), completed with 2 local objects.
remote: This repository moved. Please use the new location:
remote:    https://github.com/gitopsbook/resources.git
To https://github.com/gitops-k8s/resources
   eb1a692..70c141c  master -> master
```

4.1.2   *GitOps continuous delivery*

Figure 4.3 illustrates a comprehensive CD pipeline building on the GitOps CI/CD (chapter 2). The boxes in gray are new stages for a complete CD solution. Depending on your complexity, maturity, and compliance requirements, you can pick and choose the relevant stages for your business.

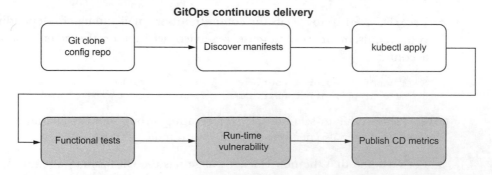

Figure 4.3   These are the stages in a GitOps CD pipeline. White boxes are from the GitOps CI pipeline from figure 2.9, and gray boxes are the additional stages for building a complete CI pipeline.

NOTE   The stages in the diagram depict the logical sequence. In practice, the GitOps stages are triggered by manifest changes in the Git repo and executed independently from the rest of the stages.

GitOps CD stages

These are logical stages performed by the GitOps operator to deploy based on manifest change.

Git clone config repo

The GitOps operator detects changes in your repo and performs a Git clone to get your Git repo's latest manifests.

Discover manifests

The GitOps Operator also determines any delta between the manifests in Kubernetes versus the latest manifests from Git repo. If there is no difference, the GitOps operator stops at this point.

Kubectl apply

If the GitOps operator determines differences between Kubernetes manifests and Git repo manifests, the GitOps operator applies the new manifests to Kubernetes using the `kubectl apply` command.

> **NOTE**   Please refer to chapter 2 for details.

Postdeployment stages

After the image is deployed, we can test the new code end to end against dependencies and run-time vulnerability.

Integration tests

Integration testing is a type of testing to check if different modules are working correctly together. Once the image is deployed in the QA environment, integration testing can test across multiple modules and other external systems like databases and services. Integration testing aims to discover issues that arise when different modules interact to perform a higher-level function that cannot be covered by unit tests.

> **NOTE**   Since the GitOps operator handles the deployment outside of the pipeline, deployment might not be completed before the functional tests execute. Exercise 4.6 discusses the steps required to make integration tests working with GitOps CD.

Run-time vulnerability

Run-time vulnerabilities are traditionally detected by penetration testing. *Penetration testing,* also called pen testing or ethical hacking, is the practice of testing a computer system, network, or web application to find security vulnerabilities that an attacker could exploit. Typical run-time vulnerabilities are SQL injection, command injection, or issuing insecure cookies. Instead of doing penetration testing in a production system (which is costly and after the fact), the QA environment can be instrumented using an agent tool like Contrast[4] while executing the integration tests to detect any run-time vulnerabilities early in the development cycle.

---

[4] https://www.contrastsecurity.com/.

Publish CD metrics

CD metrics should be stored in a separate data store for

- *Run-time issues*—Development teams need relevant data to triage issues with deployment, integration test failures, or run-time vulnerabilities.
- *Compliance requirements*—For SOC2 or PCI requirements, build information such as test results, who did the release, and what was released are required to be maintained anywhere from 14 months up to 7 years.

Exercise 4.5

Design a CD pipeline that can detect SQL injection vulnerabilities.

> **HINT**   SQL injection is a run-time vulnerability.

Exercise 4.6

This exercise covers how you can ensure changes are applied to Kubernetes and the deployment completes successfully. We will use frontend-deployment.yaml as our manifest.

Listing 4.1   frontend-deployment.yaml

```
apiVersion: apps/v1 # for versions before 1.9.0 use apps/v1beta2
kind: Deployment
metadata:
  name: frontend
  labels:
    app: guestbook
spec:
  selector:
    matchLabels:
      app: guestbook
      tier: frontend
  replicas: 3
  template:
    metadata:
      labels:
        app: guestbook
        tier: frontend
    spec:
      containers:
      - name: php-redis
        image: gcr.io/google-samples/gb-frontend:v4
        resources:
          requests:
            cpu: 100m
            memory: 100Mi
        env:
      - name: GET_HOSTS_FROM
        value: dns
        # Using `GET_HOSTS_FROM=dns` requires your cluster to
        # provide a dns service. As of Kubernetes 1.3, DNS is a built-in
        # service launched automatically. However, if the cluster you are
          using
```

```
          # does not have a built-in DNS service, you can instead
          # access an environment variable to find the master
          # service's host. To do so, comment out the 'value: dns' line
            above, and
          # uncomment the line below:
          # value: env
      ports:
      - containerPort: 80
© 2020 GitHub, Inc.
```

1 Run `kubectl diff` to determine if the frontend-deployment.yaml manifest is applied to Kubernetes. `exit status 1` means the manifest is not in Kubernetes:

```
$ kubectl diff -f frontend-deployment.yaml
diff -u -N /var/folders/s5/v3vpb73d6zv01dhxknw4yyxw0000gp/T/LIVE-
057767296/apps.v1.Deployment.gitops.frontend /var/folders/s5/
v3vpb73d6zv01dhxknw4yyxw0000gp/T/MERGED-602990303/
apps.v1.Deployment.gitops.frontend
--- /var/folders/s5/v3vpb73d6zv01dhxknw4yyxw0000gp/T/LIVE-057767296/
apps.v1.Deployment.gitops.frontend2020-01-06 14:23:40.000000000 -0800
+++ /var/folders/s5/v3vpb73d6zv01dhxknw4yyxw0000gp/T/MERGED-602990303/
apps.v1.Deployment.gitops.frontend2020-01-06 14:23:40.000000000 -0800
@@ -0,0 +1,53 @@
+apiVersion: apps/v1
+kind: Deployment
...
+status: {}
exit status 1
```

2 Apply the manifest to Kubernetes:

```
$ kubectl apply -f frontend-deployment.yaml
```

3 Rerun `kubectl diff`, and you should see the manifest applied with exit status 0. Kubernetes will start the deployment after the manifest update:

```
$ kubectl diff -f frontend-deployment.yaml
```

4 Repeatedly run `kubectl rollout status` until the deployment is fully complete:

```
$ kubectl rollout status deployment.v1.apps/frontend
Waiting for deployment "frontend" rollout to finish: 0 of 3 updated
replicas are available...
```

In production, you would automate this work using a script with a loop and sleep around the `kubectl rollout status` command.

Listing 4.2   DeploymentWait.sh

```
#!/bin/bash                          ┌── Initializes the RETRY
RETRY=0                           ◄──┘   variable to 0
STATUS="kubectl rollout status deployment.v1.apps/frontend"  ◄──┐ Defines the
                                                                 │ kubectl rollout
                                                                 │ status command
```

```
until $STATUS || [ $RETRY -eq 120 ]; do
    $STATUS
    RETRY=$((RETRY + 1))
    sleep 10
done
```

Loops exit condition when kubectl rollout status is true or the RETRY variable equals 120. This example waits up to 20 minutes (120 × 10 seconds).

Executes the kubectl rollout status command

Sleeps for 10 seconds

Increments the RETRY variable by 1

4.2   Driving promotions

Now that we have covered all the stages in the CI/CD pipeline, we can take a look at how the CI/CD pipeline can automate the promotion of code, image, and environment. An automated environment promotion's main benefit is to enable your team to deploy new code to production faster and more reliably.

4.2.1   Code vs. manifest vs. app config

In chapter 3, we started the discussion of the Git strategy consideration for working with GitOps. We discussed the benefit of keeping code and Kubernetes manifests in separate repos for more flexible deployment choices, better access control, and auditability. Where should we maintain application configuration for environment-specific dependencies such as database connection or distributed cache? There are several options for maintaining the environment configuration:

- *Docker image*—All environment-specific app config files can be bundled in the Docker image. This strategy works best to quickly package legacy applications (with all environment app config bundled) into Kubernetes. The disadvantage is that creating a new environment requires a full build and cannot reuse existing images.
- *ConfigMaps*—ConfigMaps are native resources in Kubernetes and are stored in the Kubernetes `etcd` database. The disadvantage is that Pods need to be restarted if the ConfigMap is updated.
- *Config repo*—Storing app config in a separate repo can achieve the same result as a ConfigMap. The added benefit is that the Pod can pick up changes in the application configuration dynamically (such as using Spring Cloud Config in Java).

NOTE   Given an environment consisting of code, manifest, and app config, any error in the repo changes could result in a production outage. Any changes to the code, manifest, or app config repo should follow strict pull request/code review to ensure correctness.

Exercise 4.7

Assume the code, manifest, and app config are kept in a single repo. You need to update the manifest for one of the environment's replicas from X to Y. How can you commit the change only for GitOps deployment without building another image?

4.2.2 Code and image promotion

Promotion is defined as "the act or fact of being raised in position or rank." Code promotion means the code changes are committed to a feature branch and merged (promoted) with the master branch through a pull request. Once a new image is built and published by CI, it is then deployed (promoted) by the GitOps CD operator (section 4.1).

> **NOTE** Imagine you are building a math library with addition and subtraction functions. You will first clone the master branch to create a new branch called addition. Once you complete implementing the addition functionality, you commit the code to the addition branch and generate a pull request to merge to the master branch. GitOps CI will create a new image and update the manifest. The GitOps operator will eventually deploy the new image. Then you can repeat the process to implement the subtraction functionality.

The code repo branching strategy has a direct impact on the image-promotion process. Next, we discuss the pros and cons of a single- versus multibranching strategy for the image-promotion process.

SINGLE-BRANCH STRATEGY

Single-branch strategy is also called feature-branch workflow.[5] In this strategy, the master branch is the official project history. Developers create short-lived feature branches for development. Once developers finish the feature, the changes are merged back to the master branch through the PR process. The CI build will be triggered when the PR is approved to bundle the new code into a new Docker image.

With single-branch development, every image from the CI build can be promoted to any environment and used for a production release. If you need to roll back, you can redeploy with any older images from the Docker registry. This strategy is excellent and works best if your service can be deployed independently (aka microservice) and enables your team to do frequent production releases.

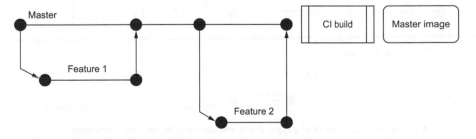

Figure 4.4 In the single-branch strategy, only the master branch is long-lived, and all feature branches will be short-lived. There is only one CI build for the master branch.

---

[5] https://www.atlassian.com/git/tutorials/comparing-workflows/feature-branch-workflow.

MULTIBRANCH STRATEGY

A *multibranch strategy* is typically for larger projects that require close coordination of external dependencies and release planning. There are many variations of the multibranch strategy. For this discussion, we use the Gitflow workflow[6] as an example. With Gitflow, the develop branch has the official project history, and the master branch has the last production release history. The CI build is configured for the develop branch for C. For feature development, developers create short-lived feature branches and merge changes to the develop branch once the feature is complete.

When a release is planned, a short-lived release branch is forked from the latest development branch, and testing and bug fixing continue in this branch until the code is ready for production deployment. Hence, a separate CI build needs to be configured to build new Docker images from the release branch. Once the release is complete, all changes are merged into the develop and master branches.

Unlike the single-branch strategy, only the release CI build images can ever be deployed to production. All images from the develop branch can only be used for preprod testing and integration. If rollback is needed, only images built from the release branch can be used. If roll-forward (or hotfix) is required for a production issue, a hotfix branch must be forked from the master branch, and a separate CI build created for the hotfix image.

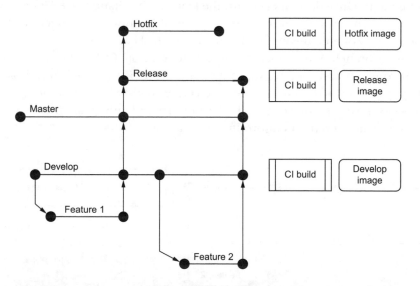

Figure 4.5 In the multibranch strategy, there will be multiple long-lived branches, and each long-lived branch will have its own CI pipeline. In this example, the long-lived branches are develop, master, and hotfix.

---

[6] https://www.atlassian.com/git/tutorials/comparing-workflows/gitflow-workflow.

Exercise 4.8

Your service needs to release a feature on a specific date. Using a multibranch strategy, design a successful release.

Using a single-branch strategy, design a successful release for the specific date.

HINT   Feature flag.

4.2.3 Environment promotion

In this section, we will discuss how to promote an image from preproduction to our production environment. The reason for having multiple environments and promoting the change is to shift as much testing as possible in the lower environment (shifting left), so we can detect and correct errors early in the development cycle.

There are two aspects to environment promotion. The first one is the environment infrastructure. As we discussed in chapter 3, Kustomize is the preferred config management tool to promote the new image to each environment, and the GitOps operator will do the rest!

The second aspect is the application itself. Since the Docker image is the immutable binary, injecting the environment-specific app config will configure the application to behave for the specific environment.

In chapter 3, we introduced QA, E2E, Stage, and Prod environments and discussed each environment's unique purpose in the development cycle. Let's review the stages that are important for each environment.

QA

The QA environment is the first environment running the new image for verifying the correctness of the code during execution with external dependencies. The following stages are critical for the QA environment:

- Functional test
- Run-time vulnerability
- Publish metrics

E2E

The E2E environment is primarily for other applications to test out existing or pre-release features. E2E environments should be monitored and operated similar to the Prod environment because E2E outage could potentially block the CI/CD pipelines of other services. An optional verification stage (sanity testing with the subset of the functional tests) is applicable for the E2E environment to ensure its correctness.

STAGE

The Stage environment will typically connect to the production dependencies to ensure all production dependencies are in place before the production release. For example, a new version might depend on DB schema updates or message queues to be configured before it can be deployed. Testing with staging can guarantee all production dependencies are correct and avoid production issues.

PROD

Canary release

Canary release[7] is a technique to reduce the risk of introducing a new software version in production by slowly rolling out the change to a small subset of users before rolling it out to the entire infrastructure and making it available to everybody. We will have an in-depth discussion in chapter 5 of canary release and how it can be implemented in Kubernetes.

Release ticket

Given the complexity and distributed nature of application services, a release ticket is crucial for your production support team in case of a production incident. A release ticket will assist the production incident team in knowing what was deployed/changed by whom and what to roll back to if needed. Besides, release tracking is a must for compliance requirements.

4.2.4 Putting it all together

This chapter started with defining the GitOps CI/CD pipeline to build a Docker image, verify the image, and deploy it to an environment. Then we discussed environment promotion with stages that are important for each environment. Figure 4.6 is an example of what a full Gitops CI/CD pipeline looks like with environment promotion.

> **SERIAL OR PARALLEL**   Even though the diagram describes each stage as serial, many modern pipelines can support running stages in parallel. For example, notification and metric publishing are mutually exclusive and can be executed in parallel to reduce the pipeline execution time.

4.3 Other pipelines

The CI/CD pipeline is primarily for your "happy path" deployment where your changes are working as expected and life is good, but we all know that's not the reality. From time to time, unexpected issues will arise in the production environment, and we will need to either roll back the environment or release hotfixes to mitigate the problem. With software-as-a-service (SaaS), the highest priority is to recover from the production issues as quickly as possible; and in most cases, a rollback is required to the previously known good state for a timely recovery.

For specific compliance standards, such as Payment Card Industry (PCI),[8] production releases require a second person's approval to ensure no single person can release changes to production. PCI also requires an annual audit that mandates reporting of the approval records. Given our original CI/CD pipeline will deploy changes to production per single PR, we need to enhance our pipeline to support compliance and auditability.

---

[7]   https://martinfowler.com/bliki/CanaryRelease.html.
[8]   https://en.wikipedia.org/wiki/Payment_card_industry.

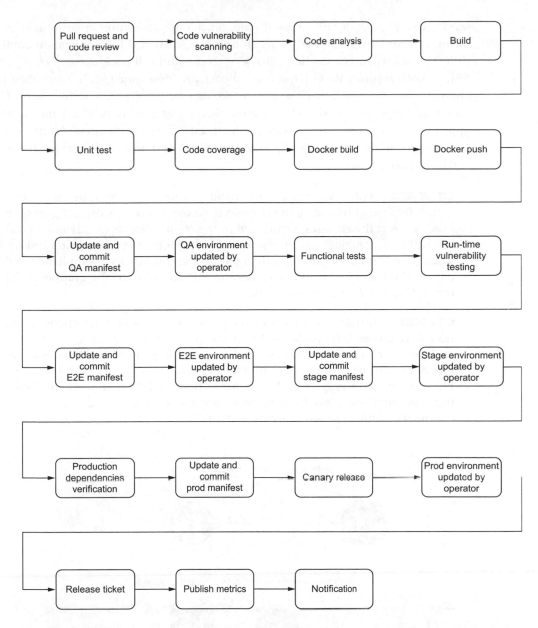

Figure 4.6 A CI/CD pipeline completes with environment promotion for single-branch development. For multibranch development, additional stages are required for branch promotion before environment promotion.

4.3.1 *Rollback*

Even if you have planned all the review, analysis, and testing stages in your CI/CD pipeline, eliminating all production issues is still impossible. Depending on the severity of the problem, you can either roll forward with fixes or roll back to restore your service to a previously known good state. Since our production environment consists of the manifest (which contains the Docker image id) and the application configuration for the environment, the rollback process could roll back the app config, manifest, or both repos. With GitOps, our rollback process is once again controlled by Git changes, and the GitOps operator will take care of the eventual deployment. (If the app config repo also needs to be rolled back, you just need to roll back the changes in app config first before rolling back the manifest since only manifest changes can trigger a deployment, not app config changes.) Git Revert and Git Reset[9] are two ways to roll back changes in Git.

GIT REVERT   The `git revert` command can be considered an undo command. Instead of removing the commit from the project history, it figures out how to invert the changes introduced by the commit and appends a new commit with the resulting inverse content. This prevents Git from losing history, which is essential for the integrity of your revision history (compliance and auditability) and for reliable collaboration. Please refer to the graphic at the top of figure 4.7 for an illustration.

GIT RESET   The `git reset` command does a couple of things, depending on how it is invoked. It modifies the index (the so-called staging area), or it changes which commit a branch head is currently pointing at. This command may alter existing history (by changing the commit that a branch references). Please refer to the graphic at the bottom of figure 4.7 for an illustration. Since this command can alter history, we do not recommend using `git reset` if compliance and auditability are important.

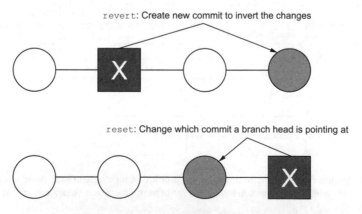

Figure 4.7   `git revert` works like an undo command with history preserved. `git reset`, on the other hand, modifies the history to reset the changes.

---

[9]   https://www.atlassian.com/git/tutorials/undoing-changes/git-reset.

Figure 4.8 is an example of a rollback pipeline. This pipeline will start with `git revert` and `git commit` to roll back the manifest to the previously known good state. After a pull request is generated from the "revert" commit, approver(s) can approve and merge the PR to the manifest master branch. Once again, the GitOps operator will do its magic and roll back the application based on the updated manifest.

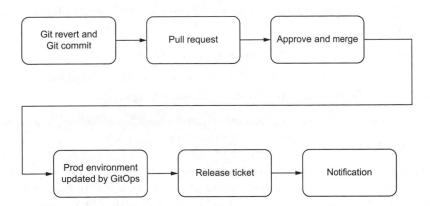

Figure 4.8   The rollback pipeline involves reverting the manifest to a previous commit, generating a new pull request, and finally approving the PR.

Exercise 4.9

This exercise will go over the steps required to revert the image id from "zzzzzz" to "yyyyyy." This exercise will use `git revert` so the commit history is preserved. Before you start, please fork the repo https://github.com/gitopsbook/resources.git. This exercise will assume your local computer is the build system:

1   Clone the repo from Git. We will assume that guestbook.yaml in the folder chapter-04/exercise4.9 is your application manifest:

```
$ git clone https://github.com/<your repo>/resources.git
```

2   Use `git config` to specify the committer user email and name. Depending on your requirement, you can use either a service account or the actual committer account:

```
$ git config --global user.email <committerEmail>
$ git config --global user.name <commmitterName>
```

NOTE   Please refer to chapter 6 for creating strong identity guarantees. The user that is specified also needs to exist in your remote Git repo.

3   Let's review the Git history:

```
$ git log --pretty=oneline
eb1a692029a9f4e4ae65de8c11135c56ff235722 (HEAD -> master) guestbook
    with image hash zzzzzz
```

```
95384207cbba2ce46ee2913c7ea51d0f4e958890 guestbook with image hash yyyyyy
4dcb452a809d99f9a1b5a24bde14116fad9a4ded (upstream/master, upstream/
   HEAD, origin/master) exercise 4.6 and 4.10
e62161043d5a3360b89518fa755741c6be7fd2b3 exercise 4.6 and 4.10
74b172c7703b3b695c79f270d353dc625c4038ba guestbook for exercise 4.4
...
```

4   From the history, you will see "eb1a692029a9f4e4ae65de8c11135c56ff23
    5722" for image hash zzzzzz. If we revert this commit, the manifest will have an
    image hash yyyyyy:

```
$ git revert eb1a692029a9f4e4ae65de8c11135c56ff235722
```

5   Now we are ready to push the revert of the manifest by pushing back to the repo
    and let the GitOps operator do its deployment magic:

```
$ git push https://<GIT_USERNAME>:<GIT_PASSWORD>@<your repo> master
```

4.3.2   *Compliance pipeline*

A compliance pipeline essentially needs to ensure second-person approval for production release and record by whom, when, and what gets released. In our case, we have created one CI/CD pipeline for preproduction development and a separate pipeline for production release. The preproduction CI/CD pipeline's last stage will generate a PR to update the production manifest with the latest image id. When the approver wants to release a particular image to production, he/she can simply approve the respective PR and the Prod environment will be updated by the GitOps operator. Figure 4.9 illustrates the stages for compliance CI/CD and production release pipelines.

Exercise 4.10

This exercise will create a new branch with your production manifest update and create a pull request back to the remote repo for approval. Before you start, please fork the repo https://github.com/gitops-k8s/resources.git. This exercise will assume your local computer is the build system:

1   Install the hub[10] CLI for pull request creation. The hub CLI tool works with
    GitHub to fork branches and create pull requests:

```
$ brew install hub
```

2   Clone the repo from Git. We will assume that guestbook.yaml in the folder
    chapter-04 is your application manifest:

```
$ git clone https://github.com/<your repo>/resources.git
```

3   Use git config to specify the committer user email and name. Depending on
    your requirement, you can use a service account or the actual committer account:

```
$ git config --global user.email <committerEmail>
$ git config --global user.name <commmitterName>
```

---

[10] https://github.com/github/hub.

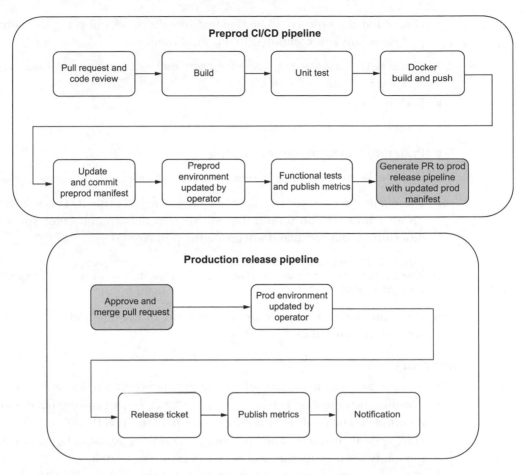

Figure 4.9 With the compliance pipeline, there is a separate production pipeline from the preprod CI/CD pipeline. At the end of the CI/CD pipeline, there is a stage to generate a new PR with the new image id to the production manifest repository. Any PR getting approved will be deployed into the production.

NOTE Please refer to chapter 6, section 6.2, for creating strong identity guarantees. The user specified also needs to exist in your remote Git repo.

4 Create a new release branch:

```
$ git checkout -b release
```

5 Let's assume that the new Docker image has the Git hashtag zzzzzz. We will update the manifest with the tag *zzzzzz*:

```
$ sed -i .bak 's+acme.com/guestbook:.*$+acme.com/guestbook:zzzzzz+'
  chapter-04/exercise4.10/guestbook.yaml
```

6 Next, we will commit the change to the manifest:

```
$ git commit -am "update container for production during build zzzzzz"
```

7 Given that the repo could be updated by others, we will run `git rebase` to pull down any new commit(s) to our local branch:

```
$ git pull --rebase https://<GIT_USERNAME>:<GIT_PASSWORD>@<your repo>
  master
```

8 Fork the repo:

```
$ hub fork --remote-name=origin
```

9 Push the changes to your new remote:

```
$ git push https://<GIT_USERNAME>:<GIT_PASSWORD>@<your repo> release
```

10 Open a pull request for the topic branch you've just pushed. This will also open up an editor for you to edit the pull request description. Once you save the description, this command will create the pull request:

```
$ hub pull-request -p
Branch 'release' set up to track remote branch 'release' from 'upstream'.
Everything up-to-date
```

11 Now you can go back to your remote repo and review and approve the pull request in your browser.

Summary

- `git rebase` can mitigate conflict due to concurrent pipeline execution.
- Continuously running `kubectl rollout status` can ensure that deployment is complete and ready for running functional tests in GitOps CD.
- Having code, manifest, and app config in separate repos will give you the best flexibility as infrastructure and code can evolve separately.
- The single-branch strategy is great for smaller projects as every CI image can be promoted to production with zero branch management.
- A multibranch strategy is excellent for larger projects with external dependencies and release planning. The downside is that multiple long-lived branches must be maintained, and only release images can be deployed to production.
- A complete CI/CD pipeline will include environment promotion and stages for static analysis, build, unit/integration testing, and publishing build metrics/notification.
- Rollback of a production environment with GitOps is simply reverting the manifest to the previous commit (image id).
- GitOps pipelines naturally support compliance and auditability because all changes are generated as pull requests with approval and history.

5

Deployment strategies

This chapter covers

- Understanding why ReplicaSet is not a good fit for GitOps
- Understanding why Deployment is declarative and a good fit for GitOps
- Implementing blue-green deployment using native Kubernetes resources and Argo Rollouts
- Implementing canary deployment using native Kubernetes resources and Argo Rollouts
- Implementing progressive delivery using Argo Rollouts

In the previous chapters, we have focused on the initial deployment of Kubernetes resources. Launching a new application can be as simple as deploying a ReplicaSet with the desired number of Pod replicas and creating a Service to route the incoming traffic to the desired Pods. But now imagine you have hundreds (or thousands) of customers sending thousands of requests per second to your application. How do you safely deploy new versions of your application? How can you limit the damage if the latest version of your application contains a critical bug? In this chapter, you will learn about the mechanisms and techniques that can be used with Kubernetes to implement multiple different deployment strategies that are critical to running applications at enterprise or internet scale.

We recommend you read chapters 1, 2, and 3 before reading this chapter.

5.1   *Deployment basics*

In Kubernetes, you can deploy a single Pod using a manifest with PodSpec only. Suppose you want to deploy a set of identical Pods with guaranteed availability. In that case, you can define a manifest with a ReplicaSet[1] to maintain a stable set of replica Pods running at any given time. A ReplicaSet is defined with the selector that specifies how to identify Pods, the number of replicas to be maintained, and a PodSpec. A ReplicaSet maintains the desired number of replicas by creating and deleting Pods as needed (figure 5.1).

> **REPLICASET IS NOT DECLARATIVE**   ReplicaSet is not declarative and hence not suitable for GitOps. Section 5.1.1 will explain how ReplicaSet works and why it is not declarative in detail. Even though ReplicaSet is not declarative, it is still an important concept because the Deployment resource uses ReplicaSet objects to manage Pods.

Deployment[2] is a higher-level concept that leverages multiple ReplicaSets (figure 5.1) to provide declarative updates to Pods along with a lot of other useful features (section 5.1.2). Once you define the desired state in a Deployment manifest, the Deployment controller will continue to observe the actual states and update the existing state to the desired state if they are different.

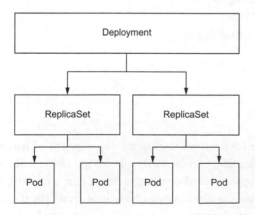

Figure 5.1   Deployments leverage one or more ReplicaSets to provide a declarative update of the application. Each ReplicaSet manages the actual number of Pods based on PodSpec and the number of replicas.

---

[1]   https://kubernetes.io/docs/concepts/workloads/controllers/replicaset/.

[2]   https://kubernetes.io/docs/concepts/workloads/controllers/deployment/.

5.1.1 Why ReplicaSet is not a good fit for GitOps

The ReplicaSet manifest includes a selector that specifies how to identify Pods it manages, the number of replicas of Pods to maintain, and a Pod template defining how new Pods should be created to meet the desired number of replicas. A ReplicaSet controller will then create and delete Pods as needed to match the desired number specified in the manifest. As we mentioned early, ReplicaSet is not declarative, and we will use a tutorial to give you an in-depth understanding of how ReplicaSet works and why it is not declarative:

1 Deploy a ReplicaSet with two Pods.
2 Update the image id in the manifest.
3 Apply the updated manifest and observe the ReplicaSet.
4 Update `replicas` to 3 in the manifest.
5 Apply the updated manifest and observe the ReplicaSet.

If ReplicaSet is declarative, you should see three Pods with the updated image id.

First, we will apply the ReplicaSet.yaml, which will create two Pods with image id `argoproj/rollouts-demo:blue` and a service:

```
$ kubectl apply -f ReplicaSet.yaml
replicaset.apps/demo created
service/demo created
```

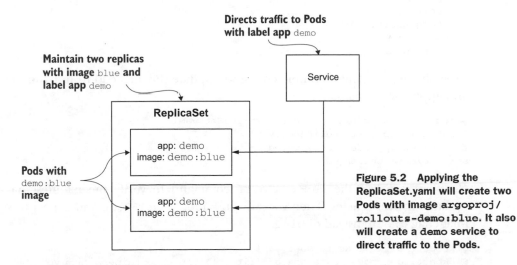

Figure 5.2 Applying the ReplicaSet.yaml will create two Pods with image `argoproj/rollouts-demo:blue`. It also will create a `demo` service to direct traffic to the Pods.

Listing 5.1 ReplicaSet.yaml

```
apiVersion: apps/v1
kind: ReplicaSet
metadata:
  name: demo
```

```
    labels:
      app: demo
spec:
  replicas: 2                    ⊲———  Updates replicas
  selector:                            from 2 to 3
    matchLabels:
      app: demo
  template:
    metadata:
      labels:
        app: demo
    spec:
      containers:
      - name: demo
        image: argoproj/rollouts-demo:blue    ⊲———  Updates image tag
        imagePullPolicy: Always                       from blue to green
        ports:
        - containerPort: 8080
---
apiVersion: v1
kind: Service
metadata:
  name: demo
  labels:
    app: demo
spec:
  ports:
  - protocol: TCP
    port: 80
    targetPort: 8080
  selector:
    app: demo
```

After the deployment is completed, we will update the image id from `blue` to `green` and apply the changes:

```
$ sed -i .bak 's/blue/green/g' ReplicaSet.yaml
$ kubectl apply -f ReplicaSet.yaml
replicaset.apps/demo configured
service/demo unchanged
```

Next, we can use the `kubectl diff` command to verify the manifest has been updated in Kubernetes. Then we can run `kubectl get Pods` and expect to see the image tag `green` instead of `blue`:

```
$ kubectl diff -f ReplicaSet.yaml
$ kubectl get pods -o jsonpath="{.items[*].spec.containers[*].image}"
argoproj/rollouts-demo:blue argoproj/rollouts-demo:blue
```

Even though the updated manifest has been applied, the existing Pods did not get updated to green. Let's update the `replicas` number from 2 to 3 and apply the manifest:

```
$ sed -i .bak 's/replicas: 2/replicas: 3/g' ReplicaSet.yaml
$ kubectl apply -f ReplicaSet.yaml
replicaset.apps/demo configured
```

```
service/demo unchanged
$ kubectl get pods -o jsonpath="{.items[*].spec.containers[*].image}"
argoproj/rollouts-demo:blue argoproj/rollouts-demo:green
argoproj/rollouts-demo:blue
$ kubectl describe rs demo
Name:         demo
Namespace:    default
Selector:     app=demo
Labels:       app=demo
Annotations:  kubectl.kubernetes.io/last-applied-configuration:
                {"apiVersion":"apps/
    v1","kind":"ReplicaSet","metadata":{"annotations":{},"labels":{"app":"de
    mo"},"name":"demo","namespace":"default"},"spe...
Replicas:     3 current / 3 desired
Pods Status:  3 Running / 0 Waiting / 0 Succeeded / 0 Failed
Pod Template:
  Labels:  app=demo
  Containers:
   demo:
    Image:        argoproj/rollouts-demo:green
    Port:         8080/TCP
    Host Port:    0/TCP
    Environment:  <none>
    Mounts:       <none>
  Volumes:        <none>
Events:
  Type    Reason           Age   From                    Message
  ----    ------           ----  ----                    -------
  Normal  SuccessfulCreate 13m   replicaset-controller   Created pod: demo-gfd8g
  Normal  SuccessfulCreate 13m   replicaset-controller   Created pod: demo-gxl6j
  Normal  SuccessfulCreate 10m   replicaset-controller   Created pod: demo-vbx9q
```

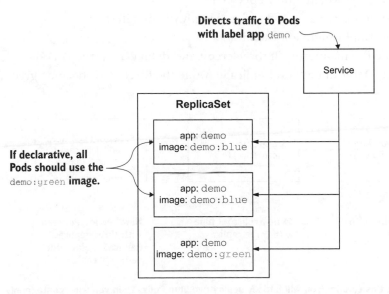

Figure 5.3   After applying the changes, you will see that only two Pods are running the blue image. If ReplicaSet is declarative, all three Pods should be green.

Surprisingly, the third Pod's image tag is green, but the first two Pods remain blue because the ReplicaSet controller's job is only to guarantee the number of running Pods. If ReplicaSet were truly declarative, the ReplicaSet controller should detect the changes with image tag/replicas and update all three Pods to green. In the next section, you will see how Deployment works and why it is declarative.

5.1.2 *How Deployment works with ReplicaSets*

Deployment is fully declarative and perfectly complements GitOps. Deployment performs rolling updates to deploy services with zero downtime. Let's go through a tutorial to examine how Deployment achieves rolling updates using multiple ReplicaSets.

> **ROLLING UPDATES** Rolling updates allow Deployments to update with zero downtime by incrementally updating Pod instances with new ones. Rolling updates work great if your service is stateless and backward compatible. Otherwise, you will have to look into other deployment strategies, like blue-green, which will be covered in section 5.1.3.

Let's imagine a real-life scenario of how this would be applicable. Suppose you run a payments service for small businesses to process credit cards. The service needs to be available 24/7, and you have been running two Pods (blue) to handle the current volume. You notice the two Pods are maxing out, so you decide to scale up to three Pods (blue) to support the increased traffic. Next, your product manager wants to add debit card support, so you need to deploy a version with three Pods (green) with zero downtime:

1 Deploy two credit card (blue) Pods using Deployment.
2 Review Deployment and ReplicaSet.
3 Update `replicas` from 2 to 3 and apply the manifest.
4 Review Deployment and ReplicaSet.
5 Update the manifest with three credit and debit card (green) Pods.
6 Review Deployment and ReplicaSet while the three Pods become green.

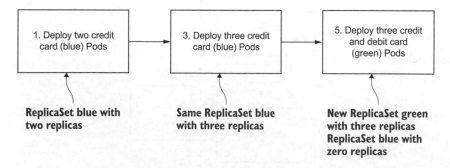

Figure 5.4   In this tutorial, you will initially deploy two blue Pods. Then you will update/apply the manifest to three replicas. Finally, you will update/apply the manifest to three green Pods.

Let's start with creating the initial Deployment. As you can see from listing 5.2, the YAML is practically the same as listing 5.1, with changes only to line 2 to use Deployment instead of ReplicaSet:

```
$ kubectl apply -f deployment.yaml
deployment.apps/demo created
service/demo created
```

Listing 5.2   deployment.yaml

```
apiVersion: apps/v1
kind: Deployment
metadata:
  name: demo
  labels:
    app: demo
spec:
  replicas: 2                              ◁─── replicas initially
  selector:                                      set to 2
    matchLabels:
      app: demo
  template:
    metadata:
      labels:
        app: demo
    spec:
      containers:
      - name: demo
        image: argoproj/rollouts-demo:blue   ◁─── Image tag initially
        imagePullPolicy: Always                    set to blue
        ports:
        - containerPort: 8080
---
apiVersion: v1
kind: Service
metadata:
  name: demo
  labels:
    app: demo
spec:
  ports:
  - protocol: TCP
    port: 80
    targetPort: 8080
  selector:                     Service demo initially set to send traffic
    app: demo        ◁───       only to Pods with label app:demo
```

Let's review what was created after we applied the Deployment manifest:

```
                                                         Two running
                                                     ◁── Pods
$ kubectl get pods
NAME                   READY   STATUS             RESTARTS   AGE
demo-8656dbfdc5-97slx   0/1    ContainerCreating   0         7s
demo-8656dbfdc5-sbl6p   1/1    Running             0         7s
```

```
$ kubectl get Deployment                          ◄──┐  One demo
NAME    READY   UP-TO-DATE   AVAILABLE   AGE          │  Deployment
demo    2/2     2            2           61s

                                                      ┌── One ReplicaSet
$ kubectl get rs                                  ◄───┘  demo-8656dbfdc5
NAME              DESIRED   CURRENT   READY   AGE
demo-8656dbfdc5   2         2         2       44s     ┌── The demo Deployment
                                                      │  creates the ReplicaSet
$ kubectl describe rs demo-8656dbfdc5 |grep Controlled ◄┘ demo-8656dbfdc5.
Controlled By:  Deployment/demo

$ kubectl describe rs demo-8656dbfdc5 |grep Replicas  ◄──┐ ReplicaSet demo-8656dbfdc5
Replicas:        2 current / 2 desired                   │ uses image id
                                                         │ argoproj/rollouts-demo:blue.
$ kubectl describe rs demo-8656dbfdc5 |grep Image        #F
    Image:          argoproj/rollouts-demo:blue
```

As expected, we have one Deployment and one ReplicaSet demo-8656dbfdc5 created
and controlled by the demo deployment. ReplicaSet demo-8656dbfdc5 manages two
replicas of Pods with the blue image. Next, we will update the manifest with three
replicas and review the changes:

```
$ sed -i .bak 's/replicas: 2/replicas: 3/g' deployment.yaml

$ kubectl apply -f deployment.yaml
deployment.apps/demo configured
service/demo unchanged

$ kubectl get pods
NAME                    READY   STATUS           RESTARTS   AGE
demo-8656dbfdc5-97slx   1/1     Running   0      98s
demo-8656dbfdc5-sbl6p   1/1     Running   0      98s
demo-8656dbfdc5-vh76b   1/1     Running   0      4s

$ kubectl get Deployment
NAME    READY   UP-TO-DATE   AVAILABLE   AGE
demo    3/3     3            3           109s

$ kubectl get rs
NAME              DESIRED   CURRENT   READY   AGE
demo-8656dbfdc5   3         3         3       109s

$ kubectl describe rs demo-5c5575fb88 |grep Replicas
Replicas:        3 current / 3 desired

$ kubectl describe rs demo-8656dbfdc5 |grep Image
    Image:          argoproj/rollouts-demo:blue
```

After the update, we should see the same Deployment and ReplicaSet that now manages the three blue Pods. At this point, the Deployment looks precisely as is depicted
in figure 5.5. Next, we will update the manifest to image green and apply the changes.
Since the image id has changed, Deployment will then create a second ReplicaSet to
deploy the green image.

DEPLOYMENT AND REPLICASETS A Deployment will create one ReplicaSet per image id and set the number of replicas to the desired value in the ReplicaSet with the matching image id. For all other ReplicaSets, Deployment will set those ReplicaSets' replica numbers to 0 to terminate all nonmatching image id Pods.

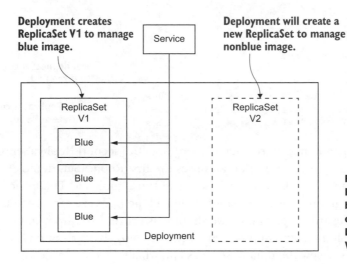

Figure 5.5 **Deployment uses ReplicaSet V1 to maintain the blue deployment. If there is a change to the nonblue image, Deployment will create ReplicaSet V2 for the new deployment.**

Before you apply the change, you can open up a new terminal with the following command to monitor the status of ReplicaSets. You should see one ReplicaSet (blue) with three Pods:

```
$ kubectl get rs --watch
NAME                DESIRED   CURRENT   READY   AGE
demo-8656dbfdc5     3         3         3       60s
```

Go back to the original terminal, update the deployment, and apply the changes:

```
$ sed -i .bak 's/blue/green/g' deployment.yaml
$ kubectl apply -f deployment.yaml
deployment.apps/demo configured
service/demo unchanged
```

Now switch to the terminal, and you should see the ReplicaSet demo-8656dbfdc5 (blue) scaled down to 0 and a new ReplicaSet demo-6b574cb9dd (green) scaled up to 3:

```
$ kubectl get rs --watch
NAME                DESIRED   CURRENT   READY   AGE
demo-8656dbfdc5     3         3         3       60s      ◁── Blue ReplicaSet began
demo-6b574cb9dd     1         0         0       0s       ◁── with three Pods
demo-6b574cb9dd     1         0         0       0s           Green ReplicaSet scaled
demo-6b574cb9dd     1         1         0       0s           up with one Pod
demo-6b574cb9dd     1         1         1       3s
```

```
demo-8656dbfdc5    2          3          3          102s
demo-6b574cb9dd    2          1          1          3s
demo-8656dbfdc5    2          3          3          102s
demo-6b574cb9dd    2          1          1          3s
demo-8656dbfdc5    2          2          2          102s
demo-6b574cb9dd    2          2          1          3s
demo-6b574cb9dd    2          2          2          6s
demo-8656dbfdc5    1          2          2          105s
demo-8656dbfdc5    1          2          2          105s
demo-6b574cb9dd    3          2          2          6s
demo-6b574cb9dd    3          2          2          6s
demo-8656dbfdc5    1          1          1          105s
demo-6b574cb9dd    3          3          2          6s      ⌐ Green ReplicaSet completed
demo-6b574cb9dd    3          3          3          9s      ◄    with three Pods
demo-8656dbfdc5    0          1          1          108s
demo-8656dbfdc5    0          1          1          108s    ⌐ Blue ReplicaSet completed
demo-8656dbfdc5    0          0          0          108s    ◄    with zero Pods
```

Let's review what is happening here. Deployment uses the second ReplicaSet, demo-6b574cb9dd, to bring up one green Pod and uses the first ReplicaSet, demo-8656dbf-dc5, to terminate one of the blue Pods, as depicted in figure 5.6. This process will repeat until all three green Pods are created while all blue Pods are terminated.

While we are discussing Deployment, we should also cover two important configuration parameters with the rolling-update strategy in Deployment: max unavailable and max surge. Let's review the default settings and what they mean according to the Kubernetes documentation:

```
$ kubectl describe Deployment demo |grep RollingUpdateStrategy
RollingUpdateStrategy:  25% max unavailable, 25% max surge
```

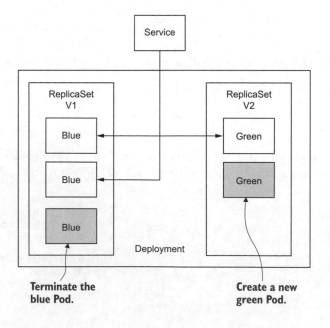

Figure 5.6   Deployment scales down ReplicaSet V1 and scales up ReplicaSet V2. ReplicaSet V1 will have zero Pods, and ReplicaSet V2 will have three green Pods when the process is complete.

Deployment ensures that only a certain number of Pods are down while they are being updated. By default, it ensures that at least 75% of the desired number of Pods are up (25% max unavailable).

Deployment also ensures that only a certain number of Pods are created above the desired number of Pods. By default, it ensures that at most 125% of the desired number of Pods are up (25% max surge).

Let's see how it works in action. We will change the image id back to blue and configure max unavailable to 3 and max surge to 3:

```
$ kubectl apply -f deployment2.yaml
deployment.apps/demo configured
service/demo unchanged
```

Now you can switch back to the terminal with ReplicaSet monitoring:

```
$ kubectl get rs --watch
NAME               DESIRED   CURRENT   READY   AGE
demo-8656dbfdc5    3         3         3       60s
demo-6b574cb9dd    1         0         0       0s
demo-6b574cb9dd    1         0         0       0s
demo-6b574cb9dd    1         1         0       0s
demo-6b574cb9dd    1         1         1       3s
demo-8656dbfdc5    2         3         3       102s
demo-6b574cb9dd    2         1         1       3s
demo-8656dbfdc5    2         3         3       102s
demo-6b574cb9dd    2         1         1       3s
demo-8656dbfdc5    2         2         2       102s
demo-6b574cb9dd    2         2         1       3s
demo-6b574cb9dd    2         2         2       6s
demo-8656dbfdc5    1         2         2       105s
demo-8656dbfdc5    1         2         2       105s
demo-6b574cb9dd    3         2         2       6s
demo-6b574cb9dd    3         2         2       6s
demo-8656dbfdc5    1         1         1       105s
demo-6b574cb9dd    3         3         2       6s
demo-6b574cb9dd    3         3         3       9s
demo-8656dbfdc5    0         1         1       108s
demo-8656dbfdc5    0         1         1       108s
demo-8656dbfdc5    0         0         0       108s
demo-8656dbfdc5    0         0         0       14m
demo-8656dbfdc5    3         0         0       14m
demo-6b574cb9dd    0         3         3       13m
demo-6b574cb9dd    0         3         3       13m
demo-8656dbfdc5    3         0         0       14m
demo-6b574cb9dd    0         0         0       13m
demo-8656dbfdc5    3         3         0       14m
demo-8656dbfdc5    3         3         1       14m
demo-8656dbfdc5    3         3         2       14m
demo-8656dbfdc5    3         3         3       14m
```

Green ReplicaSet immediately went to zero Pods.

Blue ReplicaSet scaled up three Pods at once.

As you can see from the ReplicaSet change status, ReplicaSet demo-8656dbfdc5 (green) immediately went to zero Pods and ReplicaSet demo-6b574cb9dd (blue) immediately went to three instead of one at a time.

Listing 5.3   deployment2.yaml

```
apiVersion: apps/v1
kind: Deployment
metadata:
  name: demo
  labels:
    app: demo
spec:
  replicas: 3
  selector:
    matchLabels:
      app: demo
  strategy:
    type: RollingUpdate
    rollingUpdate:
      maxSurge: 3                    ◁──┐  Creates up to three
      maxUnavailable: 3                  │  Pods at once
  template:                         ◁─   Terminates up to
    metadata:                            three Pods at once
      labels:
        app: demo
      spec:
        containers:
        - name: demo
          image: argoproj/rollouts-demo:blue
          imagePullPolicy: Always
          ports:
          - containerPort: 8080
---
apiVersion: v1
kind: Service
metadata:
  name: demo
  labels:
    app: demo
spec:
  ports:
  - protocol: TCP
    port: 80
    targetPort: 8080
  selector:                         ┐  Service demo will send traffic to
    app: demo                   ◁───   all Pods with label app:demo.
```

By now, you can see that Deployment achieves deployment with zero downtime by leveraging one ReplicaSet for blue and another ReplicaSet for green. As you learn about other deployment strategies in the rest of the chapter, you will discover that they are all implemented similarly using two different ReplicaSets to achieve the desired motivation.

5.1.3   *Traffic routing*

In Kubernetes, a Service is an abstraction that defines a logical set of Pods and a policy to access them. The set of Pods targeted by a Service is determined by a selector that is a field within the Service manifest. Service will then forward traffic to Pods with the matching labels as specified by the selector (also see listings 5.2 and 5.3). Service does round-robin load balancing and works great for rolling updates if the underlying Pods are stateless and backward compatible. If you need to customize load balancing for your deployment, you will need to explore other routing alternatives.

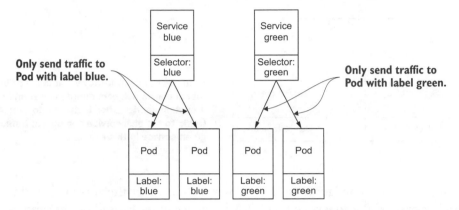

Figure 5.7 A service will only route traffic to Pods with matching labels. In this example, Service blue will only route traffic to Pods with the label blue. Service green will only route traffic to Pods with the label green.

NGINX Ingress Controller[3] can be used for many use cases and supports various balancing and routing rules. Ingress Controller can be configured as the front load balancer to perform custom routing such as TLS termination, URL rewrite, or routing traffic to any number of services by defining the custom rules. Figure 5.8 illustrates the NGINX controller configured with rules to send 40% of incoming traffic to service blue and 60% of incoming traffic to service green.

Istio Gateway[4] is a load balancer operating at the Kubernetes cluster's edge, receiving incoming or outgoing HTTP/TCP connections. The specification describes a set of ports that should be exposed, the type of protocol to use, and

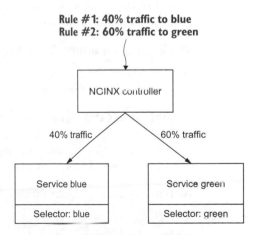

Figure 5.8 NGINX Ingress Controller can provide advanced traffic control. In this example, NGINX Ingress Controller is configured with one rule to send 40% of traffic to service blue and a second rule to send 60% of traffic to service green.

---

[3] https://kubernetes.github.io/ingress-nginx/user-guide/basic-usage/.
[4] https://istio.io/latest/docs/reference/config/networking/gateway/.

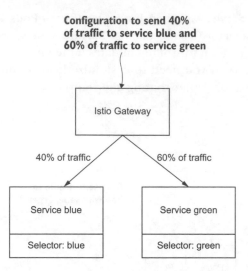

**Configuration to send 40%
of traffic to service blue and
60% of traffic to service green**

Istio Gateway

40% of traffic   60% of traffic

Service blue   Service green

Selector: blue   Selector: green

**Figure 5.9   Istio Gateway is another load balancer
that supports rich configuration for traffic routing.
A custom configuration is defined to send 40% of
traffic to the blue service and 60% of traffic to the
green service in this example.**

custom routing configuration. Istio Gateway will direct the incoming traffic to the
back services (40% to service blue, 60% to service green) based on the custom configuration (figure 5.9).

> **NOTE**   Both NGINX Ingress Controller and Istio Gateway are advanced topics
> and beyond the scope of this book. Please refer to the links in the footnotes
> for additional information.

5.1.4   *Configuring minikube for other strategies*

For the rest of the tutorial, you will need to enable NGINX ingress and Argo Rollouts[5]
support in your Kubernetes cluster.

> **ARGO ROLLOUTS**   The Argo Rollouts controller uses the Rollout custom
> resource to provide additional deployment strategies such as blue-green and
> canary to Kubernetes. The Rollout custom resource provides feature parity
> with the deployment resource but with additional deployment strategies.

With minikube,[6] you can enable NGINX ingress support simply by running the following command:

```
$ minikube addons enable ingress
✸ The 'ingress' addon is enabled
```

---

[5] https://github.com/argoproj/argo-rollouts.
[6] https://kubernetes.io/docs/tasks/access-application-cluster/ingress-minikube/.

To install Argo Rollouts in your cluster, you need to create an `argo-rollouts` Namespace and run install.yaml. For other environments, please refer to the Argo Rollouts Getting Started guide:[7]

```
$ kubectl create ns argo-rollouts
namespace/argo-rollouts created
$ kubectl apply -n argo-rollouts -f https://raw.githubusercontent.com/
    argoproj/argo-rollouts/stable/manifests/install.yaml
customresourcedefinition.apiextensions.k8s.io/analysisruns.argoproj.io
    created
customresourcedefinition.apiextensions.k8s.io/analysistemplates.argoproj.io
    created
customresourcedefinition.apiextensions.k8s.io/experiments.argoproj.io created
customresourcedefinition.apiextensions.k8s.io/rollouts.argoproj.io created
serviceaccount/argo-rollouts created
role.rbac.authorization.k8s.io/argo-rollouts-role created
clusterrole.rbac.authorization.k8s.io/argo-rollouts-aggregate-to-admin
    created
clusterrole.rbac.authorization.k8s.io/argo-rollouts-aggregate-to-edit created
clusterrole.rbac.authorization.k8s.io/argo-rollouts-aggregate-to-view created
clusterrole.rbac.authorization.k8s.io/argo-rollouts-clusterrole created
rolebinding.rbac.authorization.k8s.io/argo-rollouts-role-binding created
clusterrolebinding.rbac.authorization.k8s.io/argo-rollouts-clusterrolebinding
    created
service/argo-rollouts-metrics created
deployment.apps/argo-rollouts created
```

5.2 *Blue-green*

As you learned in section 5.1, Deployment's Rolling Update is a great way to update applications because your app will use about the same amount of resources during a deployment with zero downtime and minimal impact on performance. However, there are many legacy applications out there that don't work well with rolling updates due to backward incompatibility or statefulness. Some applications may also require deploying a new version and cutting over to it right away or fast rollback in case of issues.

For these use cases, a blue-green deployment will be the appropriate deployment strategy. Blue-green deployment accomplishes these motivations by having two deployments fully scale at the same time, but only direct incoming traffic to one of the two deployments.

> **NOTE** In this tutorial, we will use NGINX Ingress Controller to route 100% of traffic to either the blue or green deployment since the built-in Kubernetes Service[8] only manipulates the iptables[9] and does not reset the existing connection to the Pods and therefore is not suitable for blue-green deployment.

---

[7] https://argoproj.github.io/argo-rollouts/getting-started/.
[8] https://kubernetes.io/docs/concepts/services-networking/service/.
[9] https://en.wikipedia.org/wiki/Iptables.

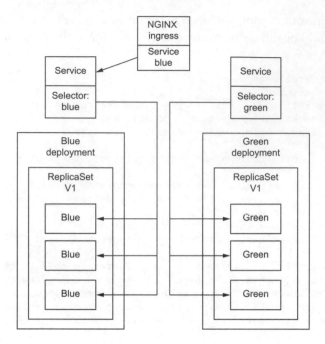

Figure 5.10   The initial deployment will configure NGINX Controller to send all traffic to the blue service. The blue service will in turn send traffic to the blue Pods.

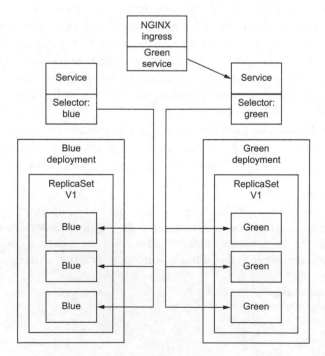

Figure 5.11   After the configuration update in the NGINX controller, all traffic will be sent to the green service. The green service will in turn send traffic to the green Pods.

5.2.1 *Blue-green with Deployment*

In this tutorial, we will perform a blue-green deployment using native Kubernetes Deployment and Service.

> **NOTE** Please refer to section 5.1.4 on how to enable ingress and install Argo Rollouts in your Kubernetes cluster prior to this tutorial.

1 Create a blue deployment and service.
2 Create ingress to direct traffic to the blue service.
3 View the application in the browser (blue).
4 Deploy a green deployment and service, and wait for all Pods to be ready.
5 Update ingress to direct traffic to the green service.
6 View the web page again in the browser (green).

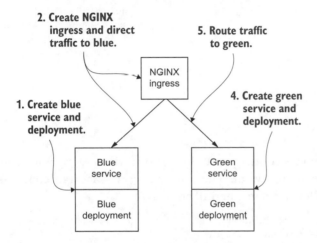

Figure 5.12 Create the initial state with a blue service and deployment along with NGINX Ingress Controller directing traffic to the blue service. Then create the green service and deployment with the configuration change to NGINX Ingress Controller to direct traffic to the green service.

We will first create the blue deployment by applying the blue_deployment.yaml:

```
$ kubectl apply -f blue_deployment.yaml
deployment.apps/blue created
service/blue-service created
```

Listing 5.4 blue_deployment.yaml

```
apiVersion: apps/v1
kind: Deployment
metadata:
  name: blue
  labels:
    app: blue
spec:
  replicas: 3
```

```
      selector:
        matchLabels:
          app: blue
      template:
        metadata:
          labels:
            app: blue
        spec:
          containers:
          - name: demo
            image: argoproj/rollouts-demo:blue
            imagePullPolicy: Always
            ports:
            - containerPort: 8080
---
apiVersion: v1
kind: Service
metadata:
  name: blue-service
  labels:
    app: blue
spec:
  ports:
  - protocol: TCP
    port: 80
    targetPort: 8080
  selector:
    app: blue
  type: NodePort
```

Now we can expose an ingress controller, so the `blue` service is accessible from your browser by applying blue_ingress.yaml. The `kubectl get ingress` command will return the ingress controller hostname and IP address:

```
$ kubectl apply -f blue_ingress.yaml
ingress.extensions/demo-ingress created
configmap/nginx-configuration created
$ kubectl get ingress
NAME            HOSTS        ADDRESS          PORTS    AGE
demo-ingress    demo.info    192.168.99.111   80       60s
```

NOTE NGINX Ingress Controller will only intercept traffic with the hostname defined in the custom rule. Please make sure you add demo.info and its IP address to your /etc/hosts.

Listing 5.5   blue_ingress.yaml

```
apiVersion: extensions/v1beta1
kind: Ingress
metadata:
  name: demo-ingress
spec:
  rules:                         ⟵──┐ Assigns the hostname demo.info
  - host: demo.info                 ┘ for the ingress controller
```

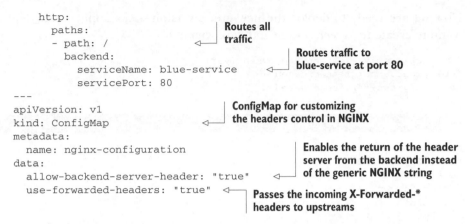

```
http:
  paths:
  - path: /                  ⟵  Routes all
    backend:                      traffic
      serviceName: blue-service  ⟵  Routes traffic to
      servicePort: 80               blue-service at port 80
---
apiVersion: v1                ⟵  ConfigMap for customizing
kind: ConfigMap                   the headers control in NGINX
metadata:
  name: nginx-configuration
data:                             Enables the return of the header
  allow-backend-server-header: "true"  ⟵  server from the backend instead
  use-forwarded-headers: "true"  ⟵  of the generic NGINX string
```

Passes the incoming X-Forwarded-*
headers to upstreams

Once you have the ingress controller, blue service, and deployment created and have updated /etc/hosts with demo.info and the correct IP address, you can enter the URL demo.info and see the blue service running.

> **NOTE** The demo app will continue to call the active service in the background and show the latest results on the right side. Blue (darker gray in print) is the running version, and green (lighter gray in print) is the new version.

Service selector to view
latency and error rate

Latency and error rate
of the selected service

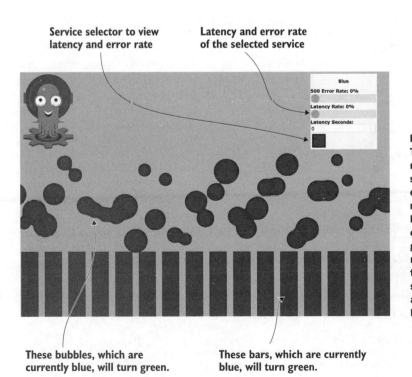

Figure 5.13
The HTML page will refresh every two seconds in the bar chart and every 100 milliseconds in the bubble chart to show either the blue or green service responding. Initially, the HTML page will show all blue because all traffic goes to the blue deployment.

These bubbles, which are currently blue, will turn green.

These bars, which are currently blue, will turn green.

Now we are ready to deploy the new green version. Let's apply green_deployment
.yaml to create the green service and deployment:

```
$ kubectl apply -f green_deployment.yaml
deployment.apps/green created
service/green-service created
```

Listing 5.6   green_deployment.yaml

```
apiVersion: apps/v1
kind: Deployment
metadata:
  name: green
  labels:
    app: green
spec:
  replicas: 3
  selector:
    matchLabels:
      app: green
  template:
    metadata:
      labels:
        app: green
    spec:
      containers:
      - name: green
        image: argoproj/rollouts-demo:green
        imagePullPolicy: Always
        ports:
        - containerPort: 8080
---
apiVersion: v1
kind: Service
metadata:
  name: green-service
  labels:
    app: green
spec:
  ports:
  - protocol: TCP
    port: 80
    targetPort: 8080
  selector:
    app: green
  type: NodePort
```

With the green service and deployment ready, we can now update the ingress controller to route traffic to the green service:

```
$ kubectl apply -f green_ingress.yaml
ingress.extensions/demo-ingress configured
configmap/nginx-configuration unchanged
```

Listing 5.7   green_ingress.yaml

```
apiVersion: extensions/v1beta1
kind: Ingress
metadata:
  name: demo-ingress
spec:
  rules:
  - host: demo.info
    http:
      paths:
      - path: /
        backend:
          serviceName: green-service      ◁──  Routes traffic to green-service
          servicePort: 80                        instead of blue-service
---
apiVersion: v1
kind: ConfigMap
metadata:
  name: nginx-configuration
data:
  allow-backend-server-header: "true"
  use-forwarded-headers: "true"
```

If you go back to your browser, you should see the service turning green!

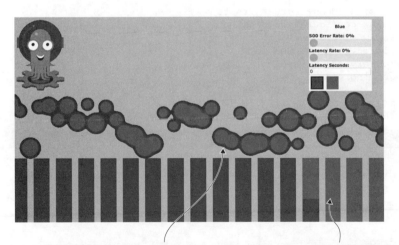

Figure 5.14   After the green deployment is complete and NGINX Ingress Controller is updated to direct traffic to the green deployment, the HTML page will start showing both the bubble and bar charts in green.

These bubbles, which were initially blue, are turning green.

These bars, which were initially blue, are turning green.

If you are happy with the deployment, you can either delete the blue service and deployment or scale down the blue deployment to 0.

Exercise 5.1

How would you scale down the blue deployment in a declarative way?

Exercise 5.2

If you want a fast rollback, should you delete the deployment or scale it down to 0?

5.2.2   *Blue-green with Argo Rollouts*

Blue-green deployment is definitely doable in production using the native Kubernetes Deployment with additional process and automation. A better approach is to make the entire blue-green deployment process fully automated and declarative; hence, Argo Rollouts is born.

Argo Rollouts introduces a new custom resource called `Rollout` to provide additional deployment strategies such as blue-green, canary (section 5.3), and progressive delivery (section 5.4) to Kubernetes. The `Rollout` custom resource provides feature parity with the Deployment resource with additional deployment strategies. In the next tutorial, you will see how simple it is to deploy blue-green with Argo Rollouts.

> **NOTE**   Please refer to section 5.1.4 on how to enable ingress and install Argo Rollouts in your Kubernetes cluster prior to this tutorial.

1   Deploy the NGINX Ingress Controller.
2   Deploy the production service and (blue) deployment using Argo Rollouts.
3   Update the manifest to use the green image.
4   Apply the updated manifest to deploy the new green version.

First, we will create the ingress controller, `demo-service`, and blue deployment:

```
$ kubectl apply -f ingress.yaml
ingress.extensions/demo-ingress created
configmap/nginx-configuration created
$ kubectl apply -f bluegreen_rollout.yaml
rollout.argoproj.io/demo created
service/demo-service created
$ kubectl get ingress
NAME           HOSTS        ADDRESS          PORTS   AGE
demo-ingress   demo.info    192.168.99.111   80      60s
```

Listing 5.8   ingress.yaml

```
apiVersion: extensions/v1beta1
kind: Ingress
metadata:
  name: demo-ingress
spec:
  rules:
  - host: demo.info
    http:
      paths:
      - path: /
        backend:
          serviceName: demo-service
          servicePort: 80
---
apiVersion: v1
data:
  allow-backend-server-header: "true"
  use-forwarded-headers: "true"
```

```
kind: ConfigMap
metadata:
  name: nginx-configuration
```

Listing 5.9   bluegreen_rollout.yaml

```
apiVersion: argoproj.io/v1alpha1
kind: Rollout                          ⟵┐ Specifies the kind to be
metadata:                                │ Rollout instead of Deployment
  name: demo
  labels:
    app: demo
spec:
  replicas: 3
  selector:
    matchLabels:
      app: demo
  template:
    metadata:
      labels:
        app: demo
    spec:
      containers:
      - name: demo                       ┌ Sets initial deployment
        image: argoproj/rollouts-demo:blue ⟵┘ with blue image
        imagePullPolicy: Always
        ports:
        - containerPort: 8080        ┌ Uses blue-green instead
  Strategy:                          │ of rolling updates as      ┌ Automatically updates the
    bluegreen:                  ⟵────┘ deployment strategy        │ selector in the demo-service to
      autoPromotionEnabled: true                            ⟵────┘ send all traffic to green Pods
      activeService: demo-service  ⟵┐ Specifies the demo-service to front
---                                  │ traffic for this rollout object
apiVersion: v1
kind: Service
metadata:
  name: demo-service
  labels:
    app: demo
spec:
  ports:
  - protocol: TCP
    port: 80
    targetPort: 8080
  selector:
    app: demo
  type: NodePort
```

NOTE Argo Rollouts internally will maintain one ReplicaSet for blue and one ReplicaSet for green. It will also ensure that the green deployment is fully scaled before updating the service selector to send all traffic over to green. (Hence, only one service is required in this case.) In addition, Argo Rollouts will also wait 30 seconds for all blue traffic to complete and scale down the blue deployment.

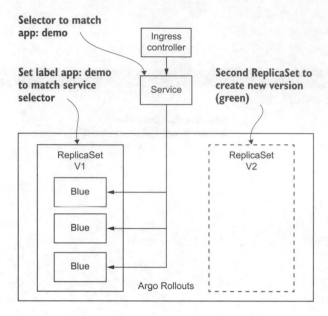

Selector to match app: demo

Set label app: demo to match service selector

Second ReplicaSet to create new version (green)

Ingress controller

Service

ReplicaSet V1

Blue

Blue

Blue

Argo Rollouts

ReplicaSet V2

Figure 5.15   Argo Rollouts is similar to a Deployment that uses one or more ReplicaSets to fulfill deployment requests. In the initial state, Argo Rollouts creates ReplicaSet V1 for blue Pods.

Once you have the ingress controller, service, and deployment created and updated /etc/hosts, you can enter the URL demo.info and see the blue service running.

NOTE   NGINX Ingress Controller will only intercept traffic with the hostname defined in the custom rule. Please make sure you add demo.info and its IP address to your /etc/hosts.

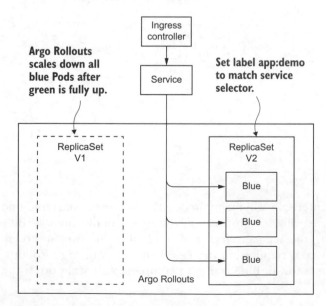

Ingress controller

Service

Argo Rollouts scales down all blue Pods after green is fully up.

Set label app:demo to match service selector.

ReplicaSet V1

ReplicaSet V2

Blue

Blue

Blue

Argo Rollouts

Figure 5.16   Argo Rollouts creates ReplicaSet V2 for green Pods. Once all green Pods are up and running, Argo Rollouts automatically scales down all blue Pods.

Now we will update the manifest to deploy the new version, green. Once you have applied the updated manifest, you can go back to your browser and see all bars and dots turning green (figure 5.16):

```
$ sed -i .bak 's/demo:blue/demo:green/g' bluegreen_rollout.yaml
$ kubectl apply -f bluegreen_rollout.yaml
deployment.apps/demo configured
service/demo-service unchanged
```

5.3   Canary

Canary deployment is a technique to reduce the risk of introducing a new software version in production by rolling out the change to a small subset of users for a short period before making it available to everybody. Canary acts as an early indicator for failures to avoid problematic deployments having a full impact on all customers at once. If one canary deployment fails, the rest of your servers aren't affected, and you can simply terminate the canary and triage the problems.

> **NOTE** Based on our experience, most production incidents are due to a change in the system, such as a new deployment. Canary deployment is another opportunity to test your new release before the new release reaches all user populations.

Our canary example is similar to the blue-green example.

With Canary running and getting production traffic, we can then monitor the canary health (latency, error, and so on) for a fixed period (such as one hour) to determine whether to scale up green deployment and route all traffic to the green

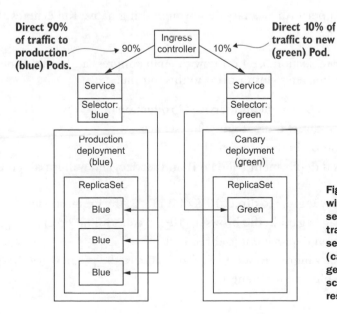

Figure 5.17 The ingress controller will front both blue and green services, but in this case, 90% of traffic will go to the blue (production) service, and 10% will go to the green (canary) service. Since green is only getting 10% of the traffic, we will only scale up one green Pod to minimize resource usage.

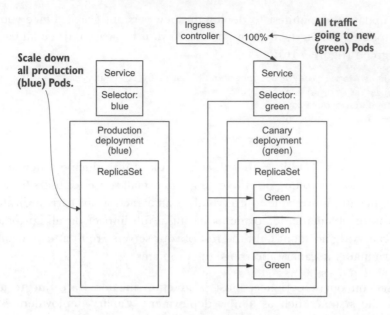

Figure 5.18   If there is no error with the canary Pod, green deployment will scale up to three Pods and receive 100% of the production traffic.

service or route all traffic back to the blue service and terminate the green Pod in case of issues.

5.3.1   *Canary with Deployment*

In this tutorial, we will perform a canary deployment using native Kubernetes Deployment and Service.

> **NOTE**   Please refer to section 5.1.4 on how to enable ingress and install Argo Rollouts in your Kubernetes cluster prior to this tutorial.

1 Create the blue deployment and service (Production).
2 Create ingress to direct traffic to the blue service.
3 View the application in the browser (blue).
4 Deploy the green deployment (one Pod) and service, and wait for all Pods to be ready.
5 Create the canary ingress to direct 10% of traffic to the green service.
6 View the web page again in the browser (10% green with no error).
7 Scale up the green deployment to three Pods.
8 Update the canary ingress to send 100% of traffic to the green service.
9 Scale down the blue deployment to 0.

We can create the production deployment by applying blue_deployment.yaml (listing 5.4):

```
$ kubectl apply -f blue_deployment.yaml
deployment.apps/blue created
service/blue-service created
```

Now we can expose an ingress controller so the blue service is accessible from our browser by applying the blue_ingress.yaml (listing 5.5). The `kubectl get ingress` command will return the ingress controller hostname and IP address:

```
$ kubectl apply -f blue_ingress.yaml
ingress.extensions/demo-ingress created
configmap/nginx-configuration created
$ kubectl get ingress
NAME           HOSTS        ADDRESS          PORTS   AGE
demo-ingress   demo.info    192.168.99.111   80      60s
```

> **NOTE** NGINX Ingress Controller will only intercept traffic with the hostname defined in the custom rule. Please make sure you add demo.info and its IP address to your /etc/hosts.

Once you have the ingress controller, blue service, and deployment created and have updated /etc/hosts with demo.info and the correct IP address, you can enter the URL demo.info and see the blue service running.

Now we are ready to deploy the new green version. Let's apply green_deployment.yaml to create the green service and deployment:

```
$ kubectl apply -f green_deployment.yaml
deployment.apps/green created
service/green-service created
```

Listing 5.10 green_deployment.yaml

```
apiVersion: apps/v1
kind: Deployment
metadata:
  name: green
  labels:
    app: green
spec:
  replicas: 1          ◁—┐ ReplicaSet is set to 1 for the
  selector:               │ initial green deployment.
    matchLabels:
      app: green
  template:
    metadata:
      labels:
        app: green
    spec:
      containers:
```

```
          - name: green
            image: argoproj/rollouts-demo:green
            imagePullPolicy: Always
            ports:
            - containerPort: 8080
---
apiVersion: v1
kind: Service
metadata:
  name: green-service
  labels:
    app: green
spec:
  ports:
  - protocol: TCP
    port: 80
    targetPort: 8080
  selector:
    app: green
  type: NodePort
```

Next, we will create the `canary_ingress` so 10% of the traffic is routed to the canary (green) service:

```
$ kubectl apply -f canary_ingress.yaml
ingress.extensions/canary-ingress configured
configmap/nginx-configuration unchanged
```

Listing 5.11   canary_ingress.yaml

```
apiVersion: extensions/v1beta1
kind: Ingress
metadata:
  name: canary-ingress
  annotations:
    nginx.ingress.kubernetes.io/canary: "true"          ◁── Tells NGINX Ingress
                                                              Controller to mark this one
                                                              as canary and associates this
                                                              ingress with the main ingress
                                                              by matching host and path
    nginx.ingress.kubernetes.io/canary-weight: "10"     ◁── Routes 10% of traffic
                                                              to green-service
spec:
  rules:
  - host: demo.info
    http:
      paths:
      - path: /
        backend:
          serviceName: green-service
          servicePort: 80
---
apiVersion: v1
data:
  allow-backend-server-header: "true"
  use-forwarded-headers: "true"
kind: ConfigMap
metadata:
  name: nginx-configuration
```

Now you can go back to the browser and monitor the green service.

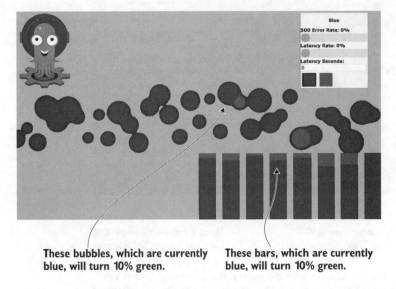

These bubbles, which are currently blue, will turn 10% green.

These bars, which are currently blue, will turn 10% green.

Figure 5.19   The HTML page will show a mix of blue and green in both the bubble and bar charts because 10% of the traffic is going to green Pods.

If you are able to see the correct result (healthy canary), you are ready to complete the canary deployment (green service). We will then scale up the green deployment, send all traffic to the green service, and scale down the blue deployment:

```
$ sed -i .bak 's/replicas: 1/replicas: 3/g' green_deployment.yaml
$ kubectl apply -f green_deployment.yaml
deployment.apps/green configured
service/green-service unchanged
$ sed -i .bak 's/10/100/g' canary_ingress.yaml
$ kubectl apply -f canary_ingress.yaml
ingress.extensions/canary-ingress configured
configmap/nginx-configuration unchanged
$ sed -i .bak 's/replicas: 3/replicas: 0/g' blue_deployment.yaml
$ kubectl apply -f blue_deployment.yaml
deployment.apps/blue configured
service/blue-service unchanged
```

Now you should be able to see all green bars and dots as 100% of the traffic is routed to the green service.

> **NOTE**   In true production, we will need to ensure all green Pods are up before we can send 100% of the traffic to the canary service. Optionally, we can incrementally increase the percentage of traffic to the green service while the green deployment is scaling up.

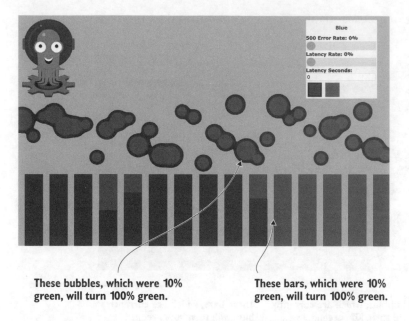

These bubbles, which were 10% green, will turn 100% green.

These bars, which were 10% green, will turn 100% green.

Figure 5.20   **If there is no error with the canary, the green deployment will scale up, and the blue deployment will scale down. After the blue deployment fully scales down, both the bubble and bar charts will show 100% green.**

5.3.2   *Canary with Argo Rollouts*

As you can see in section 5.3.1, using a canary deployment can help detect issues early to prevent problematic deployment but will involve many additional steps in the deployment process. In the next tutorial, we will use Argo Rollouts to simplify the process of canary deployment.

> **NOTE**   Please refer to section 5.1.4 on how to enable ingress and install Argo Rollouts in your Kubernetes cluster prior to this tutorial.

1 Create the ingress, production deployment, and service (blue).
2 View the application in the browser (blue).
3 Apply the manifest with the green image with 10% of the canary traffic for 60 seconds.
4 Create the canary ingress to direct 10% of the traffic to the green service.
5 View the web page again in the browser (10% green with no error).
6 Wait 60 seconds.
7 View the application again in the browser (all green).

First, we will create the ingress controller (listing 5.8), `demo-service`, and blue deployment (listing 5.12):

```
$ kubectl apply -f ingress.yaml
ingress.extensions/demo-ingress created
configmap/nginx-configuration created
$ kubectl apply -f canary_rollout.yaml
rollout.argoproj.io/demo created
service/demo-service created
$ kubectl get ingress
NAME            HOSTS        ADDRESS          PORTS   AGE
demo-ingress    demo.info    192.168.99.111   80      60s
```

Listing 5.12 canary_rollout.yaml

```yaml
apiVersion: argoproj.io/v1alpha1
kind: Rollout                          ◁── When a Rollout is first deployed,
metadata:                                  the strategy is ignored, and a
  name: demo                               regular deployment is performed.
  labels:
    app: demo
spec:
  replicas: 3
  selector:
    matchLabels:
      app: demo
  template:
    metadata:
      labels:
        app: demo
    spec:
      containers:
      - name: demo
        image: argoproj/rollouts-demo:blue
        imagePullPolicy: Always
        ports:
        - containerPort: 8080
  strategy:                            ◁── Deploys with
    canary:                                canary strategy
      maxSurge: "25%"
      maxUnavailable: 0
      steps:
      - setWeight: 10                  ◁──
      - pause:
          duration: 60                 ◁──
---
apiVersion: v1
kind: Service
```

Scales out enough Pods to service 10% of the traffic. In this example, Rollout will scale up one green Pod along with the three blue Pods resulting in the green Pod getting 25% of the traffic. Argo Rollouts can work with service mesh or NGINX Ingress Controller for fine-grain traffic routing.

Waits 60 seconds. If no error or user interruption happens, scales up green to 100%.

```
metadata:
  name: demo-service
  labels:
    app: demo
spec:
  ports:
  - protocol: TCP
    port: 80
    targetPort: 8080
  selector:
    app: demo
  type: NodePort
```

> **NOTE**   For the initial deployment (blue), `Rollout` will ignore the canary setting and perform a regular deployment.

Once you have the ingress controller, service, and deployment created and updated /etc/hosts with the demo.info and the correct IP address, you can enter the URL demo.info and see the blue service running.

> **NOTE**   NGINX Ingress Controller will only intercept traffic with the hostname defined in the custom rule. Please make sure you add demo.info and its IP address to your /etc/hosts.

Once the blue service is fully up and running, we can now update the manifest with the green image and apply the manifest:

```
$ sed -i .bak 's/demo:blue/demo:green/g' canary_rollout.yaml
$ kubectl apply -f canary_rollout.yaml
rollout.argoproj.io/demo configured
service/demo-service unchanged
```

Once the canary starts, you should see something similar to figure 5.19 in section 5.3.1. After one minute, the green ReplicaSet will scale up while the blue deployment scales down with all bars and dots going green (figure 5.20 in section 5.3.1).

5.4   *Progressive delivery*

Progressive delivery can also be viewed as a fully automated version of canary deployment. Instead of monitoring for a fixed period (such as one hour) before scaling up the canary deployment, progressive delivery will continuously monitor the Pods' health and scale up until fully scaled.

5.4.1   *Progressive delivery with Argo Rollouts*

Kubernetes does not provide an analysis tool to determine the correctness of the new deployment. In this tutorial, we will use Argo Rollouts to implement progressive delivery. Argo Rollouts uses the canary strategy along with `AnalysisTemplate` to achieve progressive delivery.

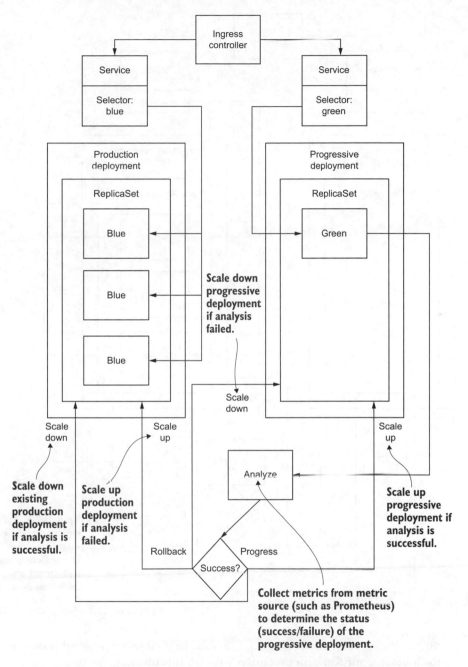

Figure 5.21 Progressive delivery continuously collects and analyzes the health of the new Pods; scales up the progressive deployment (green); and scales down the production deployment (blue), as long as the analysis is determined to be successful.

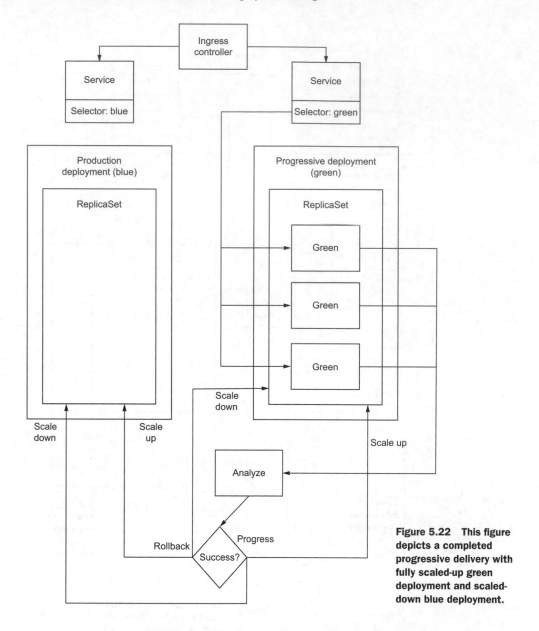

Figure 5.22   This figure depicts a completed progressive delivery with fully scaled-up green deployment and scaled-down blue deployment.

NOTE   Please refer to section 5.1.4 on how to enable ingress and install Argo Rollouts in your Kubernetes cluster prior to this tutorial.

1   Create the `AnalysisTemplate`.
2   Create the ingress, production deployment, and service (blue).
3   Create ingress to direct traffic to the production service.
4   View the application in the browser (blue).

5 Update and apply the manifest with the green image with the Pass template.
6 View the web page again in the browser (grccn).
7 Update and apply the manifest with the green image with the Fail template.
8 View the application again in the browser. Still blue!

First, we will create the AnalysisTemplate (listing 5.13) for Rollout to collect metrics and determine the health of the Pods. For simplicity, we will create one AnalysisTemplate pass, which will always return 0 (healthy), and an Analysis-Template fail, which will always return 1 (unhealthy). In addition, Argo Rollouts internally maintains multiple ReplicaSets, so there is no need for multiple services. Next, we will create the ingress controller (listing 5.8), demo-service, and blue deployment (listing 5.14):

```
$ kubectl apply -f analysis-templates.yaml
analysistemplate.argoproj.io/pass created
analysistemplate.argoproj.io/fail created
$ kubectl apply -f ingress.yaml
ingress.extensions/demo-ingress created
configmap/nginx-configuration created
$ kubectl apply -f rollout-with-analysis.yaml
rollout.argoproj.io/demo created
service/demo-service created
$ kubectl get ingress
NAME            HOSTS         ADDRESS          PORTS   AGE
demo-ingress    demo.info     192.168.99.111   80      60s
```

> **NOTE** For production, AnalysisTemplate has support for Prometheus, Wavefront, and Netflix Kayenta or can be extended for other metric stores.

Listing 5.13 analysis-templates.yaml

```
apiVersion: argoproj.io/v1alpha1
kind: AnalysisTemplate
metadata:
  name: pass
spec:
  metrics:
  - name: pass
    interval: 15s            ◁── Runs for 15 seconds
    failureLimit: 1
    provider:
      job:
        spec:
          template:
            spec:
              containers:
              - name: sleep
                image: alpine:3.8
                command: [sh, -c]
                args: [exit 0]   ◁── Returns 0 (always pass)
                restartPolicy: Never
          backoffLimit: 0
```

```
---
apiVersion: argoproj.io/v1alpha1
kind: AnalysisTemplate
metadata:
  name: fail
spec:
  metrics:
  - name: fail
    interval: 15s            ◄─┘  Runs for
    failureLimit: 1               15 seconds
    provider:
      job:
        spec:
          template:
            spec:
              containers:
              - name: sleep
                image: alpine:3.8
                command: [sh, -c]
                args: [exit 1]    ◄─┘  Returns 1
              restartPolicy: Never      (always fail)
          backoffLimit: 0
```

Listing 5.14   rollout-with-analysis.yaml

```
apiVersion: argoproj.io/v1alpha1
kind: Rollout
metadata:
  name: demo
spec:
  replicas: 3
  revisionHistoryLimit: 1
  selector:
    matchLabels:
      app: demo
  strategy:              Deploys with
    Canary:          ◄─┘ strategy Canary
      analysis:                Specifies the
        templateName: pass  ◄─┘ AnalysisTemplate pass
      steps:
      - setWeight: 10  ◄─┐  Scales out enough Pods to service 10% of the traffic. In this
      - pause:            example, Rollout will scale up one green Pod along with the
          duration: 20  ◄─ three blue Pods resulting in the green Pod getting 25% of the
  template:                 traffic. Argo Rollouts can work with Service Mesh or NGINX
    metadata:               Ingress Controller for fine-grain traffic routing.
      labels:
        app: demo        Waits 20 seconds before
    spec:                full scale-up
      containers:
      - image: argoproj/rollouts-demo:blue
        imagePullPolicy: Always
        name: demo
        ports:
        - containerPort: 8080
---
apiVersion: v1
```

```
kind: Service
metadata:
  name: demo-service
  labels:
    app: demo
spec:
  ports:
  - protocol: TCP
    port: 80
    targetPort: 8080
  selector:
    app: demo
  type: NodePort
```

NOTE For the initial deployment (blue), `Rollout` will ignore the `Canary` setting and perform a regular deployment.

Once you have the ingress controller, service, and deployment created and updated /etc/hosts with the demo.info and the correct IP address, you can enter the URL demo.info and see the blue service running.

Once the blue service is fully up and running, we can now update the manifest with the green image and apply the manifest. You should see the blue progressively turning green and completely green after 20 seconds:

```
$ sed -i .bak 's/demo:blue/demo:green/g' rollout-with-analysis.yaml
$ kubectl apply -f rollout-with-analysis.yaml
rollout.argoproj.io/demo configured
service/demo-service unchanged
```

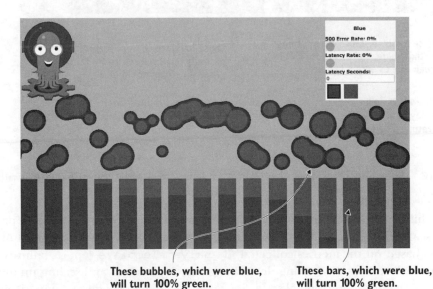

These bubbles, which were blue, will turn 100% green.

These bars, which were blue, will turn 100% green.

Figure 5.23 As the green deployment progressively scales up, both the bubble and bar charts will gradually become all green if there is no error.

Now let's deploy again and go back to the blue image. This time we will also switch to the "Fail" `AnalysisTemplate` that will return a failure status after 15 seconds. We should see the blue progressively appear in the browser but turn back to green after 15 seconds:

```
$ sed -i .bak 's/demo:green/demo:blue/g' rollout-with-analysis.yaml
$ sed -i .bak 's/templateName: pass/templateName: fail/g' rollout-with-
    analysis.yaml
$ kubectl apply -f rollout-with-analysis.yaml
rollout.argoproj.io/demo configured
service/demo-service unchanged
```

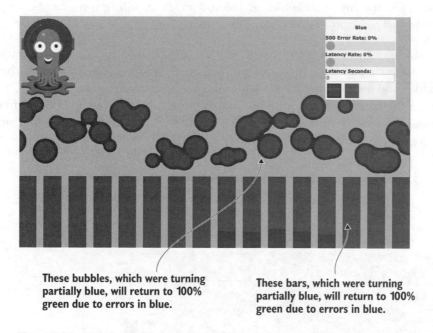

These bubbles, which were turning partially blue, will return to 100% green due to errors in blue.

These bars, which were turning partially blue, will return to 100% green due to errors in blue.

Figure 5.24   The blue deployment progressively scales up but returns errors. The blue deployment will get scaled down during failure, and both the bubble and bar charts return to green.

NOTE   The demo rollout will be marked as aborted after the failure and will not deploy again until the abort state is set to `false`.

From this tutorial, you can see that Argo Rollouts uses the canary strategy to progressively scale up the green deployment if the `AnalysisTemplate` continues to report success based on the metrics collected. If `AnalysisTemplate` reports failures, Argo Rollouts will roll back by scaling down the green deployment and scaling up the blue deployment back to its original state. See table 5.1 for a deployment comparison.

Table 5.1 Deployment strategy comparison

	Pros	Cons
Deployment	Built into Kubernetes Rolling updates Minimal hardware required	Backward-compatible and stateless application only
Blue-green	Works with stateful application and non-backward-compatible deployment Fast rollback	Requires additional automation Requires twice the hardware during the deployment
Canary	Verifies new releases using production traffic and dependencies with a subset of users	Requires additional automation Longer deployment process Backward-compatible and stateless application only
Progressive	Gradually deploys new releases to a subset of users and continuously scales out to all users if metrics are good; automatic rollback if metrics are bad	Requires additional automation Requires metrics collection and analysis Longer deployment process Backward-compatible and stateless application only

Summary

- ReplicaSet is not declarative and not suited for GitOps.
- Deployment is fully declarative and complementary to GitOps.
- Deployment performs rolling updates and is best for stateless and backward-compatible deployment.
- Deployment can be customized with `max surge` to specify the number of new Pods and `max unavailable` to limit the number of Pods being terminated.
- Blue-green deployment is suitable for non-backward-compatible deployment or sticky session service.
- Blue-green deployment can be implemented natively by leveraging two Deployments (each with a custom label) and updating `selector` in the Service to route 100% of the traffic to the active deployment.
- Canary acts as an early indicator for failures to avoid problematic deployments having a full impact on all customers at once.
- Canary deployment can be implemented natively by leveraging two Deployments and NGINX Ingress Controller to dial the traffic gradually.
- Progressive delivery is an advanced version of canary deployment using real-time metrics to continue or abort the deployment.
- Argo Rollouts is an open source project that can simplify blue-green, canary, and progressive deployment.
- Each deployment strategy has its pros/cons, and it is important to select the right strategy for your application.

Access control and security 6

This chapter covers

- Areas of attack when using GitOps-driven deployment
- Ensuring that critical infrastructure components are protected
- Guidelines for choosing the right configuration management pattern
- Enhancing security to avoid security pitfalls in GitOps

Access control and security topics are always essential and are especially crucial for deployment and infrastructure management. In this case, the attack surface includes expensive things like infrastructure, dangerous things like policy and compliance, and the most important things like data stores that contain user data. Modern operations methodologies enable engineering teams to move at a much quicker pace and optimize for fast iterations. However, more releases also mean more chances of introducing vulnerabilities and lead to new challenges for security teams. Traditional security processes that rely on human operational knowledge may still work but struggle to scale and meet the needs of enterprises utilizing GitOps with automated build and release infrastructure.

We recommend you read chapters 1 and 2 before reading this chapter.

6.1 Introduction to access control

The security topic is both critical and complex. Usually, it is handled by a security specialist or even a whole dedicated security team. So why do we talk about it while discussing GitOps? GitOps changes security responsibilities in the same way it has altered operational responsibility boundaries. With GitOps and Kubernetes, the engineering team is empowered to contribute to security by writing Kubernetes access configs and using Git to enforce proper configuration change processes. Given that the security team is no longer a bottleneck, it can offload some responsibilities to developers and focus on providing security infrastructure. GitOps facilitates a tighter and more productive collaboration between security engineers and DevOps engineers, allowing any proposed changes that impact an environment's security to undergo proper security reviews and approval before it affects production.

6.1.1 What is access control?

To better understand the nuances of access control in combination with GitOps, let's learn what access control is first.

Access control is a way of limiting access to a system or to physical or virtual resources. It dictates who is allowed to access the protected resources and what operations are allowed to be performed. Access control is composed of two parts: authentication, ensuring that users are who they say they are; and authorization, ensuring they have appropriate access to perform the requested action against the specified resources. Regardless of the domain area, access control includes three main components: subject, object, and reference monitor.

The most straightforward demonstration of the access control system is a physical world example: a person trying to enter the building through the door. The person is a subject who is trying to access the object, which is a building. The door is a reference monitor that will authorize the access request only if the person trying to enter has the door key.

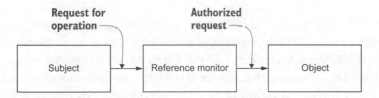

Figure 6.1 The subject is the entity that requests access to an object. The object is the entity or resource being accessed. The reference monitor is the entity controlling access to the protected object.

Exercise 6.1

An email client is trying to read emails from an email server. Can you identify what the subject, object, and reference monitor are for this scenario?

6.1.2   *What to secure*

When securing the application delivery process to a Kubernetes cluster end to end, many different components need to be secured. These include (but are not limited to)

- CI/CD pipeline
- Container registry
- Git repository
- Kubernetes cluster
- Cloud provider or data center
- The application itself
- GitOps operator (if applicable)

Each of these components has its unique security concerns, authentication mechanisms, and role-based access control (RBAC) models, and will be configured differently depending on many factors and considerations. Since security is only as strong as the weakest link, all components play an equally important role in the cluster's overall security.

Generally speaking, security choices are often a balancing act between security and convenience. A system that might be extremely secure may be so inconvenient that it becomes unusable from a user perspective. As an operator, the goal is to make the user experience as convenient as reasonably possible without compromising security.

Some considerations that factor into the security of components include

- Potential attack vectors
- Worst-case consequences if the component becomes compromised
- Who should be allowed access to the service
- What permissions (RBAC) various users have
- What protections can be put in place to mitigate risk

The next few sections describe these components and some of the unique security considerations.

CI/CD PIPELINE

The CI/CD build and deployment pipeline is the starting point for delivering freshly built software to the Kubernetes cluster. Jenkins, Circle CI, and Travis CI are examples of some popular CI/CD systems. Security is frequently an afterthought since most thought and energy is focused on protecting the production environment and production data. Still, the CI/CD is an equally important piece of the puzzle. This is because the CI/CD pipeline ultimately controls *how* new software is driven to the environment. When compromised, it has the capability of delivering *harmful* software to the cluster.

A build system is generally configured with sufficient credentials to perform its duties. For example, to publish new container images, the CI/CD pipeline might require credentials to the container registry. Traditionally, the build system is also given access and credentials to the Kubernetes cluster to perform the actual deployment. But as we will see later in this chapter, direct access to the cluster is no longer necessary with the advent of GitOps.

An attacker with access to the CI/CD build system could compromise security in many ways. For example, a pipeline could be modified to expose the container registry or cluster credentials mentioned previously. Another example is the pipeline could become hijacked such that it deploys malicious containers into the cluster instead of the intended one.

There are even some scenarios in which a bad actor might compromise security by merely using the CI system's standard functionality. For example, when a pull request is made against a code repo, it kicks off a pipeline performing a series of steps to validate and test the change. The contents of these steps are typically defined in a file contained in the code repo (such as a Jenkins' Jenkinsfile or Circle CI's .circleci/config.yml). The ability to open new pull requests is often open to the world so that anyone can propose contributions to the project. However, an attacker could simply open a pull request that modifies the pipeline to do something malicious. For this reason, many CI systems incorporate features to prevent pipelines from being executed when an untrusted source makes the PR.

CONTAINER REGISTRY

A container registry houses the container images that will be deployed in the cluster. Because the container images in the registry have the potential of running in clusters, the contents of the registry need to be trusted, as well as the users who can push to that registry. Because anyone can publish images to public registries such as DockerHub, Quay.io, and grc.io, it is a standard security measure in enterprises to block pulling images from these untrusted container registries entirely. Instead, all images would be pulled from an internal, trusted registry, which could be periodically scanned for vulnerabilities in the repositories.

An attacker with privileges to the trusted container registry could push images to the registry and overwrite existing, previously trusted images. For example, say your cluster is already running some image mycompany/guestbook:v1.0. An attacker with access to the registry could push a new image and overwrite the existing guestbook:v1.0 tag, changing the meaning of that image to something malicious. Then, the next time the container starts (perhaps due to Pod rescheduling), it would run a compromised version of the image.

This attack might go undetected since, from the perspective of Kubernetes and the GitOps system, everything is as expected; the live manifests match the configuration manifests in Git. To combat this issue, image tags (or image versions) can be designated as immutable in some registries so that once written, the meaning of that image tag can never change.

IMMUTABLE IMAGE TAGS   Some image registries (such as DockerHub) provide a feature that makes image tags immutable. This means that once an image tag already exists, no one can overwrite it, essentially preventing image tags from being reused. The use of this feature adds additional security by preventing existing deployed image tags from being modified.

GIT REPOSITORY

The Git repository, in the context of GitOps, defines *what* resources will be installed into the cluster. The Kubernetes manifests, which are stored in the Git repo, are the ones that ultimately end up in the cluster. Therefore, anyone who can access the Git repository should be trusted in deciding the cluster's makeup, including things like Deployments, container images, Roles, RoleBindings, Ingresses, and NetworkPolicies.

In the worst case, an attacker with full access to the Git repository could push a new commit to the Git repo, updating a Deployment to run a malicious container in the cluster. They might also add a Role and RoleBinding that could grant the Deployment enough privileges to read Secrets and exfiltrate sensitive information.

The good news is that since an attacker would need to push commits to the repository, the malicious actions performed would be done in plain sight and could be audited and traced. However, commit and pull request access to the Git repository should be restricted to a limited set of people who would effectively have full cluster administration access.

KUBERNETES CLUSTER

Securing a Kubernetes cluster is deserving of a book unto itself, so we will only aim to cover the topics most relevant to GitOps. As you are aware, the Kubernetes cluster is the infrastructure platform that runs your application code. An attacker who has gained access to the cluster is arguably the worst-case scenario. For this reason, Kubernetes clusters are extremely high-value targets for attackers, and the security of the cluster is paramount.

GitOps enables a whole new set of options for how you might decide to grant users access to the cluster. This will be covered in depth later in the chapter but, at a high level, GitOps gives operators a new way of providing access to the cluster (such as through Git), as opposed to the traditional method of giving users direct access to the cluster (such as with a personalized kubeconfig file).

Traditionally, before GitOps, developers would generally require direct access to the Kubernetes cluster to manage and make changes to their environment. But with GitOps, direct access to the cluster is no longer strictly required since environment management can go through a new medium, Git. And suppose all developer access to the cluster can be via Git. In that case, it also means that operators can decide to close traditional, direct access to the cluster completely (or at least write access) and enforce all changes to go through Git.

CLOUD PROVIDER OR DATA CENTER

Perhaps out of scope in the context of GitOps, but nonetheless important to the discussion of security, is the actual underlying cloud provider (such as AWS) or physical data center in which Kubernetes clusters are running. Commonly, an application that runs in Kubernetes will depend on some number of managed resources or services in the cloud for things like databases, DNSs, object storage (such as S3), message queues, and many others. Because both developers and applications need access to these resources, an operator needs to consider how creation and access to these cloud provider resources may be granted to users.

A developer will likely require access to their database to perform things like database schema migrations or generating reports. While GitOps in itself does not provide a solution for securing the database per se, GitOps does come into play when database configuration invariably starts creeping into the Kubernetes manifests (which *are* managed via GitOps). For example, one mechanism an operator might employ to help secure access to a database is IP whitelisting in a Kubernetes NetworkPolicy. And since NetworkPolicy is a standard Kubernetes resource that can be managed via Git, the *contents* (IP whitelist) of the NetworkPolicy become significant to operators as a security concern.

A second consideration is that Kubernetes resources can have a profound impact on cloud provider resources. For example, a user who is allowed to create ordinary Kubernetes Service objects could cause many costly load balancers to be created in the cloud provider and unintentionally expose services to the outside world. For these reasons, it's imperative that cluster operators have a deep understanding of the relationship between Kubernetes resources and cloud provider resources and the consequences of allowing users to manage these resources on their own.

GITOPS OPERATOR

Depending on your choice of a GitOps operator, securing the operator may or may not be an option. An elementary GitOps operator, such as our poor-man's CronJob-based GitOps operator example from chapter 2, has no other security implications since it is not a service that can be exposed externally, nor does it have any form of management aspect to it. On the other hand, a tool such as Argo CD, Helm, or Jenkins X is intended to be exposed to end users. As a result, it has additional security considerations since it could be a vector of attack.

6.1.3 *Access control in GitOps*

First of all, let's figure out the access control subjects and objects in the continuous delivery (CD) security model. As we've learned already, the objects are resources that have to be protected. The CD surface attack is large, but the idea of immutable infrastructure and Kubernetes narrow it to just two things: Kubernetes configuration and deployment artifacts.

As you already know, the Kubernetes configuration is represented by a collection of Kubernetes resources. The resource manifests are stored in Git and automatically applied to the target Kubernetes cluster. The deployment artifacts are container images. Having these two, you can shape your production in any way and even re-create it from scratch at any time.

The access control subjects, in this case, are engineers and automated processes, such as a CI pipeline. The engineers are leveraging automation to continuously produce new container images and update Kubernetes configuration to deploy them.

Unless you are using GitOps, the Kubernetes configuration is either updated manually or scripted in continuous integration. This approach, sometimes called CIOps,[1] usually makes the security team nervous.

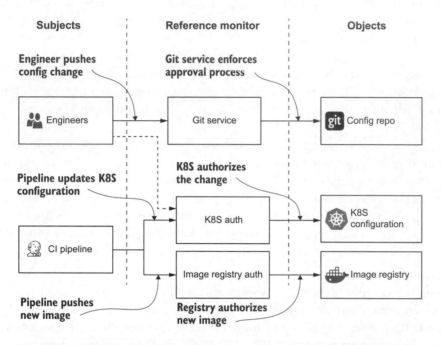

Figure 6.2   The CIOps security model is not safe since it provides cluster access to both engineers and CI systems. The problem here is that the CI system gets control over the cluster and is allowed to make arbitrary Kubernetes configuration changes. That significantly expands the attack surface and makes it difficult to secure your cluster.

So how does GitOps improve the situation? GitOps unifies the process of applying changes from the Git repo to the cluster. That allows keeping access tokens closer to the cluster and effectively moves the burden of securing access to the cluster to the Git repository.

Protecting configuration in the Git repository still requires an effort. The great thing about it is that we can use the same tools that are used to protect the application source code. Git hosting providers such as GitHub and GitLab allow us to define and enforce the change process like mandatory reviews or static analysis for every change.

---

[1]   http://mng.bz/MXB7.

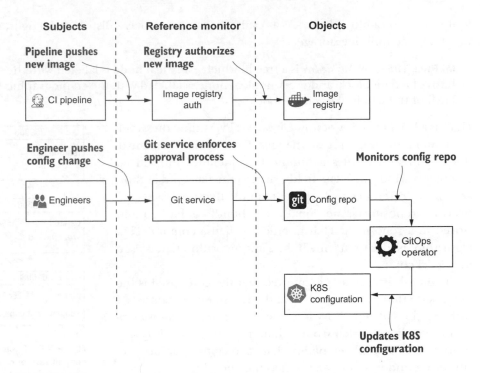

Figure 6.3 The GitOps security model limits cluster access to the GitOps operator only. The attack surface is greatly reduced, and protecting the cluster is much simpler.

Since the GitOps operator is the only subject with cluster access, it is much easier to define what can and cannot be deployed into the cluster by the engineering team and significantly improves cluster security.

Let's go ahead and learn what it takes to protect Kubernetes configs in the Git repository and how to fine-tune Kubernetes access control.

6.2   Access limitations

As discussed at the beginning of the chapter, there are many components involved in securing the cluster, including the CI/CD build system, the container registry, and the actual Kubernetes cluster. Each component implements specific access control mechanisms to allow or deny access.

6.2.1   Git repository access

Git is a completely developer-oriented tool. By default, it is configured to make it extremely easy to change anything at any time. This simplicity is what made Git so popular in the developer community.

However, Git is built on top of a solid cryptographic foundation: it uses Merkle trees as a fundamental underlying data structure. The same data structure is used as a foundation for a blockchain.[2] As a result, Git can be used as a distributed ledger, making it a great audit log storage.

> **MERKLE TREE**   A *Merkle tree* is a tree in which every leaf node is labeled with the hash of a data block, and every nonleaf node is labeled with the cryptographic hash of the labels of its child nodes.[3]

Here is a brief overview of how Git works. Every time the developer wants to save a set of changes, Git calculates an introduced diff and creates a bundle that includes introduced changes, various metadata fields, such as the date and author, as well as a reference to the parent bundle that represents the previous repository state. Finally, the bundle is hashed and stored in a repository. That bundle is called a commit. That algorithm used is pretty much the same algorithm that is used in a blockchain.

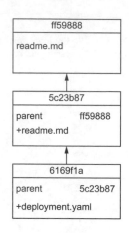

The hash is used as a guarantee that the code used is the same code that was committed, and it has not been tampered with. So the Git repository is a chain of commits that is cryptographically protected from hidden modifications. It is safe to trust the Git implementation thanks to cryptographic algorithms behind it, so we can use it as the audit log.

Figure 6.4 Each Git commit references the previous commit and forms a treelike data structure. All modifications are fully tracked in the Git repository.

CREATE DEPLOYMENT REPOSITORY

Let's create a sample deployment repository and then see what it takes to make it ready to drive GitOps deployment. For your convenience, let's use the existing deployment repository available at https://github.com/gitopsbook/sample-app-deployment. The repository contains the deployment manifests of a Kubernetes Service and a Deployment resource. The Deployment resource manifest is available in the following listing.

> **Listing 6.1   Sample app deployment (http://mng.bz/ao1z)**

```
apiVersion: apps/v1
kind: Deployment
metadata:
  name: sample-app
spec:
  replicas: 1
  revisionHistoryLimit: 3
  selector:
    matchLabels:
      app: sample-app
  template:
```

---

[2] https://en.wikipedia.org/wiki/Blockchain.
[3] https://en.wikipedia.org/wiki/Merkle_tree.

```
metadata:
  labels:
    app: sample-app
spec:
  containers:
  - image: gitopsbook/sample-app:v0.1
    name: sample-app
    command:
      - /app/sample-app
    ports:
    - containerPort: 8080
```

As has been mentioned, Git is a distributed version control system. That means every developer has a full local repository copy with full access to make changes. However, there is also a common repository that all team members use to exchange their changes. That common remote repository is hosted by a Git hosting service like GitHub or GitLab. Hosting services provide a set of security features that allow protecting the repository from unwanted modifications, enforcing commit author identity, preventing history override, and much more.

As a first step, navigate to the gitopsbook/sample-app-deployment repo and create a fork[4] in your GitHub account:

```
https://github.com/gitopsbook/sample-app-deployment
```

Once the fork is created, use the following command to clone the repository locally and get ready to make changes:

```
$ git clone https://github.com/<username>/sample-app-deployment.git
Cloning into 'sample-app-deployment'...
remote: Enumerating objects: 14, done.
remote: Total 14 (delta 0), reused 0 (delta 0), pack-reused 14
Receiving objects: 100% (14/14), done.
Resolving deltas: 100% (3/3), done.
```

Although the repository is public, that does not mean that everyone with a GitHub account can make a change without proper permission. GitHub ensures that a user is either a repository owner or invited as a collaborator.[5]

Exercise 6.2

Clone the repository using the HTTPS URL and try to push any changes without providing your GitHub username and password:

```
git clone https://github.com/<username>/sample-app-deployment.git
```

Instead of creating a personal repository, you might create an organization[6] and manage access using teams. That set of access management features is very comprehensive

---

[4] http://mng.bz/goBl.
[5] http://mng.bz/e5lz.
[6] http://mng.bz/pVPG.

and covers most use cases, starting from the single developer to the large organization. However, this is not enough.

Exercise 6.3

Create a second GitHub user and invite that user as a collaborator. Trying pushing any changes using the second GitHub user's credentials.

ENFORCING A CODE REVIEW PROCESS

Neither the cryptographic protection nor authorization setting can protect from vulnerabilities introduced intentionally by a malicious developer or simply by mistake through poor coding practices. Whether the vulnerabilities in application source code are introduced intentionally or not, the recommended solution is the same: all changes in the deployment repository must go through a code review process that is enforced by the Git hosting provider.

Let's make sure that every change to the master branch of the sample-app-deployment repository goes through the code review process and is approved by at least one reviewer. The steps to enable a mandatory review process are described at http://mng.bz/OExn:

1 Navigate to the Branches section in the repository settings.
2 Click the Add Rule button.
3 Enter the required branch name.
4 Enable the Require Pull Request Reviews Before Merging and Include Administrators settings.

Next, let's try to make a config change and push it to the master:

```
$ sed -i .bak 's/v0.1/v0.2/' deployment.yaml
$ git commit -am 'Upgrade image version'
$ git push
remote: error: GH006: Protected branch update failed for refs/heads/master.
remote: error: At least 1 approving review is required by reviewers with
    write access.
To github.com:<username>/sample-app-deployment.git
 ! [remote rejected] master -> master (protected branch hook declined)
error: failed to push some refs to 'github.com:<username>/sample-app-
    deployment.git'
```

The `git push` fails because the branch is protected and will require a pull request and a review. This guarantees that at least one additional person is going to review the change and sign off on the deployment.

Don't forget to run cleanup before moving to the next paragraph. Delete the rule that protects the master branch in GitHub and run the following command to reset local changes:

```
$ git reset HEAD^1 --hard
```

Exercise 6.4

Explore additional settings under the Require Pull Request Reviews Before Merging section. Think which settings combination is suitable for your project or organization.

ENFORCE AUTOMATED CHECKS

In addition to human judgment, pull requests allow us to incorporate an automated manifest analysis that can help to catch security issues very early. Although the ecosystem of Kubernetes security tools is still emerging, there are already several options available. Two good examples are kubeaudit[7] and kubesec.[8] Both tools are available under the Apache license and allow scanning Kubernetes manifests to find weak security parameters.

Because our repository is open source and hosted by GitHub, we can use a CI service such as https://travis-ci.org or https://circleci.com for free! Let's configure an automated kubeaudit usage and enforce successful verification for every pull request using https://travis-ci.org:

```
git add .travis.yml
git commit -am 'Add travis config'
git push
```

Listing 6.2   .travis.yml

```
language: bash
install:
  - curl -sLf -o kubeaudit.tar.gz  https://github.com/Shopify/kubeaudit/
    releases/download/v0.7.0/kubeaudit_0.7.0_linux_amd64.tar.gz
  - tar -zxvf kubeaudit.tar.gz
  - chmod +x kubeaudit
script:
  - ./kubeaudit nonroot -f deployment.yaml &> errors
  - if [ -s errors ] ; then cat errors; exit -1; fi
```

Once the configuration is ready we just need to enable CI integration at http://mng.bz/Gxyq and create a pull request:

```
$ git checkout -b change1
Switched to a new branch 'change1'

$ sed -i .bak 's/v0.1/v0.2/' deployment.yaml

$ git commit -am 'Upgrade image version'
[change1 c52535a] Upgrade image version
 1 file changed, 1 insertion(+), 1 deletion(-)

$ git push --set-upstream origin change1
Enumerating objects: 5, done.
Counting objects: 100% (5/5), done.
Delta compression using up to 8 threads
Compressing objects: 100% (3/3), done.
Writing objects: 100% (3/3), 359 bytes | 359.00 KiB/s, done.
Total 3 (delta 1), reused 0 (delta 0), pack-reused 0
remote: Resolving deltas: 100% (1/1), completed with 1 local object.
remote:
remote: Create a pull request for 'change1' on GitHub by visiting:
```

---

7 https://github.com/Shopify/kubeaudit.
8 https://kubesec.io/.

```
remote: https://github.com/<username>/sample-app-deployment/pull/new/change1
remote:
To github.com:<username>/sample-app-deployment.git
 * [new branch]      change1 -> change1
Branch 'change1' set up to track remote branch 'change1' from 'origin'.
```

The CI should be triggered as soon as the PR is created and fails with the following error message:

```
time="2019-12-17T09:05:41Z" level=error msg="RunAsNonRoot is not set in
    ContainerSecurityContext, which results in root user being allowed!
    Container=sample-app KubeType=deployment Name=sample-app"
```

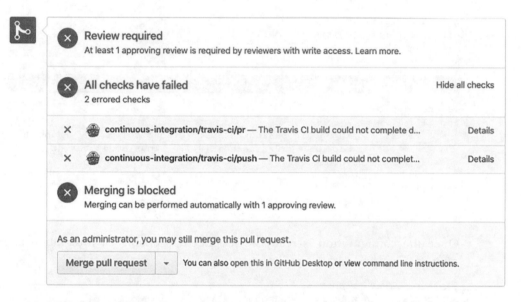

Figure 6.5 Travis runs the CI job that validates deployment manifests. The validation fails due to detected vulnerabilities.

The kubeaudit detected that the Pod security context is missing the `runAsNonRoot` property that prevents running a container with root user as part of the Pod. This is a valid security concern. To fix the security issue, change the Pod manifest as represented in the following code listing.

Listing 6.3 Sample app deployment (http://mng.bz/zxXa)

```
apiVersion: apps/v1
kind: Deployment
metadata:
  name: sample-app
spec:
  replicas: 1
```

```
  revisionHistoryLimit: 3
  selector:
    matchLabels:
      app: sample-app
  template:
    metadata:
      labels:
        app: sample-app
    spec:
      containers:
      - image: gitopsbook/sample-app:v0.1
        name: sample-app
        command:
          - /app/sample-app
        ports:
        - containerPort: 8080
+       securityContext:
+         runAsNonRoot: true
```

Commit changes and update the pull request by pushing the `change1` branch:

```
git commit -am 'Update deployment'
git push upstream change1
```

The pull request should pass verification!

Exercise 6.5
Learn which additional audits are provided by the kubeaudit application. Try using the `kubeaudit autofix -f deployment.yaml` command.

PROTECTING COMMIT AUTHOR IDENTITY
At this point, our repository is securely hosted on GitHub. We control which GitHub accounts can make changes in the repository, enforce the code review process for every change, and even run static analysis for every pull request. This is great but still not enough. As often happens, a social engineering attack can bypass all these security gates.

What would you do if your boss sent you a pull request and asked you to merge it immediately? Under pressure, an engineer might decide to take a quick look at the pull request and approve it without careful testing. Since our repository is hosted on GitHub, we know which user authored the commit. It is impossible to make a commit on behalf of someone else, right?

Unfortunately, this is not true. Git was not designed with strong identity guarantees. As we mentioned before, Git is a completely developer-oriented tool. Every bit of a commit is under the engineers' control, including information about the commit author. So an intruder can easily create a commit and put your boss's name into the commit metadata. Let's do a simple exercise to demonstrate this vulnerability.

Open a console, and create a new commit on the master branch using this command:

```
echo '# hacked' >> ./deployment.yaml
git commit --author='Joe Beda <joe.github@bedafamily.com>' -am 'evil commit'
git push upstream master
```

Open the commit history of your repository on GitHub, and check the most recent commit information. Look, Joe Beda[9] just updated our Pod manifest!

Figure 6.6   GitHub commit history contains the Joe Beda avatar. By default, GitHub does not execute any validation and uses author information stored in the commit metadata.

That looks pretty scary, but it does not mean that going forward, you need to personally verify the identity of every pull request author before approving it. Instead of manually verifying who is the commit's author, you might leverage a digital crypto signature.

The cryptographic tools like GPG allow you to inject a crypto signature into the commit metadata. Later, this signature might be verified by the Git hosting service or GitOps operator. It would take too much time to learn exactly how a GPG signature works, but we definitely can use it to protect our deployment repo.

Unfortunately, the GPG configuration process might be difficult. It includes multiple steps that might vary depending on your operating system. Refer to the steps described in appendix C and the GitHub online documentation[10] to configure the GPG key.

Finally, we are ready to make a commit and sign it. The following command creates a new change to the deployment manifest and signs it with the GPG key associated with your GitHub account:

```
echo '# signed change' >> ./deployment.yaml
git add .
git commit -S -am 'good commit'
git push upstream master
```

Now the GitHub commit history includes information about the author that is based on a GPG key and cannot be faked.

GitHub allows you to require that all commits to a particular repository be signed. The Require Signed Commits setting is available under the Protected Branches section of the repository settings.

---

[9] Joe Beda (https://www.linkedin.com/in/jbeda) is one of the principal founders of Kubernetes.

[10] https://help.github.com/en/github/authenticating-to-github/adding-a-new-gpg-key-to-your-github-account.

Figure 6.7   Signing Git cryptographically protects author identity. The GitHub user interface visualizes GPG verification results.

In addition to Git hosting service confirmation, you might configure your GitOps operator to verify GPG signatures automatically before updating the Kubernetes cluster configuration. Fortunately, some GitOps operators have built-in signature verification support and don't require complex configuration. This topic will be covered in the following chapters.

6.2.2   *Kubernetes RBAC*

As you already know, GitOps methodology assumes that a CI pipeline has no access to the Kubernetes cluster. The only automation tool with direct cluster access is the GitOps operator that lives inside the cluster. This is already a great advantage over the traditional DevOps model. However, that does not mean that GitOps should have god-level access. We still need to think carefully about which permissions level the operator should get. The operator inside of a cluster, the so-called pull model, is not the only possibility either. You might consider placing the GitOps operator inside of the protected perimeter and reduce management overhead by using a push model and managing multiple clusters using one operator. Each such consideration has some pros and cons. To make a meaningful decision, you need to have a good understanding of the Kubernetes access model. So let's step back and learn which security tools are built into Kubernetes and how we can use them.

ACCESS CONTROL TYPES

There are four well-known access control flavors:

- *Discretionary access control* (DAC)—With DAC models, the data owner decides on access. DAC is a means of assigning access rights based on rules that users specify.
- *Mandatory access control* (MAC)—MAC was developed using a nondiscretionary model, in which people are granted access based on an information clearance. MAC is a policy in which access rights are assigned based on regulations from a central authority.
- *Role-based access control* (RBAC)—RBAC grants access based on a user's role and implements key security principles, such as least privilege and separation of privilege. Thus, someone attempting to access information can only access data deemed necessary for their role.

- *Attribute-based access control* (ABAC)—ABAC, also known as policy-based access control, defines an access control paradigm whereby access rights are granted to users through the use of policies that combine attributes together.

ABAC is very flexible and probably the most powerful model in the list. Because of its power, ABAC was initially chosen as the Kubernetes security model. However, later on, the community realized that ABAC concepts and the way they were implemented in Kubernetes were hard to understand and use. As a result, a new authorization mechanism that is based on RBAC was introduced. In 2017 the RBAC-based authorization was moved into beta, and ABAC was declared deprecated. Currently, RBAC is the preferred authorization mechanism in Kubernetes and recommended to be used for every application running on Kubernetes.

The RBAC model includes the following three main elements: subjects, resources, and verbs. Subjects represent users or processes that want to access a resource, and a verb is an operation that can be executed against a resource.

So how are these elements mapped to Kubernetes API objects? The RBAC resources are represented by a regular Kubernetes resource such as Pod or Deployment. In order to represent verbs, two new sets of specialized resources were introduced in Kubernetes. The verbs are represented by Role and RoleBinding resources, and subjects are represented by User and ServiceAccount resources.

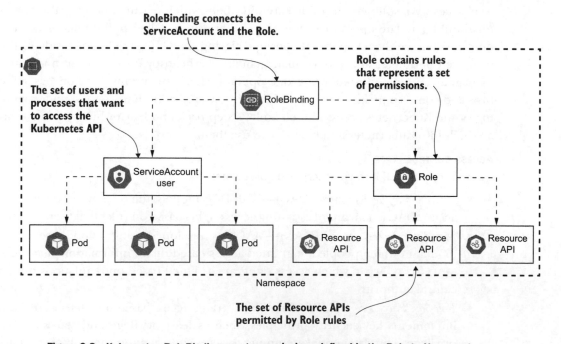

Figure 6.8   Kubernetes RoleBinding grants permissions defined in the Role to Users and ServiceAccounts. ServiceAccount provides an identity for processes that run in a Pod.

ROLE AND ROLEBINDING

The Role resource is meant to connect verbs and Kubernetes resources. A sample Role definition is represented in the following code listing.

Listing 6.4   Sample Role (http://mng.bz/0mKx)

```
apiVersion: rbac.authorization.k8s.io/v1
kind: Role
metadata:
  name: sample-role
rules:
- apiGroups:
  - ""
  resources:
  - configmaps
  verbs:
  - get
  - list
```

The verbs section contains lists of allowed actions. So altogether that Role allows listing config maps with the cluster and getting the detailed information of every config map. The advantage of a Role is that it is a reusable object and can be used for different subjects. For example, you might define the read-only Role and assign it to various subjects without duplicating the resources and verbs definitions.

It is important to know that Roles are Namespaced resources and provide access to the resources defined in the same Namespace.[11] This means that a single Role cannot provide access to the resources in multiple Namespaces or cluster-level resources. In order to provide cluster-level access, you might use an equivalent resource called ClusterRole. The ClusterRole resource has pretty much the same set of fields as a Role, with the exception of the Namespace field.

The RoleBinding enables the Role to be connected with the subjects. A sample RoleBinding definition is represented here.

Listing 6.5   Sample RoleBinding (http://mng.bz/KMeK)

```
apiVersion: rbac.authorization.k8s.io/v1
kind: RoleBinding
metadata:
  name: sample-role-binding
roleRef:
  apiGroup: rbac.authorization.k8s.io
  kind: Role
  name: sample-role
subjects:
- kind: ServiceAccount
  name: sample-service-account
```

---

[11] http://mng.bz/9MDl.

The sample RoleBinding grants a set of permissions defined in the Role named `sample-role` to the ServiceAccount named `sample-service-account`. Similarly to a Role, a RoleBinding has an equivalent object, ClusterRoleBinding, that allows connecting subjects with the ClusterRole.

USER AND SERVICEACCOUNT

Finally, Kubernetes subjects are represented by ServiceAccounts and Users.

BASIC GITOPS OPERATOR RBAC

We configured Kubernetes RBAC in chapter 2 while working on the basic GitOps operator implementation. Let's use the knowledge acquired in this chapter to tighten the operator permissions and limit what it can deploy.

To get started, make sure you've completed the basic GitOps operator tutorial. As you might remember, we have configured a CronJob along with a ServiceAccount and the ClusterRoleBinding resources. Let's take a look at a ServiceAccount and Cluster-RoleBinding definitions one more time and find what should be changed to improve security.

Listing 6.6   rbac.yaml

```
---
    apiVersion: v1
kind: ServiceAccount
metadata:
  name: gitops-serviceaccount
  namespace: gitops


---
    apiVersion: rbac.authorization.k8s.io/v1
kind: ClusterRoleBinding
metadata:
  name: gitops-operator
roleRef:
  apiGroup: rbac.authorization.k8s.io
  kind: ClusterRole
  name: admin
subjects:
- kind: ServiceAccount
  name: gitops-serviceaccount
  namespace: gitops
```

The ClusterRoleBinding defines the link between the ClusterRole with name admin and the ServiceAccount that is used by the GitOps operator CronJob. The admin ClusterRole exists by default in the cluster and provides god-level access to the whole cluster. That means that the GitOps operator has no limitations and can deploy any resource as long as it is defined in the Git repository.

So what is wrong in this RBAC configuration? The problem is that this is secure only if we assume that the developer with Git repository write permissions already has full cluster access. Since a GitOps operator can create any resource, the developer might add manifests of additional roles and role bindings and grant himself admin permissions. This is not what we want, especially in a multitenant environment.

Another consideration is human mistakes. When a cluster is used by multiple teams, we need to ensure that one team cannot touch the resources of another team. As you learned in chapter 3, teams are typically separated from each other using Kubernetes Namespaces. So it makes sense to limit GitOps operator permissions to one Namespace only.

Finally, we want to control what Namespace-level resources can be managed by a GitOps operator. While it is perfectly fine to let developers manage resources like Deployments, ConfigMaps, and Secrets, there are some resources that should be managed by the cluster administrator only. A good example of restricted network resources is NetworkPolicy. The NetworkPolicy controls what traffic is allowed to the Pods within a Namespace and is typically managed by cluster administrators.

Let's go ahead and update the RBAC configuration of the operator. We would have to make the following changes to ensure secure configuration:

- Limit GitOps operator permissions to only one Namespace.
- Remove permissions to install cluster-level resources.
- Limit operator permissions to selected Namespaced resources.

The updated RBAC configuration is represented here.

Listing 6.7   updated-rbac.yaml

```
---
apiVersion: v1
kind: ServiceAccount
metadata:
  name: gitops-serviceaccount
  namespace: gitops


---
apiVersion: rbac.authorization.k8s.io/v1
kind: Role
metadata:
  name: gitops-role
  namespace: gitops
rules:
- apiGroups:
  - ""
  resources:
  - secrets
  - configmaps
  verbs:
  - '*'
- apiGroups:
  - "extensions"
  - "apps"
  resources:
  - deployments
```

```
      - statefulsets
    verbs:
    - '*'


    ---
    apiVersion: rbac.authorization.k8s.io/v1
    kind: RoleBinding
    metadata:
      name: gitops-role-binding
      namespace: gitops
    roleRef:
      apiGroup: rbac.authorization.k8s.io
      kind: Role
      name: gitops-role
    subjects:
    - kind: ServiceAccount
      name: gitops-serviceaccount
```

Here is a summary of the applied changes:

- The ClusterRoleBinding was replaced with the RoleBinding to ensure Namespace-level access only.
- Instead of using a built-in admin role, we are using the custom Namespace `Role`.
- The Namespaced role provides access only to specified Kubernetes resources. That ensures that the operator cannot modify resources like NetworkPolicy.

6.2.3   *Image registry access*

By securing the Kubernetes cluster, we guarantee that cluster configuration describes the correct workloads that reference the correct Docker images and ultimately run the software we want. The protected deployment repository and fully automated GitOps-driven deployment process provide auditability and observability. The last missing piece that is still not protected is the Docker image itself.

We'll discuss Docker image protection last, but this is definitely not the least important topic. The image content ultimately defines what binary is going to be executed inside of a cluster. So even if everything else is secure, a breach in Docker registry protection defeats all other security gates.

So what does Docker image protection mean in practice? We would have to take care of the two following issues:

- The registry images cannot be changed without permission.
- Images are securely delivered into the Kubernetes cluster.

REGISTRY IMAGE PROTECTION

Similarly to the Git repository, Docker repository protection is provided by the hosting service. Probably the most popular Docker repository hosting service is DockerHub. The service allows accessing thousands of Docker images. The service is provided by Docker Inc. and completely free for any open source project.

To get hands-on experience with DockerHub, you need to get an account on DockerHub, create a repository, and push an image. Unless you already have an account, navigate to https://hub.docker.com/signup and create one. As a next step, you need to create a Docker repository named gitops-k8s-security-alpine, as described in the DockerHub documentation.[12] Finally, you are ready to verify if DockerHub is protecting the repository, but first you need to get a sample Docker image. The simplest way to create one is to pull an existing image and rename it. The following command pulls the Alpine Linux image from the official DockerHub repository and renames it <username>/gitops-k8s-security-alpine, where <username> is the name of your DockerHub account:

```
docker pull alpine
docker tag alpine <username>/gitops-k8s-security-alpine:v0.1
```

The next command pushes the image into the gitops-k8s-security-alpine Docker registry:

```
docker push <username>/gitops-k8s-security-alpine:v0.1
```

However, the local Docker client does not have credentials to access the DockerHub repository, so the push command should fail. To fix the error, run the following command and provide your DockerHub account username and password:

```
docker login
```

Once you have logged in successfully, the Docker client knows who you are, and the Docker push command can be executed.

SECURING IMAGE DELIVERY

The security of image delivery into the cluster means answering the question, "Do we trust the source of the image?" And trust means that we want to be sure that the image was created by an authorized author, and the image content is not being modified while transferring from the repository. So this is the problem of protecting image author identity. And the solution is very similar to the solution that protects Git commit author identity:

- The person or an automated process uses a digital signature to sign the content of the image.
- The signature is used by the consumer to verify that the image was created by a trusted author, and the content was not tampered with.

The good news is that this is already supported by the Docker client and the image registry. The Docker feature named Content Trust allows signing the image and pushing it into the registry along with the signature. The consumer can use the Content Trust feature to verify that the signed image content was not changed.

So in the perfect scenario, the CI pipeline should publish the signed image, and Kubernetes should be configured to require a valid signature for every image running

---

[12] https://docs.docker.com/docker-hub/repos.

in production. The bad news is that Kubernetes, as of version 1.17, still does not provide a configuration that enforces image signature verification. So the best we can do is verify the image signature before modifying the Kubernetes manifests.

The content trust configuration is fairly simple. You have to set the DOCKER _CONTENT_TRUST environment variable:

```
export DOCKER_CONTENT_TRUST=1
```

Once the environment variable is set, the Docker commands run and pull should verify the image signature. We can confirm that by pulling the unsigned image that we just pushed to the gitops-k8s-security-alpine repository:

```
$ docker pull <username>/gitops-k8s-security-alpine:v0.1
Error: remote trust data does not exist for docker.io/<username>/gitops-k8s-
    security-alpine: notary.docker.io does not have trust data for
    docker.io/<username>/gitops-k8s-security-alpine
```

The command fails as expected because the <username>/gitops-k8s-security-alpine:v0.1 image was not signed. Let's fix it. Make sure the DOCKER_CONTENT_TRUST environment variable is still set to 1, and create a signed image using the following command:

```
$ docker tag alpine <username>/gitops-k8s-security-alpine:v0.2
$dockerpush<username>/gitops-k8s-security-alpine:v0.2
The push refers to repository [docker.io/<username>/gitops-k8s-security-
    alpine]
6b27de954cca: Layer already exists
v0.2: digest: sha256:3983cc12fb9dc20a009340149e382a18de6a8261b0ac0e8f5fcdf
    11f8dd5937e size: 528
Signing and pushing trust metadata
You are about to create a new root signing key passphrase. This passphrase
will be used to protect the most sensitive key in your signing system. Please
choose a long, complex passphrase and be careful to keep the password and the
key file itself secure and backed up. It is highly recommended that you use a
password manager to generate the passphrase and keep it safe. There will be no
way to recover this key. You can find the key in your config directory.
Enter passphrase for new root key with ID cfe0184:
Repeat passphrase for new root key with ID cfe0184:
Enter passphrase for new repository key with ID c7eba93:
Repeat passphrase for new repository key with ID c7eba93:
Finished initializing "docker.io/<username>/gitops-k8s-security-alpine"
Successfully signed docker.io/<username>/gitops-k8s-security-alpine:v0.2
```

This time, the docker push command signs the image before pushing it. If you are pushing the signed image for the first time, Docker will generate keys in the ~/.docker/trust/ directory and prompt you for the passphrase to use for the root key and repo key. After providing the passphrase, the signed image is pushed to the Docker Hub. Finally, we can verify that the pushed image has a proper signature by running the docker pull command one more time:

```
docker pull <username>/gitops-k8s-security-alpine:v0.2
```

The command successfully completed. Our image has the proper signature, and the Docker client was able to verify it!

6.3 Patterns

OK, let's face it. Brand-new greenfield projects are not necessarily started with a perfectly secure deployment process. In fact, young projects don't even have an automated deployment process. The lead engineer may be the only one able to deploy the project, which they may do from their laptop. Typically, a team starts adding automation as it gets more and more time consuming to deploy all the application services. As the potential cost and damage from unauthorized access increases, the security of that automation becomes more and more critical.

6.3.1 Full access

The initial security model of almost every new project is based completely on trust between the team members. Every team member has full access, and deployment changes are not necessarily recorded and available for an audit later.

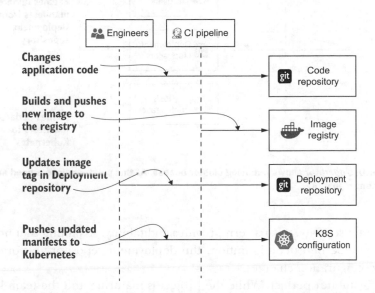

Figure 6.9 The full-access security model assumes that both engineers and CI systems have full access to the Kubernetes cluster. The trade-off is speed over security. This model is more applicable for new projects in the beginning stage.

Weak security is not necessarily a bad thing in the beginning. Full access means fewer barriers, enabling the team to be more flexible and move more quickly. While there is no important customer data in production, it is a perfect chance to focus on speed and shape the project until you are ready to move into production. But probably sooner rather than later, you will need to put proper security controls in place, not only for customer data in production but also to ensure the integrity of the code being deployed into production.

6.3.2   Deployment repo access

Disabling direct Kubernetes access for developers by default is a big step forward from a security perspective. This is the most common pattern if you are using GitOps. In this model, developers still have full access to the deployment repository but must rely on the GitOps operator to push changes to the Kubernetes cluster.

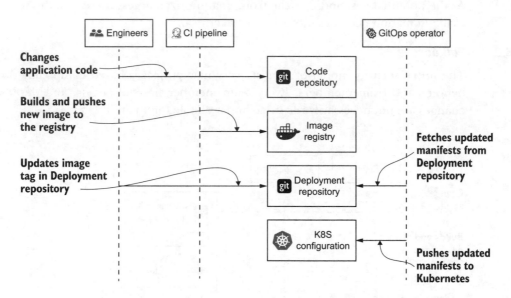

Figure 6.10   The GitOps operator allows removing cluster access. At this point, engineers need access only to the deployment repository.

In addition to better security, this pattern provides auditability. Assuming that no one has access to the Kubernetes configuration, the deployment repository history contains all cluster configuration changes.

The pattern is still not perfect. While the project is maturing and the team keeps improving the deployment configuration, it feels perfectly fine to update the deployment repository manually. However, after some time, each application release is going to require only an image tag change. At this stage, maintenance of the deployment repository is still very valuable but may feel like a lot of overhead.

6.3.3   Code access only

The code-access-only pattern is a logical continuation of the deployment-repository-access-only approach. If release changes in the deployment repository are predictable, it is possible to codify the configuration change process in the CI pipeline.

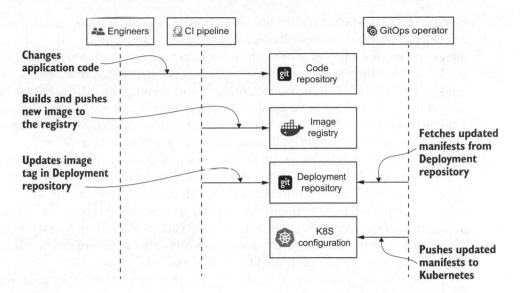

Figure 6.11 **The code-access-only model assumes that both the deployment repository and Kubernetes cluster changes are fully automated. Engineers need only code repository access.**

The pattern streamlines the development process and significantly reduces the amount of manual work. It also improves deployment security in several ways:

- The development team no longer needs access to the deployment repository. Only the dedicated automation account has permission to push into the repository.
- Since changes in the deployment repository are automated, it is much easier to configure the GPG signing process and automate it in the CI pipeline.

Exercise 6.6
Choose which pattern fits your project the best. Try to elaborate on the pros and cons of each pattern, and explain why you prefer the chosen pattern.

6.4 Security concerns

We've learned how to protect our deployment process end to end, starting from the most basic, all the way to identity protection of configuration changes and new images. Finally, let's learn important edge cases that must be covered to ensure the security of your cluster.

6.4.1 Preventing image pull from untrusted registries

In section 6.2.3, we showed how you can implement security controls on public registries, such as docker.io, to ensure images have been published by authorized users as intended and have not been tampered with when being pulled. However, the fact is that a public registry is outside of your visibility and control. You must trust that the maintainers of the public registry are following security best practices. And even if they are, the fact that they are a public registry means that anyone on the internet can push images to it. For some businesses with very high security needs, this is not acceptable.

To address this, many enterprises will maintain their own private Docker image registry for reliability, performance, privacy, and security. In this case, new images should be pushed to the private registry (such as docker.mycompany.com) instead of a public registry (such as docker.io). This can be accomplished by modifying the CI pipeline to push successfully built new images to the private registry.

Deployments to Kubernetes should also only pull images from the private registry. But how can this be enforced? What if a naive developer accidentally pulls a virus- or malware-infected image from docker.io? Or a malicious developer who doesn't have privileges to push images to the private registry tries to side-load an image from their public DockerHub repository? Of course, using GitOps will ensure that these actions are recorded in the audit trail so those responsible should be able to be identified. However, how can this be prevented in the first place?

This can be accomplished using the Open Policy Agent (OPA) and an admission webhook that rejects manifests that reference an image coming from a prohibited image registry.

6.4.2 *Cluster-level resources in a Git repository*

As you know from this chapter, the Kubernetes access settings are controlled using Kubernetes resources such as Role and ClusterRole. RBAC resources management is a perfectly valid use of a GitOps operator. It is common practice to package the definition of an application deployment together with required Kubernetes access settings. However, there is a potential security hole that can be used to escalate privileges. Because Kubernetes access settings are managed by resources, these resources can be placed into the deployment repository and delivered by the GitOps operator. The intruder might create a ClusterRole and give permissions to the service account that later on might be used as a back door.

The rule of thumb that prevents privileges escalation is to limit the GitOps operator privileges. If the development team that leverages the GitOps operator is not supposed to manage ClusterRoles, then the GitOps operator should not have that permission. If the GitOps operator is shared by multiple teams, the operator should be configured appropriately and should enforce team-specific security checks.

Exercise 6.7
Refer to the poor-man's GitOps operator tutorial. Review the RBAC configuration and check if it allows a security privileges escalation attack.

Summary

- The traditional CI Ops security model has a wide attack surface due to access by both engineers and CI systems. The GitOps security model significantly reduces the attack surface of the cluster because only the GitOps operator has access to the cluster.

- Git's underlying data structure uses the Merkle tree, which provides a treelike structure with cryptographic protection to provide a tamper-proof commit log.
- In addition to Git's data structure security advantage, the code review process using pull request and automated checks using tools such as kubeaudit and kubesec can detect security vulnerability in the manifests.
- Git natively does not protect commit author identity. Using GPG can guarantee the authenticity of the commit author by injecting a digital crypto signature in the commit metadata.
- RBAC is the preferred way to implement access control in Kubernetes. Both users and GitOps operators' access control can be provisioned through RBAC.
- Similar to Git, all Docker images should be signed with a digital signature to verify authenticity using the Content Trust feature.
- New projects can start with full access (cluster, deployment repo, and code repo) for engineers to focus on development velocity initially. As projects mature and get ready for initial production release, both cluster and deployment repo access should be restricted to put emphasis on security rather than speed.

7

Secrets

This chapter covers

- Kubernetes Secrets
- GitOps strategies for managing Secrets
- Tooling for managing Secrets

Kubernetes provides a mechanism allowing users to store small bits of sensitive information in a protected resource object, called a Secret. A Secret is anything that you want to tightly control access to. Common examples of data you would want to store in a Secret include things like username and password credentials, API keys, SSH keys, and TLS certificates. In this chapter, you will learn about different Secret management strategies when using a GitOps system. You will also have a brief introduction to several different tools that can be used for storing and managing Secrets.

We recommend you read chapters 1 and 2 before reading this chapter.

7.1 Kubernetes Secrets

A simple *Kubernetes Secret* is a data structure composed of three pieces of information:

- The name of the Secret
- The type of the Secret (optional)
- A map of field names to sensitive data, encoded in Base64

A basic Secret looks like the following.

Listing 7.1 example-secret.yaml

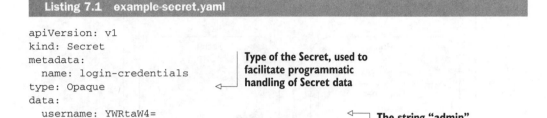

```
apiVersion: v1
kind: Secret
metadata:                          Type of the Secret, used to
  name: login-credentials          facilitate programmatic
type: Opaque                       handling of Secret data
data:
  username: YWRtaW4=                                    The string "admin"
  password: UEA1NXcwcmQ=                                Base64 encoded
                          The string "P@55w0rd"
                          Base64 encoded
```

When looking at the values of a Secret for the first time, at first glance you might mistakenly think that the Secret values were protected with encryption, since the fields are not readable by a human and are not presented in plain text. But you would be mistaken, and it is important to understand that

- Secret values are Base64 encoded.
- Base64 encoding is not the same thing as encryption.
- Viewing should be considered the same as plain text.

BASE64 ENCODING Base64 is an encoding algorithm that allows you to transform any characters into an alphabet that consists of Latin letters, digits, plus, and slash. It allows binary data to be represented in an ASCII string format. Base64 does *not* provide encryption.

The reason Kubernetes Base64 encodes the data at all is that it allows Secrets to store binary data. This is important for storing things like certificates as Secrets. Without Base64 encoding, it would be impossible to store binary configurations as a Secret.

7.1.1 Why use Secrets?

Using Secrets is optional in Kubernetes, but more convenient, flexible, and secure than other techniques, such as placing the sensitive values directly in the Pod specification or baking the values into the container image during build time. Just as with ConfigMaps, Secrets allow the separation of the configuration of an application from the build artifact.

7.1.2   *How to use Secrets*

Kubernetes Secrets, like ConfigMaps, can be used in several ways:

- As files mounted as files in the Pod
- As environment variables in the Pod
- Kubernetes API access

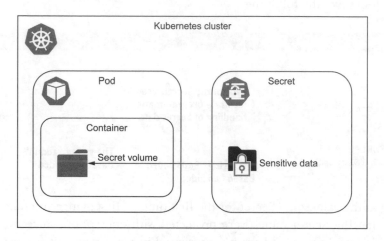

Figure 7.1   A Secret volume is used to pass sensitive information, such as passwords, to Pods. Secret volumes are backed by tmpfs (a RAM-backed filesystem) so they are never written to nonvolatile storage.

VOLUME-MOUNTING SECRETS AS FILES IN A POD

The first technique of utilizing Secrets is mounting them into a Pod as a volume. To do this, you first declare the following.

Listing 7.2   secret-volume.yaml

```
apiVersion: v1
kind: Pod
metadata:
  name: secret-volume-pod          A volume of type Secret
spec:                              is declared in the Pod,
  Volumes:                         with an arbitrary name.
  - name: foo
    secret:
      secretName: mysecret
  containers:
  - name: mycontainer              The container that needs the
    image: redis                   Secrets specifies a path for where
    volumeMounts:                  to mount the Secret data volume.
    - name: foo
      mountPath: /etc/foo
      readOnly: true
```

When projecting a Secret (or ConfigMap) into a Pod as a volume of files, changes to the underlying Secret will eventually update the files mounted in the Pod. This allows the opportunity for the application to reconfigure itself, or hot-reload, without a restart of the container/Pod.

USING SECRETS AS ENVIRONMENT VARIABLES

The second way of utilizing Kubernetes Secrets is by setting them as environment variables.

Listing 7.3   secret-environment-variable.yaml

```
apiVersion: v1
kind: Pod
metadata:
  name: secret-env-pod
spec:
  containers:
  - name: mycontainer
    image: redis
    env:
    - name: SECRET_USERNAME
      valueFrom:
        secretKeyRef:
          name: mysecret          ◁─┐
          key: username   ◁─┐        │  Name of
    - name: SECRET_PASSWORD  │        │  the Secret
      valueFrom:             │        │
        secretKeyRef:        │        │
          name: mysecret     │      ◁─┘
          key: password   ◁──┘
```

The key of the Secret data map

Exposing Secrets to containers as environment variables, while convenient, is arguably not the optimal way to consume Secrets, since it is less secure than consuming them as volume-mounted files. When a Secret is set as an environment variable, all processes in the container (including child processes) will inherit the OS environment and be able to read the environment variable values, and thus the Secret data. For example, a forked shell script would be able to read the environment variables by running the env utility.

> **DISADVANTAGE OF SECRET ENVIRONMENT VARIABLES**   A second disadvantage of using Secrets as environment variables is that, unlike Secrets projected into volumes, values of Secret environment variables will not be updated if the Secret is ever updated after the container starts. A container or Pod restart would be necessary to notice changes.

USING SECRETS FROM THE K8S API

Finally, Kubernetes Secrets can also be retrieved directly from the Kubernetes API. Suppose you had the following Secret with a password field.

Listing 7.4   secret.yaml

```yaml
apiVersion: v1
kind: Secret
metadata:
  name: my-secret
type: Opaque
data:
  password: UEA1NXcwcmQ=
```

To retrieve the Secret, the Pod itself could retrieve the Secret value directly from Kubernetes, for example, by using a `kubectl` command or REST API call. The following `kubectl` command retrieves the Secret named `my-secret`, Base64 decodes the password field, and prints the plain-text value to standard out:

```
$ kubectl get secret my-secret -o=jsonpath='{.data.password}' | base64 --decode
P@55w0rd
```

This technique requires that the Pod has privileges to retrieve the Secret.

SECRET TYPES

The Secret type field is an indication of what type of data is contained inside the Secret. It is primarily used by software programs to identify relevant Secrets they might be interested in, as well as safely make assumptions about what available fields inside the Secret are set.

The following table describes the built-in Kubernetes Secret types, as well as the required fields for each type.

Table 7.1   Built-in Secret types

Type	Description	Required fields
Opaque	The default type. Contains arbitrary user-defined data.	
kubernetes.io/service-account-token	Contains a token that identifies a service account to the Kubernetes API.	data["token"]
kubernetes.io/dockercfg	Contains a serialized ~/.dockercfg file.	data[".dockercfg"]
kubernetes.io/dockerconfigjson	Contains a serialized ~/.docker/config.json file.	data[".dockerconfigjson"]
kubernetes.io/basic-auth	Contains basic username/password credentials.	data["username"] data["password"]
kubernetes.io/ssh-auth	Contains a private SSH key needed for authentication.	data["ssh-privatekey"]
kubernetes.io/tls	Contains a TLS private key and certificate.	data["tls.key"] data["tls.crt"]

7.2   *GitOps and Secrets*

Kubernetes GitOps practitioners will invariably come to the same problem: while users are perfectly comfortable with storing configuration in Git, when it comes to sensitive data, they are unwilling to store that data in Git due to security concerns. Git was designed as a collaborative tool, making it easy for multiple people and teams to gain access to code and view each other's changes. But these same properties are also what make using Git to hold Secrets an extremely dangerous practice. There are many concerns and reasons why it is inappropriate to store Secrets in Git, which we cover next.

7.2.1   *No encryption*

As we learned earlier, Kubernetes provides no encryption on the contents of a Secret, and the Base64 encoding of the values should be considered the same as plain text. Additionally, Git alone does not provide any form of built-in encryption. So when storing Secrets in a Git repository, the Secrets are laid bare to anyone with access to the Git repository.

7.2.2   *Distributed Git repos*

With GitOps, you and your colleagues will be locally cloning the Git repository to your laptops and workstations, for the purposes of managing the configuration of the applications. But by doing so, you would also be proliferating and distributing Secrets to many systems, without adequate auditing or tracking. If any of these systems were to become compromised (hacked or even physically lost), someone would gain access to all of your Secrets.

7.2.3   *No granular (file-level) access control*

Git does not provide read protection of a subpath or subfile of a Git repository. In other words, it is not possible to restrict access to some files in the Git repository but not others. When dealing with Secrets, you ideally should be granting read access to the Secrets on a need-to-know basis. For example, if you had a temporary worker who needed partial access to the Git repository, you would want to give the least amount of access to the content as possible to that user. Unfortunately, Git does not provide any facilities to accomplish this, and it is an all-or-nothing decision when giving permissions to a repo.

7.2.4   *Insecure storage*

Git was never intended to be used in the capacity of a Secret management system. As a result, it did not design into the system standard security features such as encryption at rest. Therefore, a compromised Git server would have the potential of also leaking the Secrets of all the repositories it manages, making it a prime target for attack.

> **GIT PROVIDER FEATURES**   Although Git in itself does not provide security features such as encryption at rest, Git providers often do provide these features

on top of Git. For example, GitHub does claim to encrypt repositories at rest. But this functionality may vary from provider to provider.

7.2.5   *Full commit history*

Once a Secret is added to the Git commit history, it is very difficult to remove. If the Secret is checked into Git and then later deleted, that Secret can still be retrieved by checking out an earlier point in the repository history before the Secret was deleted. Even if the Secret is encrypted, when the key used to encrypt the Secret is later rotated and the Secret is reencrypted with a new key, the Secret encrypted with the old keys is still present in the repository history.

7.3   *Secrets management strategies*

There are many different strategies for dealing with Secrets in GitOps with trade-offs in flexibility, manageability, and security. Before going into the application of tools to implement these strategies, we'll first go over some of the strategies at a conceptual level.

7.3.1   *Storing Secrets in Git*

The first strategy of GitOps and Secrets is to not have a strategy at all. In other words, you would simply commit and manage your Secrets in Git like any other Kubernetes resource and accept the security consequences.

You might be thinking, "What is so wrong about storing my Secrets in Git?" Even if you have a private GitHub repository, which is only accessible by trusted members of your team, you might want to allow third-party access to the Git repo—CI/CD systems, security scanners, static analysis, and so on. By providing your Git repository of Secrets to these third-party software systems, you are in turn entrusting them with your Secrets.

So in practice, the only real acceptable scenarios where Secrets could be stored as is in Git are when the Secrets do not contain any truly sensitive data, such as dev and test environments.

7.3.2   *Baking Secrets into the container image*

One naive strategy that might come to mind to avoid storing Secrets in Git is to bake the sensitive data directly into the container image. In this approach, the Secret data is directly copied into the container image as part of the Docker build process.

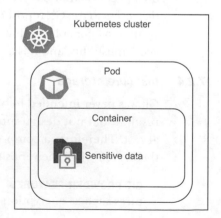

Figure 7.2   **Baking a Secret into the container image. The Docker build process bakes the sensitive data into the image (such as by copying the sensitive file into the container). No Secret store is used (Kubernetes or external), but the container registry becomes sensitive since it is effectively a Secret store.**

A simplistic Dockerfile that bakes Secrets into the image might look like this.

> **Listing 7.5 Dockerfile with a Secret**

```
FROM scratch

COPY ./my-app /my-app
COPY ./credentials.txt /credentials.txt

ENTRYPOINT ["/my-app"]
```

An advantage of this approach is that it removes Git and even Kubernetes itself from the equation. In fact, with the Secret data baked into the container image, the image can be run anywhere, not just Kubernetes, and work without any configuration.

However, baking the sensitive data directly into the container image has some very bad drawbacks, which should automatically rule it out as a viable option. The first issue is that the container image *itself* is now sensitive. Due to the fact that the sensitive data was baked into the image, anyone or anything that has access to the container image (such as via a docker pull), can now trivially copy out and retrieve the Secret.

Another problem is that because the Secret is baked into the image, updates to the Secret data are extremely burdensome. Whenever credentials need to be rotated, it will require a complete rebuild of the container image.

A third problem is that the container image is not flexible enough to accommodate when the same image needs to run using different Secret datasets. Suppose you have three environments where this container image will be deployed:

- A developer environment
- A test environment
- A production environment

Each of these environments needs a different set of credentials because it connects to three different databases. The approach of baking the Secret data into the container image would not work here, because it can choose only one of the database credentials to bake into the image.

7.3.3 Out-of-band management

A second approach for dealing with Secrets in GitOps is to manage Secrets completely *out-of-band* from GitOps. With this approach, everything *except* Kubernetes Secrets would be defined in Git and deployed via GitOps, but some other mechanism would be used for deploying Secrets, even if it was manual.

For example, a user could store their Secrets in a database, a cloud provider's managed Secret store, even a text file on their local workstation. When it came time to deploy, the user would manually run kubectl apply to deploy the Secret into the cluster and then let a GitOps operator deploy everything else.

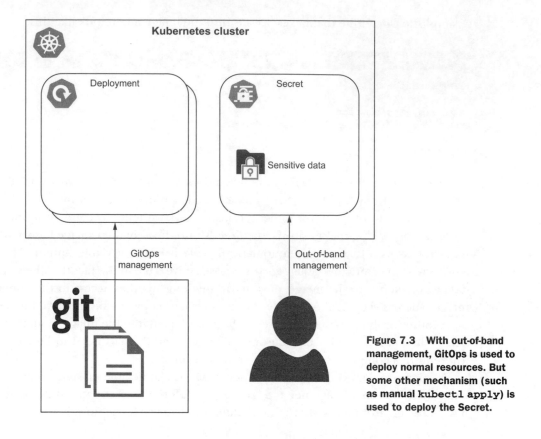

Figure 7.3   With out-of-band management, GitOps is used to deploy normal resources. But some other mechanism (such as manual `kubectl apply`) is used to deploy the Secret.

The obvious disadvantage of this approach is that you would need to have two different mechanisms for deploying resources to the cluster: one for normal Kubernetes resources via GitOps and another strictly for Secrets.

7.3.4   *External Secrets management systems*

Another strategy for dealing with Secrets in GitOps is to use an external Secret management system *other than* Kubernetes. In this strategy, rather than using the native Kubernetes features to store and load Secrets into the container, the application containers themselves retrieve the Secret values dynamically at run-time, at the point of use.

A variety of Secret management systems exist, but the most popular and widely used one is HashiCorp Vault, which is the tool that we will primarily focus on when discussing external Secret management systems. Individual cloud providers also provide their own Secret management services such as AWS Secrets Manager, Google Cloud Secret Manager, and Microsoft Azure Key Vault. The tools may differ in capabilities and feature sets, but the general principles are the same and should be applicable to all.

By choosing to use an external Secret management system (such as Vault) to manage your Secrets, you are also effectively making a decision not to use Kubernetes Secrets. This is because when using this strategy, you are relying on the external secret

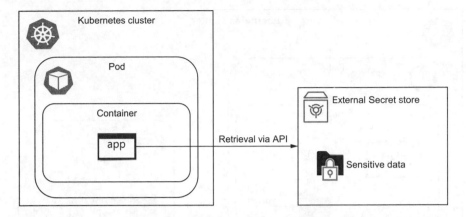

Figure 7.4   Retrieval of a Secret from an external Secret store. In this approach, sensitive data is not stored as Kubernetes Secrets. Instead, it is stored in an external system, which would be retrieved by a container at run-time (such as via an API call).

management system to store and retrieve your Secrets, and not Kubernetes. A large consequence is that you also would not be able to leverage some of the conveniences that Kubernetes Secrets provide, such as setting the value of an environment variable from a Secret or mapping the Secret as files in a volume.

When using an external Secret store, it is the responsibility of the application to retrieve the Secrets from the store securely. For example, when the application starts, it could dynamically retrieve the Secret values from the Secret store at run-time, as opposed to using the Kubernetes mechanisms (environment variables, volume mounts, and so on). This shifts the burden of safekeeping of Secrets to both the application developers who must retrieve the Secret safely and administrators of the external Secret store.

Another consequence of this technique is that because Secrets are managed in a separate database, you do not have the same history/record of when Secrets were changed as you do for your configuration managed in Git. This could even affect your ability to roll back in a predictable manner. For example, during a rollback, applying the manifests at the previous Git commit might not be enough. You would additionally have to roll back the Secret to a previous value at the same time of the Git commit. Depending on what Secret store was used, this might be inconvenient in the best case, or downright impossible in the worst.

7.3.5   *Encrypting Secrets in Git*

Since Git is considered unsafe for storing plain-text Secrets, one strategy is to encrypt the sensitive data so that it *is* safe to store in Git and then decrypt the encrypted data closer to its point of use. The actor performing the decryption would have to have the necessary keys to decrypt the encrypted Secret. This might be the application itself, an init container that populates a volume used by the application, or a controller to handle these tasks for the application seamlessly.

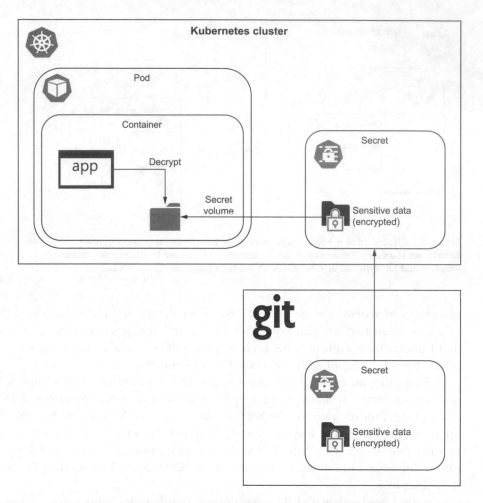

Figure 7.5   Secrets are encrypted and safely stored in Git alongside other Kubernetes resources. At run-time, the application can decrypt the contents before using.

One popular tool that aids in this technique of encrypting Secrets in Git is Bitnami SealedSecrets, which we will cover in depth later in this chapter.

The challenges of encrypting Secrets in Git is that there still is one last Secret involved, and that is the encryption key used to encrypt those Secrets. Without adequate protection of the encryption key, this technique is meaningless, as anyone with access to the encryption key now has the ability to decrypt and gain access to the sensitive data in the manifests.

7.3.6   *Comparison of strategies*

There are many different approaches to managing Secrets in Kubernetes, each with trade-offs. Consider the following advantages and disadvantages before deciding on a solution and/or tool that fits your needs.

Table 7.2 GitOps Secrets management strategies

Type	Advantages	Disadvantages
Store in Git	Simple and convenient Secrets and configuration are managed in the same place (Git)	Completely insecure
Bake into image	Simple and convenient	Container images are sensitive. Rotating Secrets requires rebuilding. Images are not portable. Secrets are not sharable across Pods.
Out-of-band management	Still able to leverage native Kubernetes Secrets faculties (such as volume mounts and environment variables)	Different processes for deploying Secrets and config Modifications to Secrets are not recorded in Git history, possibly affecting the ability to roll back.

7.4   *Tooling*

Both within and outside the Kubernetes ecosystem, numerous projects have emerged to help users deal with the problem of Secrets. All of the projects use one of the strategies to Secret management discussed previously. In this section, we cover some of the more popular tools that can complement a Kubernetes environment with a GitOps-focused approach.

7.4.1   *HashiCorp Vault*

Vault, by HashiCorp, is a purpose built, open source tool for storing and managing Secrets in a secure manner. Vault provides a CLI and a UI, as well as an API for programmatic access to the Secret data. Vault is not specific to Kubernetes and is popular as a standalone Secret management system.

VAULT INSTALLATION AND SETUP

There are many ways to install and run Vault. But if you are new to Vault, the recommended and easiest way to get started is to install Vault using the official Helm chart maintained by HashiCorp. For the purposes of simplifying our tutorial, we will be installing Vault in dev mode, which is meant for experimentation, development, and testing. Additionally, the command also installs the Vault Agent Sidecar Injector, which we will cover and use in the following section:

```
# NOTE: requires Helm v3.0+

$ helm repo add hashicorp https://helm.releases.hashicorp.com

$ helm install vault hashicorp/vault \
    --set server.dev.enabled=true \
    --set injector.enabled=true
```

> **NON-KUBERNETES INSTALLATION** Note that it is not necessary to run Vault in a Kubernetes environment. Vault is a general purpose Secret management system, useful for applications and platforms other than Kubernetes. Many enterprises choose to run a centrally managed Vault instance for their company, so a single Vault instance can service multiple Kubernetes clusters

and virtual machines, as well as be accessed by developers and operators from the corporate network and workstations.

The Vault CLI can be downloaded from https://www.vaultproject.io/downloads or (for macOS) by using the `brew` package manager:

```
$ brew install vault
```

Once installed, Vault can be accessed through standard port forwarding, and visiting the UI at http://localhost:8200:

```
# Run the following from a different terminal, or background it with '&'
$ kubectl port-forward vault-0 8200

$ export VAULT_ADDR=http://localhost:8200

# In dev mode, the token is the word: root
$ vault login
Token (will be hidden):
Success! You are now authenticated. The token information displayed below
is already stored in the token helper. You do NOT need to run "vault login"
again. Future Vault requests will automatically use this token.

Key                     Value
---                     -----
token                   root
token_accessor          o4SQvGgg4ywEv0wnGgqHhK1h
token_duration          ?
token_renewable         false
token_policies          ["root"]
identity_policies       []
policies                ["root"]


$ vault status
Key             Value
---             -----
Seal Type       shamir
Initialized     true
Sealed          false
Total Shares    1
Threshold       1
Version         1.4.0
Cluster Name    vault-cluster-23e9c708
Cluster ID      543c058a-a9d4-e838-e270-33f7e93814f2
HA Enabled      false
```

VAULT USE

Once Vault is installed in your cluster, it's time to store your first Secret in Vault:

```
$ vault kv put secret/hello foo=world
Key             Value
---             -----
created_time    2020-05-15T12:36:21.956834623Z
deletion_time   n/a
destroyed       false
version         1
```

To retrieve the Secret, run the `vault kv get` command:

```
$ vault kv get secret/hello
====== Metadata ======
Key                Value
---                -----
created_time       2020-05-15T12:36:21.956834623Z
deletion_time      n/a
destroyed          false
version            1

=== Data ===
Key    Value
---    -----
foo    world
```

By default, `vault kv get` will print Secrets in a tabular format. While this format is presented in an easy-to-read way and is great for humans, it's not as easy to parse via automation and to be consumed by an application. To aid in this, Vault provides some additional ways of formatting the output and extracting specific fields of the Secret:

```
$ vault kv get -field foo secret/hello
world

$ vault kv get -format json secret/hello
{
  "request_id": "825d85e4-8e8b-eab0-6afb-f6c63856b82c",
  "lease_id": "",
  "lease_duration": 0,
  "renewable": false,
  "data": {
    "data": {
      "foo": "world"
    },
    "metadata": {
      "created_time": "2020-05-15T12:36:21.956834623Z",
      "deletion_time": "",
      "destroyed": false,
      "version": 1
    }
  },
  "warnings": null
}
```

This makes it easy for the Vault CLI to be used in a startup script, which might

1. Run the `vault kv get` command to retrieve the value of a Secret.
2. Set the Secret value as an environment variable or file.
3. Start the main application, which can now read the Secret from env var or file.

An example of such a startup script might look like the following.

Listing 7.6   vault-startup.sh

```
#!/bin/sh

export VAULT_TOKEN=your-vault-token
export VAULT_ADDR=https://your-vault-address.com:8200
export HELLO_SECRET=$(vault kv get -field foo secret/hello)
    ./guestbook
```

To integrate this with a Kubernetes application, this startup script would be used as the entry point to the container, replacing the normal application command with the startup script, which starts the application *after* the Secret has been retrieved and set to an environment variable.

One thing to notice about this approach is that the `vault kv get` command *itself* needs privileges to access Vault. So for this script to work, `vault kv get` needs to securely communicate with the Vault server, typically using a Vault token. Another way of saying this is that you still need a Secret to get more Secrets. This presents a chicken-and-egg problem, where you now need to somehow securely configure and store the Vault secret needed to retrieve the application Secrets. The solution lies in a Kubernetes-Vault integration, which we will cover in the next section.

7.4.2   *Vault Agent Sidecar Injector*

Due to Vault's popularity, many Vault and Kubernetes integrations have been created to make it easier to use. The official Kubernetes integration, developed and supported by HashiCorp, is the Vault Agent Sidecar Injector.

As explained in the previous section, for an application to retrieve Secrets from Vault, a specialized script was used, which performed some prerequisite steps before launching the application. This involved retrieving and preparing the application Secrets. There were a few problems with that approach:

- Although application Secret(s) were retrieved in a secure manner, the technique still needed to deal with protecting the Vault Secret used to access the application Secrets.
- The container needed to be Vault aware, in the sense that the container needed to be built with a specialized script that understood how to retrieve a specific Vault Secret and pass it to the application.

To solve this problem, HashiCorp developed the Vault Agent Sidecar Injector, which solves these two problems in a generic way. The Vault Agent Sidecar Injector automatically modifies Pods that are annotated a specific way, and securely retrieves annotated Secret references (application Secrets) and renders those values into a shared volume accessible to the application container. By rendering Secrets to a shared volume, containers within the Pod can consume Vault Secrets without being Vault aware.

HOW IT WORKS

The Vault Agent Injector alters Pod specifications to include Vault Agent containers that populate Vault Secrets to a shared memory volume accessible to the application. To achieve this, you use a feature in Kubernetes called *mutating admission webhooks*.

> **MUTATING ADMISSION WEBHOOKS**   Mutating admission webhooks are one of the many ways to extend the Kubernetes API server with additional functionality. Mutating webhooks are implemented as HTTP callbacks, which intercept admission requests (create, update, patch requests) and modify the object in some way.

Figure 7.6 explains how the Vault Agent Injector works.

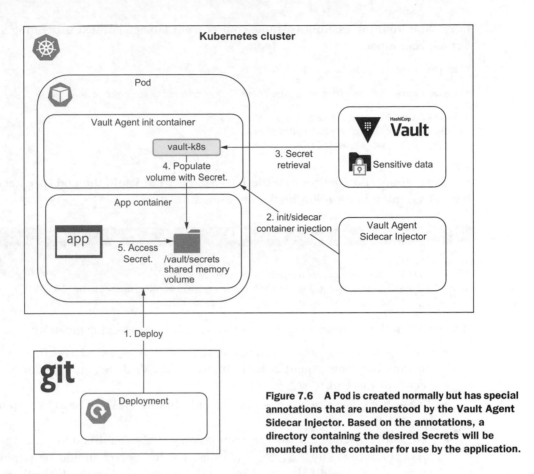

Figure 7.6 A Pod is created normally but has special annotations that are understood by the Vault Agent Sidecar Injector. Based on the annotations, a directory containing the desired Secrets will be mounted into the container for use by the application.

The series of steps involved in this approach are as follows:

1 A workload resource (Deployment, Job, ReplicaSet, and so on) is deployed to the cluster. This eventually creates a Kubernetes Pod.

2 As the Pod is being created, the Kubernetes API server invokes a mutating webhook call to the Vault Agent Sidecar Injector. The Vault Agent Sidecar Injector modifies the Pod by injecting an init container to the Pod (and, optionally, a sidecar).

3 When the Vault Agent Init Container runs, it securely communicates with Vault to retrieve the Secret.

4 The Secret is written to a shared memory volume, which is shared between the init container and the application container.

5 When the application container runs, it is now able to retrieve the Secret from the shared memory volume.

VAULT AGENT SIDECAR INJECTOR INSTALLATION AND SETUP

Earlier in the chapter, we describe how to install Vault using the official Helm chart. This chart also includes the Agent Sidecar Injector. The instructions are repeated here. Note that the examples assume your current kubectl context is pointing at the default Namespace:

```
# NOTE: requires Helm v3.0+

$ helm repo add hashicorp https://helm.releases.hashicorp.com

$ helm install vault hashicorp/vault \
    --set server.dev.enabled=true \
    --set injector.enabled=true
```

USE

When an application desires to retrieve its Secrets from Vault, the Pod spec needs to have at a minimum the following Vault agent annotations.

Listing 7.7   vault-agent-inject-annotations.yaml

```
annotations:
      vault.hashicorp.com/agent-inject: "true"
  vault.hashicorp.com/agent-inject-secret-hello.txt: secret/hello
  vault.hashicorp.com/role: app
```

Breaking this down, these annotations convey several pieces of information:

- The annotation key `vault.hashicorp.com/agent-inject:` `"true"` informs the Vault Agent Sidecar Injector that Vault Secret injection should occur for this Pod.
- The annotation value `secret/hello` indicates which Vault Secret key to inject into the Pod.
- The suffix `hello.txt` of the annotation, `vault.hashicorp.com/agent-inject-secret-hello.txt`, indicates that the Secret should be populated under a file named hello.txt in the shared memory volume with the final path being /vault/secrets/hello.txt.
- The annotation value from the `vault.hashicorp.com/role` indicates which Vault role should be used when retrieving the Secret.

Now let's try with a real example. To run all the Vault commands in this tutorial, you will need to first gain console access inside Vault. Run `kubectl exec` to access the interactive console of the Vault server:

```
$ kubectl exec -it vault-0 -- /bin/sh
/ $
```

If you haven't already, follow the earlier guide on creating your first Secret named "hello" in Vault:

```
$ vault kv put secret/hello foo=world
Key                Value
---                -----
created_time       2020-05-15T12:36:21.956834623Z
deletion_time      n/a
destroyed          false
version            1
```

Next, we need to configure Vault to allow Kubernetes Pods to authenticate and retrieve Secrets. To do so, run the following Vault commands to enable the Kubernetes auth method:

```
$ vault auth enable kubernetes
Success! Enabled kubernetes auth method at: kubernetes/

$ vault write auth/kubernetes/config \
    token_reviewer_jwt="$(cat /var/run/secrets/kubernetes.io/serviceaccount/
     token)" \
    kubernetes_host="https://$KUBERNETES_PORT_443_TCP_ADDR:443" \
    kubernetes_ca_cert=@/var/run/secrets/kubernetes.io/serviceaccount/ca.crt
Success! Data written to: auth/kubernetes/config
```

These two commands configure Vault to use the Kubernetes authentication method to use the service account token, the location of the Kubernetes host, and its certificate.

Next, we define a policy named "app," as well as a role named "app," which will have read privileges to the "hello" Secret:

```
# Create a policy "app" which will have read privileges to the "secret/hello"
    secret
$ vault policy write app - <<EOF
path "secret/hello" {
  capabilities = ["read"]
}
EOF

# Grants a pod in the "default" namespace using the "default" service account
# privileges to read the "hello" secret
$ vault write auth/kubernetes/role/app \
    bound_service_account_names=default \
    bound_service_account_namespaces=default \
    policies=app \
    ttl=24h
```

Now it's time to deploy a Pod that will automatically get our injected Vault Secret. Apply the following Deployment manifest, which has the Vault annotations we described earlier on the Pod.

Listing 7.8 vault-agent-inject-example.yaml

```
apiVersion: apps/v1
kind: Deployment
metadata:
  name: vault-agent-inject-example
spec:
  selector:
    matchLabels:
      app: vault-agent-inject-example
  template:
    metadata:
      labels:
        app: vault-agent-inject-example
      annotations:
```

```
        vault.hashicorp.com/agent-inject: "true"
        vault.hashicorp.com/agent-inject-secret-hello.txt: secret/hello
        vault.hashicorp.com/role: app
     spec:
       containers:
       - name: debian
         image: debian:latest
         command: [sleep, infinity]
```

When the deployment is up and running, we can access the console of the Pod and verify that the Pod does indeed have the Secret mounted in it:

```
$ kubectl exec deploy/vault-agent-inject-example -it -c debian -- bash
root@vault-agent-inject-example-5c48967c97-hgzds:/# cat /vault/secrets/
    hello.txt
data: map[foo:world]
metadata: map[created_time:2020-10-14T17:58:34.5584858Z deletion_time:
    destroyed:false version:1]
```

Aso you can see, using the Vault Agent Sidecar Injector is one of the easiest ways to get Vault Secrets seamlessly into your Pods in a secure manner.

7.4.3 *Sealed Secrets*

Sealed Secrets, by Bitnami, is another solution to the GitOps Secret problem and aptly describes the problem as "I can manage all my K8s config in Git, except Secrets." While not the only tool, currently Sealed Secrets is the most popular and widely used tool for teams who would prefer to encrypt their Secrets in Git. This allows everything, including Secrets, to be completely and wholly managed in Git.

Sealed Secrets follows the strategy of encrypting the sensitive data so that it can be safely stored in Git, and decrypting it inside the cluster. What makes it unique is that it provides a controller and command-line interface, which help automate this process.

HOW IT WORKS

Sealed Secrets consists of the following:

- A new CustomResourceDefinition, called a SealedSecret, which will produce a normal Secret
- A controller that runs in the cluster responsible for decrypting a SealedSecret, and produces a normal Kubernetes Secret with the decrypted data
- A command-line tool, kubeseal, which encrypts sensitive data into a Sealed-Secret for safe storage in Git

When a user wishes to manage a Secret using Git, they will seal or encrypt the Secret into a SealedSecret custom resource using the kubeseal CLI, which they will store in Git alongside other application resources (Deployments, ConfigMaps, and so on). The SealedSecret is deployed like any other Kubernetes resource.

When a SealedSecret is deployed, the `sealed-secrets-controller` will decrypt the data and produce a normal Kubernetes Secret with the same name. At this point, there is no difference in the experience with a SealedSecret and a normal Kubernetes Secret, since a regular Kubernetes Secret is available to be used by Pods.

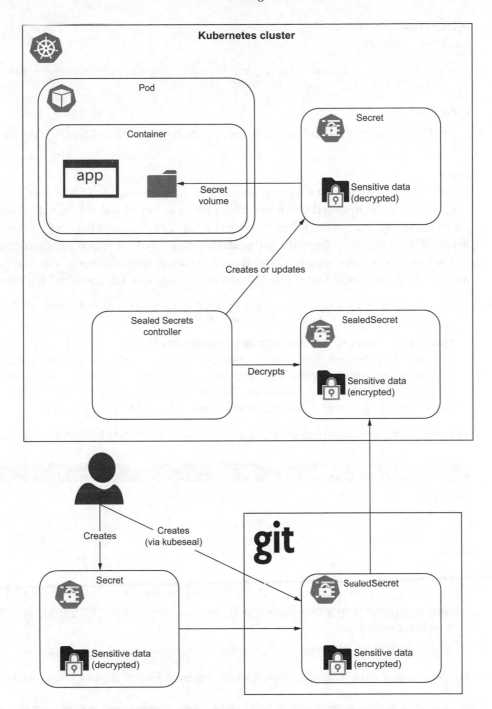

Figure 7.7 A user will encrypt a Secret into a SealedSecret to store in Git. The Sealed Secrets controller decrypts the SealedSecret and formulates a corresponding Kubernetes Secret to be used by a Pod using normal Kubernetes faculties.

INSTALLATION

CRD and controller:

```
$ kubectl apply -f https://github.com/bitnami-labs/sealed-secrets/releases/
    download/v0.12.4/controller.yaml
```

Kubeseal CLI:

- Download the binary from https://github.com/bitnami-labs/sealed-secrets/releases.

USE

To use SealedSecrets, you first create a regular Kubernetes Secret like you normally would using your preferred technique, and place it at some local file path. For this simple example, we will use the `kubectl create secret` command to create a password Secret. The `--dry-run` flag is used to print the value to stdout, which is then redirected to a temporary file. We store it in a temporary location, since the Secret containing the unencrypted data should be discarded and not persisted in Git (or anywhere else).

```
$ kubectl create secret generic my-password --from-literal=password=Pa55Word1
    --dry-run -o yaml > /tmp/my-password.yaml
```

> **DON'T USE KUBECTL CREATE SECRET --FROM-LITERAL** The use of `--from-literal` in the previous example is only for demo and exercise purposes, and it should never be used with any sensitive data. This is because your shell records recently run commands into a history file for convenient retrieval. If you wish to use kubectl to generate a Secret, consider using `--from-file` instead.

The preceding command will produce the following temporary Kubernetes Secret file.

Listing 7.9   my-password.yaml

```
apiVersion: v1
kind: Secret
metadata:
  name: my-password
data:
  password: UGE1NVdvcmQx
```

The next step is to seal or encrypt the temporary Secret using the kubeseal CLI. The following command creates a SealedSecret object, based on the temporary Secret file that we just created:

```
$ kubeseal -o yaml </tmp/my-password.yaml > my-sealed-password.yaml
```

This will produce the following SealedSecret resource, which can be safely stored in Git.

Listing 7.10   my-sealed-password.yaml

```
apiVersion: bitnami.com/v1alpha1
kind: SealedSecret
metadata:
  creationTimestamp: null
```

```
    name: my-password
    namespace: default
spec:
  encryptedData:
    password: AgAF7r6v4LG/
      JPU7TiOi77bhd1NJ9ua9g1dvzNw7wBKK2LLJyndSR8GShF3f1zRY+cNM0iOGTkcaFrNRCG/
      CMrLiwNltQv1gZKqryFugjcp7tiM0dwmmi4M0aIeqRfXq3+vL/Mmdc/xEsK/FtuKOg18rWoG/
      wEhvNhtvXult4kXHTSVL5xa4KmYD8Hn8p8CNZrGATLfy6rIlZsydM9DoB1nSFDsfG5kHlE++
      RbyXxd6Y6vckK1DPl6oqI5GidnrEQlQmkhEr+h/YuUrajAxMFNZpqzs9yaTkURdc0xDp2w
      MiycBooEn7eRzTt2aTohO4q9rgoiWwjztCyXdOCyCt+eisoG0QsqC697PiQV35IFuNbkpty
      FUU04nfMtxYfb2aZEHfVt8/j3xl9JlqKQl6zy9g0jhj1QLxhBjmRK9EyqTxqVGRTfrHaHqqz
      7mzSy/x2H6lkfBBVFLWSvwOFkYD82wdQRfTYBF5Uu/cnjeB2Uob8JkM91nEtXhLWAwtl2K5
      w0LYyUd3qOaNEEXgyv+dN/4pTHK1V+LF6IHNDOFau8QVNmqJrxrXv8yEnRGzBYg60J99Kl9
      vhp8pfbHAYfn2Tb9o8WxWjWD0YAc+pAuFAGjUmJKEJmaPr0vUo0k67BlXj77LVuHPH6
      Ei6JxGYOZA0B2WElmOwILHzDl7unWXnI+Q7Hmk2TEYSeEo81x+I9mLd8D6EpunG2lFndo=
  template:
    metadata:
      creationTimestamp: null
      name: my-password
      namespace: default
```

The SealedSecret can now be stored alongside your other application manifests and deployed like a normal resource without any special treatment.

SEALING SECRETS WITHOUT CLUSTER ACCESS By default, kubeseal will encrypt the Secret using the certificate of the `sealed-secrets-controller`. To do so, it needs access to the Kubernetes cluster to retrieve the certificate directly from the `sealed-secrets-controller`. It is possible to seal Secrets offline without direct access to the cluster. Alternatively, the certificate could be provided using different means, by using the `kubeseal --cert` flag, which allows you to specify a local path to a certificate or even URL.

One thing you might have noticed when comparing the original Kubernetes Secret and the SealedSecret is that the SealedSecret has a Namespace specified in the metadata, whereas the original Secret does not. This means that the SealedSecret is much less portable than the original Secret, since it cannot be deployed in different Namespaces. This is actually a security feature of SealedSecrets, in what is referred to as a *strict scope*. With a strict scope, SealedSecrets encrypts the Secret in such a way that it can only be used for the Namespace that it was encrypted for, and also with the exact same Secret name (my-password, in our example). This feature prevents an attack where an attacker could deploy a SealedSecret to a different Namespace or name that the attacker has privileges to, in order to view the sensitive data of the resulting Secret.

In non-multitenant environments, the strict scope can be relaxed so that the same SealedSecret can be used in any Namespace in the cluster. To do so, you can specify the `--scope cluster-wide` flag during the sealing process:

```
$ kubeseal -o yaml --scope cluster-wide </tmp/my-password.yaml > my-cluster-
    sealed-password.yaml
```

This produces a slightly different cluster-scope SealedSecret, which now no longer contains the Namespace.

Listing 7.11   my-clusterwide-sealed-password.yaml

```
apiVersion: bitnami.com/v1alpha1
kind: SealedSecret
metadata:
  annotations:
    sealedsecrets.bitnami.com/cluster-wide: "true"
  creationTimestamp: null
  name: my-password
spec:
  encryptedData:
    password: AgBjcpeaU2SKqOTMQ2SxYnxoJgy19PR7uzi1qrP5e3PqCPRi7yWD6TvozJE2r9O
      rey0zLL0/yTuIHn0Z5S7FBQT6p7FA19FGxcCu+Xdd1p/purofibL5xR8Zfk/VxEAH2RSVPS
      UGdMwpMRqhKFrsK2rZujjrDjOdC/7zTRgueSMJ6RTIWSCctXZ5htaWIBvN3nUJKGAWsrG/
      cF1xA6pPANE6eZTjyX3+pEQ3YPmPqkc4chseU/aUqk3fXN5tEcwuLWFXFkihN5hMnhKUH8
      CePk7IWB/BXATxLNYlGRzrcYAoXZOyYGkUlw24yVMl0AbpmlmqYiCdlnQMEhTilc9iyKKT3
      ASplH+T/WMr7DdKcDpbTcgL0wI0EeBtUXV2zBWdNWquVA6oPCJmo4TruiBtLDZjeu6xj9fV
      tlZD/HETGLgeDuBSw/BN7fUqi6GuRObFMiZUhoN4ynm2jNHTe0bVDV6QOidbTvy6FcPjHV
      qjwKsLu2jN/TYhLTkbzHjL9Or2dZX8gI/BrmMOtoRDzSK2C4T9KqyAxipRgYkSH9cImdT9
      ChCPA9jIQUZRZGMS48Yg/SDRvA/d+QaGdMhhbhtmApWPWMaA/0+adxnPcoKBnVtuzAlPla
      YN64JCBzyJkKDVutm/wvMYtoZ95vMnLDG1d/b9CmYobAyeuz9AGZ5UeZWoZ32DMMhc5kXecR/
      FsnfMWeCaHiT+6423nJU=
  template:
    metadata:
      annotations:
        sealedsecrets.bitnami.com/cluster-wide: "true"
      creationTimestamp: null
      name: my-password
```

One of the consequences of a clusterwide SealedSecret scope is that the SealedSecret can now be deployed and decrypted in *any* Namespace of the cluster. This means that anyone with privileges to a single Namespace in the cluster can simply deploy the SealedSecret in their Namespace for the purposes of viewing the sensitive data.

One challenge to using SealedSecrets is that the encryption key that is used to encrypt the Secrets is different for every cluster. When a `sealed-secrets-controller` converts and encrypts a normal Kubernetes Secret into a SealedSecret, that SealedSecret object is only valid for the signing controller, and nowhere else. This means that there is a different SealedSecret object in Git for every cluster. If you are dealing with a single cluster, this challenge may not be an issue for you. However, if the same Secret needs to be deployed to more clusters, then this becomes a configuration management problem, since the SealedSecret would need to be produced for each environment.

Although it is possible to use the same encryption key for multiple clusters, this presents a different challenge: it then becomes difficult to safely distribute, manage, and secure that key in all clusters. The encryption key would be distributed across many locations, presenting more opportunities for it to become compromised, and ultimately allowing an attacker to gain access to every Secret in every cluster.

7.4.4   *Kustomize Secret generator plugin*

Users who are managing their Kubernetes configurations using Kustomize have a unique feature available to them, Kustomize plugins, which can be leveraged for retrieving Secrets. Kustomize's plugin feature allows Kustomize to invoke user-defined logic to generate or transform Kubernetes resources during the build process. Plugins are very powerful, and could be written to retrieve Secrets from an external source,

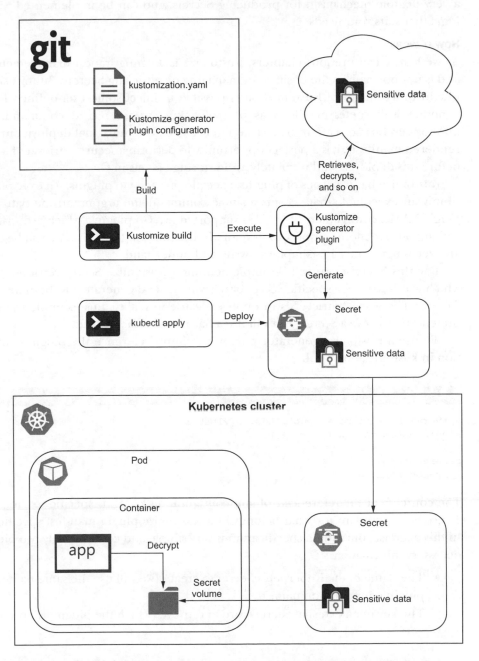

Figure 7.8 Instead of storing a Secret in Git, the recipe for formulating or retrieving that Secret is stored (as a Kustomize Secret generator). This approach implies the rendered Secret will be applied to the cluster immediately after rendering (the Kustomize build).

such as a database, RPC calls, or even an external Secret store such as Vault. The plugin could even be written to perform decryption of encrypted data and transform it into a Kubernetes Secret. The important takeaway is that Kustomize plugins provide a very flexible mechanism for producing Secrets, and can be implemented with any logic that suits your needs.

HOW IT WORKS

As we learned in previous chapters, Kustomize is a configuration management tool, and is not normally in the business of managing or retrieving Secrets. But by using the plugin functionality of Kustomize, it is possible to inject some user-defined logic to generate Kubernetes manifests as part of a `kustomize build` command. Since `kustomize build` is often the last step to occur before the actual deployment of the rendered manifests, it is a perfect opportunity to perform a secure retrieval of a Secret before it is deployed, and ultimately avoid storing Secrets in Git.

Kustomize has two types of plugins: exec plugins and Go plugins. An exec plugin is simply an executable that accepts a single command-line argument: the path of the plugin YAML configuration file. Also supported are Go plugins, which are written in Golang but are more complex to develop. In the following exercise, we will be writing an exec plugin, since it is simpler to write and understand.

For this exercise, we will be implementing a Kustomize Secret retriever plugin, which will "retrieve" a specific Secret by a key name and generate a Kubernetes Secret from it. The word "retrieve" is in quotes because in reality, this example will simply pretend to retrieve a Secret, and will use a hardwired value instead.

To use a Kustomize generator plugin, we simply reference the plugin configuration in kustomization.yaml.

Listing 7.12   kustomization.yaml

```
apiVersion: kustomize.config.k8s.io/v1beta1
kind: Kustomization

generators:
- my-password.yaml
```

The contents of the referenced plugin configuration YAML is specific to the plugin. There is no standard for what belongs in a Kustomize plugin manifest specification. In this exercise, our plugin specification is very simple and contains only two pieces of necessary information:

- The name of the Kubernetes Secret to create (we will use the same name as the plugin configuration name)
- The key in an external Secret store to retrieve (which the plugin will pretend to get)

Listing 7.13   my-password.yaml

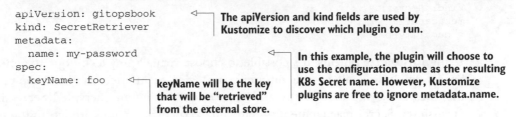

```
apiVersion: gitopsbook
kind: SecretRetriever
metadata:
  name: my-password
spec:
  keyName: foo
```

The apiVersion and kind fields are used by Kustomize to discover which plugin to run.

In this example, the plugin will choose to use the configuration name as the resulting K8s Secret name. However, Kustomize plugins are free to ignore metadata.name.

keyName will be the key that will be "retrieved" from the external store.

Finally, we get to the actual plugin implementation, which we will be writing as a shell script. This plugin accepts the path of the plugin configuration and parses out the Secret name and key to retrieve to generate a final Kubernetes Secret to deploy.

Listing 7.14   gitopsbook/secretretriever/SecretRetriever

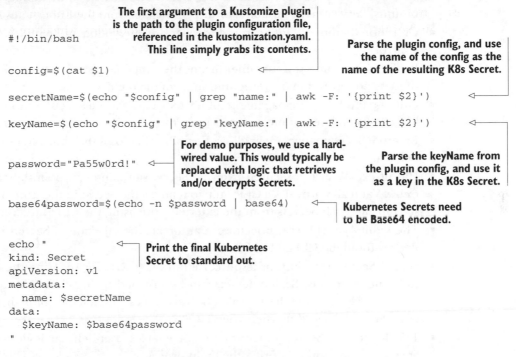

```
#!/bin/bash

config=$(cat $1)

secretName=$(echo "$config" | grep "name:" | awk -F: '{print $2}')

keyName=$(echo "$config" | grep "keyName:" | awk -F: '{print $2}')

password="Pa55w0rd!"

base64password=$(echo -n $password | base64)

echo "
kind: Secret
apiVersion: v1
metadata:
  name: $secretName
data:
  $keyName: $base64password
"
```

The first argument to a Kustomize plugin is the path to the plugin configuration file, referenced in the kustomization.yaml. This line simply grabs its contents.

Parse the plugin config, and use the name of the config as the name of the resulting K8s Secret.

Parse the keyName from the plugin config, and use it as a key in the K8s Secret.

For demo purposes, we use a hard-wired value. This would typically be replaced with logic that retrieves and/or decrypts Secrets.

Kubernetes Secrets need to be Base64 encoded.

Print the final Kubernetes Secret to standard out.

This example can also be run from the GitOps resources Git repository:

```
$ git clone https://github.com/gitopsbook/resources

$ cd resources/chapter-07/kustomize-secret-plugin

$ export KUSTOMIZE_PLUGIN_HOME=$(pwd)/plugin

$ kustomize build ./config --enable_alpha_plugins
apiVersion: v1
```

```
data:
  foo: UGE1NXcwcmQh
kind: Secret
metadata:
  name: my-password
```

Using Kustomize plugins, it's possible to choose virtually any technique to generate a Secret, including all of the different strategies mentioned in this chapter. This includes retrieving a Secret by a reference, decrypting an encrypted Secret in Git, accessing a Secret management system, and so on. The options are left to the user to decide which strategy makes the most sense for their situation.

Summary

- Kubernetes Secrets are simple data structures that allow the separation of the configuration of an application from the build artifact.
- Kubernetes Secrets can be used by Pods in various ways, including volume mounts, environment variables, or direct retrieval from the Kubernetes API.
- Git is not appropriate for Secrets due to lack of encryption and path-level access control.
- Baking Secrets into the container means the container itself is also sensitive and there is no separation of configuration from the build artifact.
- Out-of-band Secret management allows native Kubernetes faculties to be used, but results in different mechanisms to manage/deploy Secrets and config.
- External Secret management allows flexibility, but loses the ability to use Kubernetes native Secret faculties.
- HashiCorp Vault is a secured external Secret store and can be installed using `brew`. Vault also provides a CLI `vault` to manage the Secret in the store. Pods on startup can fetch Secrets from the external store using the CLI and scripting.
- The Vault Agent Sidecar Injector can automate the injection of Secrets into the Pods without the CLI and scripting.
- Sealed Secrets is a CustomResourceDefinition (CRD) for securing the data in Kubernetes Secrets. Sealed Secrets can be installed to the cluster by applying the Sealed Secrets manifest. Sealed Secrets comes with a CLI tool, kubeseal, to encrypt the data in Kubernetes Secrets.
- The Kustomize Secret generator plugin enables user-defined logic to inject Secrets in the manifest during the build process.

Observability

8

> ## This chapter covers
> - Relating GitOps to observability
> - Providing observability of Kubernetes to a cluster operator
> - Enabling GitOps through Kubernetes observability
> - Improving the observability of the system with GitOps
> - Using tools and techniques to ensure your cloud-native applications are also observable

Observability is vital to manage a system properly, determine if it is working correctly, and decide what changes are needed to fix, change, or improve its behavior (such as how to control the system). Observability has been an area of interest in the cloud-native community for some time, with many projects and products being developed to allow observability of systems and applications. The Cloud Native Computing Foundation recently formed a Special Interest Group (SIG) dedicated to observability.[1]

---

[1] https://github.com/cncf/sig-observability.

In this chapter, we will discuss observability in the context of GitOps and Kubernetes. As was mentioned earlier, GitOps is implemented by a GitOps operator (or controller) or Service that must manage and control the Kubernetes cluster. The key functionality of GitOps is comparing the desired state of the system (which is stored in Git) to the current actual state of the system and performing the required operations to converge the two. This means GitOps relies on the observability of Kubernetes and the application to do its job. But GitOps is also a system that must provide observability. We will explore both aspects of GitOps observability.

We recommend you read chapters 1 and 2 before reading this chapter.

8.1 *What is observability?*

Observability is a system capability, like reliability, scalability, or security, that must be designed and implemented into the system during system design, coding, and testing. In this section, we will explore the various ways GitOps and Kubernetes provide observability for a cluster. For example, what version of an application was most recently deployed to the cluster? Who deployed it? How many replicas were configured for the application a month ago? Can a decrease in application performance be correlated to changes to the application or Kubernetes configuration?

When managing a system, the focus is on controlling that system and applying changes that *improve* the system in some way, whether through additional functionality, increasing performance, improving stability, or some other beneficial change. But how do you know how to control the system and what changes to make? Once the changes are applied, how do you know that they improved the system and didn't make it worse?

Remember back to the earlier chapters. We previously discussed how GitOps stores the desired state of a system in a declarative format in Git. A GitOps operator (or service) changes (controls) the system's running state to match the system's desired state. The GitOps operator must be able to observe the system being managed, which in our case is Kubernetes and the applications running on Kubernetes. What's more, the GitOps operator itself must also provide observability so that ultimately the user can control GitOps.

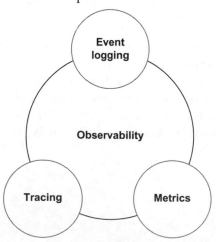

OK, but in practical terms, what does that really mean?

As was mentioned earlier, observability is a capability of a system that encompasses multiple aspects. Each of these aspects must be designed and built into the system. Let's briefly examine each of these three aspects: event logging, metrics, and tracing.

Figure 8.1 Observability is composed of three primary aspects: event logging, metrics, and tracing. These aspects combine to provide operational insights that enable the proper management of the system.

8.1.1 Event logging

Most developers are familiar with the concept of logging. As the code executes, log messages can be output that indicate significant events, errors, or changes. Each event log is timestamped and is an immutable record of a particular system component's internal operation. When rare or unpredictable failures occur, the event log may provide context at a fine level of granularity, indicating what went wrong.

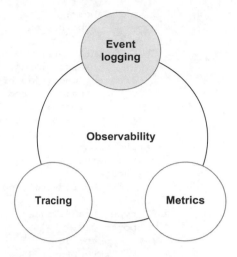

Often the first step in debugging an improperly behaving application is to look at the application's log for clues. Logging is an invaluable tool for developers to observe and debug the system and applications. Logging and the retention of records may also be required for compliance with applicable industry standards.

Figure 8.2 Event logs are timestamped and provides an immutable record of a particular system component's internal operation.

For Kubernetes, a fundamental aspect of observability is displaying the log output of all the various Pods in the cluster. Applications output debug information about their running state to stdout (standard out), captured by Kubernetes and saved to a file on the Kubernetes node that the Pod/container is running on. The logs of a particular Pod can be displayed with the `kubectl logs <pod_name>` command.

To illustrate various aspects of logging, metrics, and tracing, we will be using an example ride-sharing application called Hot ROD.[2] Let's launch the application in our minikube cluster so we can take a look at its logs. Here is the manifest for the application deployment.

Listing 8.1 Hot ROD application deployment (http://mng.bz/vzPJ)

```
apiVersion: v1
kind: List
items:
  - apiVersion: apps/v1
    kind: Deployment
    metadata:
      name: hotrod
    spec:
      replicas: 1
      selector:
        matchLabels:
          app: hotrod
      template:
        metadata:
```

---

[2] http://mng.bz/4Z6a.

```
            labels:
              app: hotrod
          spec:
            containers:
              - args: ["-m", "prometheus", "all"]
                image: jaegertracing/example-hotrod:latest
                name: hotrod
                ports:
                  - name: frontend
                    containerPort: 8080
    - apiVersion: v1
      kind: Service
      metadata:
        name: hotrod-frontend
      spec:
        type: LoadBalancer
        ports:
          - port: 80
            targetPort: 8080
        selector:
          app: hotrod
```

Deploy the Hot ROD application using the following commands:

```
$ minikube start
$ kubectl apply -f hotrod-app.yaml
deployment.apps/hotrod created
service/hotrod-frontend created
```

Now let's look at the log messages of the Pod:

```
$ kubectl get pods
NAME                       READY   STATUS    RESTARTS   AGE
hotrod-59c88cd9c7-dxd55    1/1     Running   0          6m4s

$ kubectl logs hotrod-59c88cd9c7-dxd55
2020-07-10T02:19:56.940Z   INFO   cobra@v0.0.3/command.go:792   Using Prometheus
                                                                 as metrics
                                                                 backend
2020-07-10T02:19:56.940Z   INFO   cobra@v0.0.3/command.go:762   Starting all
                                                                 services
2020-07-10T02:19:57.048Z   INFO   route/server.go:57   Starting {"service":
     "route", "address": "http://0.0.0.0:8083"}
2020-07-10T02:19:57.049Z   INFO   frontend/server.go:67   Starting {"service":
     "frontend", "address": "http://0.0.0.0:8080"}
2020-07-10T02:19:57.153Z   INFO   customer/server.go:55   Starting {"service":
     "customer", "address": "http://0.0.0.0:8081"}
```

The output tells us that each of the microservices (route, frontend, and customer) is "Starting." But at this point, there is not too much information in the log. And it may not be entirely clear if each of the microservices was successfully started.

Use the `minikube service hotrod-frontend` command to create a tunnel on your workstation to the `hotrod-frontend` service and open the URL in a web browser:

```
$ minikube service hotrod-frontend
|-----------|------------------|-------------|------------------------|
| NAMESPACE |       NAME       | TARGET PORT |          URL           |
|-----------|------------------|-------------|------------------------|
| default   | hotrod-frontend  |          80 | http://172.17.0.2:31725 |
|-----------|------------------|-------------|------------------------|
🏃 Starting tunnel for service hotrod-frontend.
|-----------|------------------|-------------|------------------------|
| NAMESPACE |       NAME       | TARGET PORT |          URL           |
|-----------|------------------|-------------|------------------------|
| default   | hotrod-frontend  |             | http://127.0.0.1:53457 |
|-----------|------------------|-------------|------------------------|
🎉 Opening service default/hotrod-frontend in default browser...
```

This will open a web browser to the application. When it opens, click on each of the buttons to simulate requesting a ride for each customer.

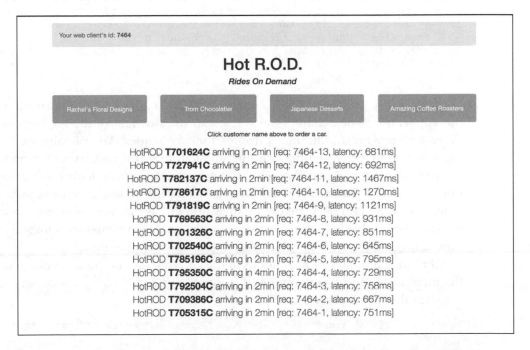

Figure 8.3 A screenshot of the Hot ROD example application that simulates a ride-sharing system. Clicking the buttons at the top of the page initiates a process that invokes multiple microservices to match a customer with a driver and a route.

Now, in another terminal window, let's look at the logs for the application:

```
$ kubectl logs hotrod-59c88cd9c7-dxd55
:
2020-07-10T03:02:13.012Z  INFO  frontend/server.go:81  HTTP request received
    {"service": "frontend", "method": "GET", "url": "/
    dispatch?customer=567&nonse=0.6850439192313089"}
2020-07-10T03:02:13.012Z  INFO  customer/client.go:54  Getting customer
    {"service": "frontend", "component": "customer_client", "customer_id":
    "567"}
http://0.0.0.0:8081/customer?customer=567
2020-07-10T03:02:13.015Z  INFO  customer/server.go:67  HTTP request received
    {"service": "customer", "method": "GET", "url": "/
    customer?customer=567"}
2020-07-10T03:02:13.015Z  INFO  customer/database.go:73  Loading customer
    {"service": "customer", "component": "mysql", "customer_id": "567"}
2020-07-10T03:02:13.299Z  INFO  frontend/best_eta.go:77  Found customer
    {"service": "frontend", "customer": {"ID":"567","Name":"Amazing Coffee
    Roasters","Location":"211,653"}}
2020-07-10T03:02:13.300ZINFO  driver/client.go:58  Finding nearest drivers
    {"service": "frontend", "component": "driver_client", "location":
    "211,653"}
2020-07-10T03:02:13.301Z  INFO  driver/server.go:73  Searching for nearby
    drivers  {"service": "driver", "location": "211,653"}
2020-07-10T03:02:13.324Z  INFO  driver/redis.go:67  Found drivers
    {"service": "driver", "drivers": ["T732907C", "T791395C", "T705718C",
    "T724516C", "T782991C", "T703350C", "T771654C", "T724823C", "T718650C",
    "T785041C"]}
:
```

Logging is very flexible in that it can also be used to infer a lot of information about the application. For example, you can see in the first line of the log snippet `HTTP request received`, indicating a frontend service request. You can also see log messages related to loading customer information, locating the nearest drivers, and so on. There is also a timestamp on each log message so you can calculate the amount of time taken for a particular request by subtracting the ending time from the starting time. You could also calculate the number of requests that were processed in a given interval. To do this type of log analysis at scale, you need cluster-level logging[3] and a central logging backend like Elasticsearch plus Kibana[4] or Splunk.[5]

Click on a few more of the buttons in the Hot ROD application. We can determine the number of requests by counting the number of `HTTP request received` messages for the frontend service:

```
$ kubectl logs hotrod-59c88cd9c7-sdktk | grep -e "received" | grep frontend |
    wc -l
    7
```

---

[3] https://kubernetes.io/docs/concepts/cluster-administration/logging/.
[4] https://www.elastic.co/what-is/elk-stack.
[5] https://www.splunk.com/.

From this output, we can see that there have been seven frontend requests received since the Pod was started.

However, as critical and flexible as logging is, it is sometimes not the best tool to observe certain aspects of the system. Logs are a very low-level aspect of observability. Using log messages to derive metrics such as count of requests processed, requests per second, and so on, can be quite expensive and may not give all the information you need. Also, it is quite tricky, if not impossible, to determine the state of the system at any given moment by parsing log messages without a deep understanding of the code. Often log messages are coming from different threads and subprocesses of the system and must be correlated to one another to follow the system's current state. So, while important, Pod logs are just barely scratching the surface of the observability capabilities of Kubernetes.

In the next section, we will see how metrics can be used to observe the system's properties, instead of low-level log parsing.

Exercise 8.1

Use the `kubectl logs` command to display the Hot ROD Pod's log messages and look for any error messages (hint: `grep` for the string ERROR). If so, what are the types of errors you see?

8.1.2 Metrics

Another critical aspect of observability is metrics that measure the performance and operation of the system or application. At a fundamental level, metrics are a set of key-value pairs that provide information about the system's operation. You can think of metrics as the observable properties of each component of the system. Some core resource metrics that apply to all components are CPU, memory, disk, and network utilization. Other metrics may be specific to the application, like the number of a particular type of error that has been encountered or the count of items in a queue waiting to be processed.

Kubernetes provides basic metrics using an optional component called the `metrics-server`. The `metrics-server` can be enabled in minikube by running the following command:

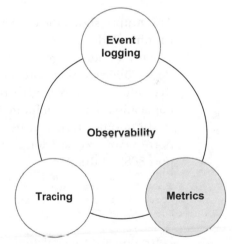

Figure 8.4 Metrics are a set of key-value pairs that provide information about the system's operation.

```
$ minikube addons enable metrics-server
❄ The 'metrics-server' addon is enabled
```

Once the `metrics-server` is enabled and you wait a few minutes for enough metrics to be collected, you can access the `metrics-server` data using the commands `kubectl top nodes` and `kubectl top pods`.

Listing 8.2   Output of `kubectl top nodes` and `kubectl top pods`

```
$ kubectl top nodes
NAME        CPU(cores)   CPU%    MEMORY(bytes)    MEMORY%
minikube    211m         5%      805Mi            40%


$ kubectl top pods --all-namespaces
NAMESPACE      NAME                              CPU(cores)   MEMORY(bytes)
default        hotrod-59c88cd9c7-sdktk           0m           4Mi
kube-system    coredns-66bff467f8-gk4zp          4m           8Mi
kube-system    coredns-66bff467f8-qqxdv          4m           20Mi
kube-system    etcd-minikube                     28m          44Mi
kube-system    kube-apiserver-minikube           62m          260Mi
kube-system    kube-controller-manager-minikube  26m          63Mi
kube-system    kube-proxy-vgzw2                   0m           22Mi
kube-system    kube-scheduler-minikube           5m           12Mi
kube-system    metrics-server-7bc6d75975-lc5h2   0m           9Mi
kube-system    storage-provisioner               0m           35Mi
```

This output shows the CPU and memory utilization of the node (minikube) and the running Pods.

In addition to general CPU and memory utilization that is common across all Pods, applications can provide their own metrics by exposing an HTTP *metrics endpoint* that returns a list of metrics in the form of key-value pairs. Let's look at the Hot ROD application metrics endpoint that we used in the previous section.

In another terminal, use the `kubectl port-forward` command to forward a port on your workstation to the metrics endpoint of Hot ROD, which is exposed on port 8083 of the Pod:

```
$ kubectl port-forward hotrod-59c88cd9c7-dxd55 8083
Forwarding from 127.0.0.1:8083 -> 8083
Forwarding from [::1]:8083 -> 8083
```

Once the port forward connection is established, open http://localhost:8083/metrics in your web browser or run `curl http://localhost:8083/metrics` from the command line.

Listing 8.3   Output of Hot ROD metrics endpoint

```
$ curl http://localhost:8083/metrics
# HELP go_gc_duration_seconds A summary of the GC invocation durations.
# TYPE go_gc_duration_seconds summary
go_gc_duration_seconds{quantile="0"} 6.6081e-05
go_gc_duration_seconds{quantile="0.25"} 8.1335e-05
go_gc_duration_seconds{quantile="0.5"} 0.000141919
```

```
go_gc_duration_seconds{quantile="0.75"} 0.000197202
go_gc_duration_seconds{quantile="1"} 0.000371112
go_gc_duration_seconds_sum 0.000993336
go_gc_duration_seconds_count 6
# HELP go_goroutines Number of goroutines that currently exist.
# TYPE go_goroutines gauge
go_goroutines 26
# HELP go_info Information about the Go environment.
# TYPE go_info gauge
go_info{version="go1.14.4"} 1
:
:
```

By themselves, metrics provide a snapshot of a system component's performance and operation at a particular point in time. Often, metrics are collected periodically and stored in a time-series database to observe the metrics' historical trends. In Kubernetes, this is typically done by a Cloud Native Computing Foundation (CNCF) open source project called Prometheus (https://prometheus.io).

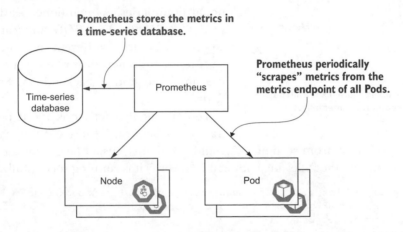

Figure 8.5 A single Prometheus deployment can scrape the metric endpoints of both nodes and Pods of a cluster. Metrics are scraped at a configurable interval and stored in a time-series database.

As was mentioned earlier in the chapter, some metrics can be inferred through the examination of log messages. Still, it is more efficient to have the system or application measure its metrics directly and provide programmatic access to query the metric values.

Exercise 8.2
Find out the number of different HTTP requests. (Hint: search for metrics named `http_requests`). How many `GET /dispatch`, `GET /customer`, and `GET /route` requests have been processed by the application? How would you get similar information from the application's logs?

8.1.3   *Tracing*

Typically, distributed tracing data requires an application-specific agent that knows how to collect the detailed execution paths of the code being traced. A distributed tracing framework captures detailed data of how the system runs internally, from the initial end user request on through possibly dozens (hundreds?) of calls to different microservices and other external dependencies, perhaps hosted on another system. Whereas metrics typically give an aggregated view of the application in a particular system, tracing data usually provides a detailed picture of an individual request's execution flow, potentially across multiple services and systems. This is particularly important in the age of microservices where an "application" may utilize functionality from tens or hundreds of services and cross multiple operational boundaries. As mentioned earlier in section 8.1.1, the Hot ROD application is composed of four different microservices (frontend, customer, driver, and route) and two simulated storage backends (MySql and Redis).

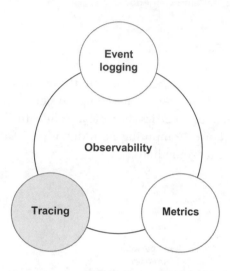

Figure 8.6   Tracing captures detailed data of how the system runs internally.

To illustrate this, let's look at one popular tracing framework, Jaeger, and the example Hot ROD application from sections 8.1.1 and 8.1.2. First, install Jaeger on the minikube cluster and use the following commands to verify it is running successfully:

```
$ kubectl apply -f https://raw.githubusercontent.com/gitopsbook/resources/
    master/chapter-08/jaeger/jaeger-all-in-one.yaml
deployment.apps/jaeger created
service/jaeger-query created
service/jaeger-collector created
service/jaeger-agent created
service/zipkin created

$ kubectl get pods -l app=jaeger
NAME                      READY    STATUS     RESTARTS    AGE
jaeger-f696549b6-f7c9h    1/1      Running    0           2m33s
```

Now that Jaeger is running, we need to update the Hot ROD application deployment to send tracing data to Jaeger. This is done simply by adding the `JAEGER_AGENT`_HOST environment variable to the `hotrod` container, indicating the `jaeger-agent` service deployed by jaeger-all-in-one.yaml in the previous step:

```
$ diff --context=4 hotrod-app.yaml hotrod-app-jaeger.yaml
*** hotrod-app.yaml              2020-07-20 17:57:07.000000000 -0700
```

```
--- hotrod-app-jaeger.yaml  2020-07-20 17:57:07.000000000 -0700
***************
*** 22,29 ****
--- 22,32 ----
                    #- "--fix-disable-db-conn-mutex"
                    - "all"
                  image: jaegertracing/example-hotrod:latest
                  name: hotrod
+                 env:
+                 - name: JAEGER_AGENT_HOST
+                   value: "jaeger-agent"
                  ports:
                  - name: frontend
                    containerPort: 8080
                  - name: customer
***************
*** 41,45 ****
          - port: 80
            targetPort: 8080
        selector:
          app: hotrod
!       type: LoadBalancer
\ No newline at end of file
--- 44,48 ----
          - port: 80
            targetPort: 8080
        selector:
          app: hotrod
!       type: LoadBalancer
```

Since we have configured the `hotrod-app` to send data to Jaeger, we need to generate some trace data by opening the `hotrod-app` UI and clicking a few buttons as we did in the event-logging section.

Use the `minikube service hotrod-frontend` command to create a tunnel on your workstation to the `hotrod-frontend` service and open the URL in a web browser:

```
$ minikube service hotrod-frontend
|-----------|-----------------|-------------|------------------------|
| NAMESPACE |      NAME       | TARGET PORT |          URL           |
|-----------|-----------------|-------------|------------------------|
| default   | hotrod-frontend |             | http://127.0.0.1:52560 |
|-----------|-----------------|-------------|------------------------|
🎉 Opening service default/hotrod-frontend in default browser...
```

This will open a web browser to the application. When it opens, click on each of the buttons to simulate requesting a ride for each customer.

Now that we should have some trace data, open the Jaeger UI by running `minikube service jaeger-query`:

```
$ minikube service jaeger-query
|-----------|--------------|--------------|----------------------------|
| NAMESPACE |     NAME     | TARGET PORT  |            URL             |
|-----------|--------------|--------------|----------------------------|
|  default  | jaeger-query |  query-http  | http://192.168.99.120:30274 |
|-----------|--------------|--------------|----------------------------|
```
🐙 Opening service default/jaeger-query in default browser...

This will open the Jaeger UI in your default browser. Or, you can open the URL yourself that is listed in the previous output (such as http://127.0.0.1:51831). When you are finished with the Jaeger exercises in this chapter, you can press Ctrl-C to close the tunnel to the `jaeger-query` service.

From the Jaeger UI, you can choose the service "frontend" and the operation "HTTP GET /dispatch," and then click Find Traces to get a list of all the GET /dispatch call graph traces.

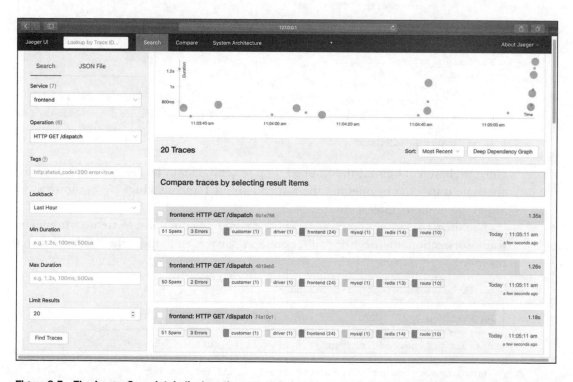

Figure 8.7   The Jaeger Search tab displays the `GET /dispatch` requests from the frontend service that occurred in the last hour. A graph at the top right shows each request's duration over time, with each circle's size representing the number of spans in each request. The bottom-right lists of all the requests, and each row can be clicked for additional detail.

From there, you can select the trace to examine. The following screenshot shows a call graph of the frontend GET /dispatch request in the Jaeger UI.

Log messages for
SQL SELECT

Duration of SQL
SELECT call

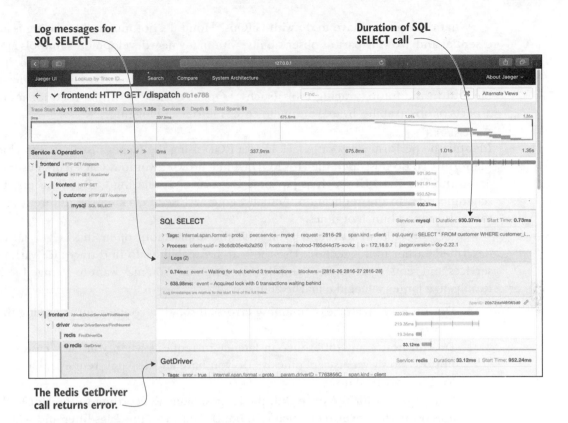

Figure 8.8 In this detailed view of a GET /dispatch trace, Jaeger displays all the call spans initiated from the originating request. This example shows such details as the duration and logs of an SQL SELECT call and the Redis GetDriver call's return error.

The Redis GetDriver
call returns error.

As you can see from figure 8.8, there is a lot of valuable information regarding the GET /dispatch request processing. From this, you can see the breakdown of what code is being called, what its response is (success or failure), and how long it took. For example, in the screenshot, it appears that the SQL query used by this request took 930.37 ms. Is that good? The application developer can do more testing and dig deeper to see if that query can be optimized or if there is a different area of the code that would benefit from additional optimization.

Again, as was mentioned earlier, a developer may sprinkle their code with log statements to have "tracing data" in their application logs, but this is a costly and inefficient approach. Using a proper framework for tracing is much more desirable and will provide a much better result in the long run.

As you can imagine, tracing data can be quite large, and it may not be feasible to collect the data for every single request. Tracing data is often sampled at a configured rate and may have a much shorter retention period than, for example, application logs or metrics.

What does tracing have to do with GitOps? Honestly, not much. But tracing is an essential and growing part of observability, with many new developments in tools and services that help provide, manage, and analyze distributed tracing data, so it's important to understand how it fits in the overall observability system. It is also possible that in the future, tracing tools (such as OpenTelemetry) will be used for more aspects of observability by expanding to cover metrics and logging.

Exercise 8.3

Identify the performance bottleneck in Hot ROD using the Jaeger distributed tracing platform.[6] To do this, open the Hot ROD UI in a browser window. Click a few customers in the Hot ROD UI (such as Japanese Desserts and Amazing Coffee Roasters) to schedule rides in the application. Actually, go crazy! Keep clicking the different customer buttons a bunch of times.

Once you've played around a bit with the application, open the Jaeger UI as described earlier in this section. Use the search capabilities to find traces for various services and requests to answer the following questions. You may want to change Limit Results to a larger value, like maybe 200:

1   Do you have any traces containing errors? If so, what component is causing the errors?

2   Do you notice any difference in latency in requests when you click customer buttons slowly versus very quickly? Do you have any dispatch requests that take longer than 1000 ms?

3   Search Jaeger for the trace with the longest latency according to the Hot ROD app using the driver ID (which is in bold). Hint: Use the Tags filter and search for "driver=T123456C," where "T123456C" is the driver ID of your longest latency request.

4   Where is the application spending the most time? What span is the longest?

5   What do the logs of the longest span say? Hint: The log message starts with `Waiting for…`

6   Based on what you discovered in the previous question, what might be impacting the performance of the Hot ROD application? Examine the code at this link:

http://mng.bz/QmRw

Exercise 8.4

Fix the Hot ROD application's performance bottleneck by adding the `--fix-disable-db-conn-mutex` argument to the `hotrod` container and updating the deployment. (Hint: Look at the GitHub hotrod-app-jaeger.yaml file, and uncomment the appropriate line.) This simulates fixing a database lock contention in the code:

1   Update the `hotrod` container by adding the `--fix-disable-db-conn-mutex` argument.

2   Redeploy the updated hotrod-app-jaeger.yaml file.

---

[6]   https://github.com/jaegertracing/jaeger/tree/master/examples/hotrod.

3   Test the `hotrod` UI. Do you notice a difference in the latency of each dispatch? Can you get a dispatch request to take longer than 1000 ms?

4   Look at the Jaeger UI. Do you notice the difference in the traces? What is different after adding the `--fix-disable-db-conn-mutex` argument?

To dive deeper into Jaeger and the Hot ROD sample application, refer to the blog and video links at the top of the README page.[7]

8.1.4   *Visualization*

All of the discussed aspects of observability are really about the system providing data about itself. And it adds up to a lot of data that can be difficult to make sense of. The last aspect of observability is visualization tools that help convert all that observability data into information and insights.

Many tools provide visualization of observability data. In the previous section, we discussed Jaeger, which provides visualization of trace data. But now, let's look at another tool that provides visualization of the current running state of your Kubernetes cluster, the K8s Dashboard.

You can enable the K8s Dashboard minikube add-on[8] using the following command:

```
$ minikube stop
🖐 Stopping "minikube" in docker ...        Stops minikube if it
⬤ Powering off "minikube" via SSH ...       is already running
⬤ Node "minikube" stopped.
$ minikube addons enable dashboard          Enables the
✳ The 'dashboard' addon is enabled          dashboard add-on
```

Once enabled, you can start your minikube cluster and display the Dashboard:

```
$ minikube start
😄 minikube v1.11.0 on Darwin 10.15.5
✨ Using the docker driver based on existing profile
🎛 Starting control plane node minikube in cluster minikube
🎉 minikube 1.12.0 is available! Download it: https://github.com/kubernetes/
    minikube/releases/tag/v1.12.0
💡 To disable this notice, run: 'minikube config set WantUpdateNotification
    false'

🔄 Restarting existing docker container for "minikube" ...
🐳 Preparing Kubernetes v1.18.3 on Docker 19.03.2 ...
    ? kubeadm.pod-network-cidr=10.244.0.0/16
🔎 Verifying Kubernetes components...
✳ Enabled addons: dashboard, default-storageclass, metrics-server, storage-
    provisioner                                 Dashboard add-on is
🏄 Done! kubectl is now configured to use "minikube"   started with minikube.
$ minikube dashboard
```

---

[7] http://mng.bz/XdqG.
[8] https://minikube.sigs.k8s.io/docs/tasks/addons/.

The command `minikube dashboard` will open a browser window that looks similar to figure 8.9.

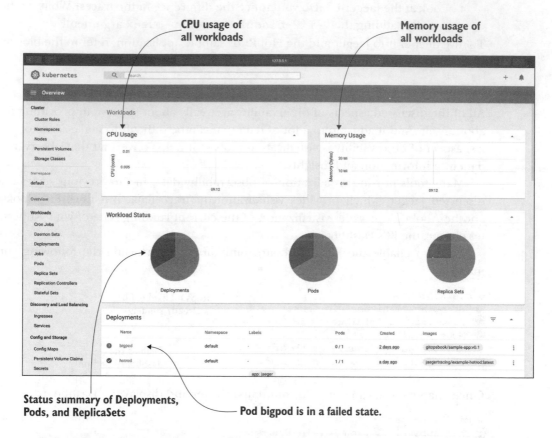

Figure 8.9   The Overview page of the Kubernetes Dashboard shows the CPU and memory usages of the workloads currently running on the cluster, along with a summary chart of each type of workload (Deployments, Pods, and ReplicaSets). The page's bottom-right pane shows a list of each workload `GET /dispatch`, and each row can be clicked for additional detail.

The Kubernetes Dashboard provides visualization of many different aspects of your Kubernetes cluster, including the status of your Deployments, Pods, and ReplicaSets. We can see that there is a problem with the `bigpod` deployment. Upon seeing this, the Kubernetes administrator should take action to bring this deployment back into a healthy state.

Exercise 8.5
Install the Dashboard add-on on minikube. Open the Dashboard UI, explore the different panels available, and perform the following actions:

1   Switch the view to All Namespaces. How many total Pods are running on minikube?

2 Select the Pod panel. Filter the Pods list to those containing "dns" in the name by clicking on the filter icon in the top right of the Pod panel. Delete one of the DNS-related Pods by clicking the action icon for that Pod and choosing Delete. What happens?

3 Click on the plus icon (+) in the top right of the Dashboard UI, and select "Create from form." Create a new NGINX deployment containing three Pods using the `nginx` image. Experiment with the "Create from input" and "Create from file" options, perhaps using code listings from earlier chapters.

8.1.5 Importance of observability in GitOps

Okay, so now you know what observability is and that it is generally a good thing, but you may wonder why a book on GitOps would devote a whole chapter to observability. What does observability have to do with GitOps?

As was discussed in chapter 2, using the declarative configuration of Kubernetes allows the desired state of the system to be precisely defined. But how do you know if the running state of the system has converged with the desired state? How do you know if a particular deployment was successful? More broadly, how can you tell if your system is working as intended? These are critical questions that GitOps and observability should help answer.

There are several aspects of observability in Kubernetes that are critical for the GitOps system to function well and answer critical questions about the system:

- *Application health*—Is the application operating correctly? If a new version of the application is deploying using GitOps, is the system "better" than before?
- *Application sync status*—Is the running state of the application the same as the desired state defined in the deployment Git repo?
- *Configuration drift*—Has the application's configuration been changed outside of the declarative GitOps system (such as either manually or imperatively)?
- *GitOps change log*—What changes were recently made to the GitOps system? Who made them, and for what reason?

The remainder of this chapter will cover how the observability of the Kubernetes system and the application allow these questions to be answered by the GitOps system and how, in turn, the GitOps system provides observability capabilities.

8.2 Application health

The first and most important way observability relates to GitOps is in the ability to observe application health. At the beginning of the chapter, we talked about how operating a system is really about managing that system so that overall it improves and gets better over time instead of getting worse. GitOps is key where the desired state of the system (one that presumably is "better" than the current state) is committed to the Git repo, and then the GitOps operator applies that desired state to the system, making it become the current state.

For example, imagine that when the Hot ROD application discussed earlier in this chapter was initially deployed, it had relatively small operating requirements. However, over time, as the application becomes more popular, the dataset grows and the memory allocated to the Pod is no longer enough. The Pod periodically runs out of memory and is terminated (an event called "OOMKilled"). The application health of the Hot ROD application would show that it is periodically crashing and restarting. The system operator could check-in a change to the Git deployment repository for the Hot ROD application that increases its requested memory. The GitOps operator would then apply that change, increasing the memory of the running Hot ROD application.

Perhaps we could leave things there. After all, someone committed a change to the system, and GitOps should just do what it's been told. But what if the committed change actually makes things worse? What if the application comes back up after deploying the latest change but then starts returning more errors than it did before? Or even worse, what if it doesn't come back up at all? What if, in this example, the operator increased the memory for the Hot ROD application too much, causing other applications running on the cluster to run out of memory?

With GitOps, we would at least like to detect those conditions where, after a deployment, the system is "worse" than before and, at a minimum, alert the users that perhaps they should consider rolling back the most recent change. This is only possible if the system and application have strong observability characteristics that the GitOps operator can, well, observe.

8.2.1   *Resource status*

At a basic level, a key feature of Kubernetes that enables observability of its internal state is how, with a declarative configuration, the desired configuration and active state are both maintained. This allows every Kubernetes resource to be inspected at any time to see whether or not the resource is in the desired state. Each component or resource will be in a particular operational state at any given time. For example, a resource might be in an INITIALIZED or NOT READY state. It also might be in a PENDING, RUNNING, or COMPLETED state. Often the status of a resource is specific to its type.

The first aspect of application health is determining that all the Kubernetes resources related to the application are in a good state. For example, have all the Pods been successfully scheduled, and are they in a Running state? Let's take a look at how this can be determined.

Kubernetes provides additional information for each Pod that indicates if a Pod is healthy or not. Let's run the kubectl describe command on the etcd Pod:

```
$ kubectl describe pod etcd-minikube -n kube-system
Name:                 etcd-minikube
Namespace:            kube-system
Priority:             2000000000
Priority Class Name:  system-cluster-critical
Node:                 minikube/192.168.99.103
Start Time:           Mon, 10 Feb 2020 22:54:14 -0800
```

```
  :
Status:            Running
IP:                192.168.99.103
IPs:
  IP:              192.168.99.103
Controlled By:     Node/minikube
Containers:
  etcd:
    :
    Command:
      :
    State:           Running
      Started:       Mon, 10 Feb 2020 22:54:05 -0800
    Ready:           True
    Restart Count:   0
    Liveness:        http-get http://127.0.0.1:2381/health delay=15s
      timeout=15s period=10s #success=1 #failure=8
    Environment:     <none>
    Mounts:
      :
Conditions:
  Type            Status
  Initialized     True
  Ready           True
  ContainersReady True
  PodScheduled    True
Volumes:
  :
QoS Class:         BestEffort
Node-Selectors:    <none>
Tolerations:       :NoExecute
Events:            <none>
```

This output has been truncated for brevity, but take a closer look at it and compare it to the output from your minikube. Do you see any properties of the Pod that may help with observability? One very important (and obvious) one near the top is `Status:` `Running`, which indicates the phase the Pod is in. The Pod phase is a simple, high-level summary of where the Pod is in its life cycle. The conditions array, the reason and message fields, and the individual container status arrays contain more detail about the Pod's status.

Table 8.1 Pod phases

Phase values	Description
Pending	The Kubernetes system has accepted the Pod, but one or more container images have not been created. This includes time before being scheduled as well as time spent downloading images over the network, which could take a while.
Running	The Pod has been bound to a node, and all of the containers have been created. At least one container is still running or is in the process of starting or restarting.
Succeeded	All containers in the Pod have terminated in success and will not be restarted.

Table 8.1   Pod phases *(continued)*

Phase values	Description
Failed	All containers in the Pod have completed, and at least one container has terminated in failure. The container either exited with non-zero status or was terminated by the system.
Unknown	For some reason, the Pod state could not be obtained, typically due to an error in communicating with the Pod's host.

This is observability: the internal state of a Pod can be easily queried so decisions can be made about controlling the system. For GitOps, if a new version of an application is deployed, it is important to look at the resulting new Pod's state to ensure its success.

But the Pod state (phase) is only a summary, and, to understand why a Pod is in a particular state, you need to look at the Conditions. A Pod has four conditions that will be True, False, or Unknown.

Table 8.2   Pod conditions

Phase values	Description
PodScheduled	The Pod has been successfully scheduled to a node in the cluster.
Initialized	All init containers have started successfully.
ContainersReady	All containers in the Pod are ready.
Ready	The Pod can serve requests and should be added to the load-balancing pools of all matching Services.

Exercise 8.6

Use the kubectl describe command to display the information of other Pods running in the kube-system Namespace.

An elementary example of how a Pod may get into a bad state is submitting a Pod with a manifest that requests more resources than are available in the cluster. This will cause the Pod to go into a Pending state. The status of the Pod can be "observed" by running kubectl describe pod <pod_name>.

Listing 8.4   http://mng.bz/yYZG

```
apiVersion: v1
kind: Pod
metadata:
  name: bigpod
spec:
  containers:
    - command:
        - /app/sample-app
```

```
    image: gitopsbook/sample-app:v0.1
    name: sample-app
    ports:
      - containerPort: 8080
    resources:
      requests:
        memory: "999Gi"      ←——┐ Requests an impossible
        cpu: "99"                  amount of memory          ┐ Requests an impossible
                                                        ←——┘ number of CPU cores
```

If you apply this YAML and check the Pod status, you will notice that the Pod is Pend-ing. When you run kubectl describe, you will see that the Pod is in a Pending state since the minikube cluster can't satisfy the resource request for 999 GB of RAM or the request for 99 CPUs:

```
$ kubectl apply -f bigpod.yaml
deployment.apps/bigpod created


$ kubectl get pod
NAME                         READY   STATUS     RESTARTS   AGE
bigpod-7848f56795-hnpjx      0/1     Pending    0          5m41s


$ kubectl describe pod bigpod-7848f56795-hnpjx
Name:           bigpod-7848f56795-hnpjx
Namespace:      default
Priority:       0
Node:           <none>
Labels:         app=bigpod
                pod-template-hash=7848f56795
Annotations:    <none>
Status:         Pending        ←——┐ Pod status
IP:                                │ is Pending.
IPs:            <none>
Controlled By:  ReplicaSet/bigpod-7848f56795
Containers:
  bigpod:
    Image:      gitopsbook/sample-app:v0.1
    Port:       8080/TCP
    Host Port:  0/TCP
    Command:
      /app/sample-app
    Requests:
      cpu:      99
      memory:   999Gi
    Environment: <none>
    Mounts:
      /var/run/secrets/kubernetes.io/serviceaccount from default-token-8dzwz
      (ro)
Conditions:
  Type          Status
  PodScheduled  False         ←——┐ PodScheduled condition
                                  │ is False.
```

```
Volumes:
  default-token-8dzwz:
    Type:         Secret (a volume populated by a Secret)
    SecretName:   default-token-8dzwz
    Optional:     false
QoS Class:        Burstable
Node-Selectors:   <none>
Tolerations:      node.kubernetes.io/not-ready:NoExecute for 300s
                  node.kubernetes.io/unreachable:NoExecute for 300s
Events:
  Type     Reason            Age         From              Message        ◁────────┐
  ----     ------            ----        ----              -------                 │
  Warning  FailedScheduling  <unknown>   default-scheduler  0/1 nodes are          │
     available: 1 Insufficient cpu, 1 Insufficient memory.                         │
  Warning  FailedScheduling  <unknown>   default-scheduler  0/1 nodes are          │
     available: 1 Insufficient cpu, 1 Insufficient memory.                         │
```

No node is available with sufficient
memory or CPU to schedule the Pod.

Exercise 8.7

Update bigpod.yaml with a more reasonable request for CPU and memory, and redeploy the Pod. (Hint: Change CPU to `99m` and memory to `999Ki`.) Run `kubectl describe` on the updated Pod, and compare the output with the output before your changes. What are the `Status`, `Conditions`, and `Events` of the updated Pod?

8.2.2 *Readiness and liveness*

If you look carefully at the Pod `Conditions` listed in table 8.2, something might stand out. The `Ready` state claims that "the Pod can serve requests." How does it know? What if the Pod has to perform some initialization? How does Kubernetes know that the Pod is ready? The answer is that the Pod itself notifies Kubernetes when it is ready based on its own application-specific logic.

Kubernetes uses readiness probes to decide when the Pod is available for accepting traffic. Each container in the Pod can specify a readiness probe, in the form of a command or an HTTP request, that will indicate when the container is `Ready`. It is up to the container to provide this observability about its internal state. Once all the Pod containers are `Ready`, then the Pod itself is considered `Ready` and can be added to load balancers of matching Services and begin handling requests.

Similarly, each container can specify a liveness probe that indicates if the container is alive and not, for example, in some sort of deadlock situation. Kubernetes uses liveness probes to know when to restart a container that has entered a bad state.

So here again is an aspect of observability that is built into Kubernetes. Application Pods provide visibility to their internal state through readiness and liveness probes so that the Kubernetes system can decide how to control them. Application developers must properly implement these probes so that the application provides the correct observability of its operation.

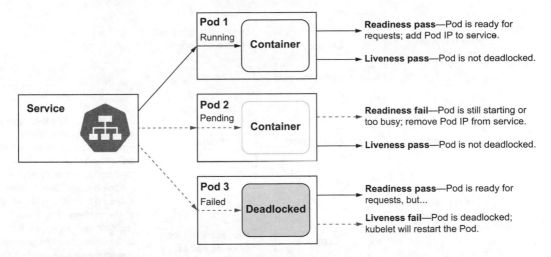

Figure 8.10   Kubernetes uses readiness and liveness probes to determine which Pods are available to accept traffic. Pod 1 is in a `Running` state, and both the readiness and liveness probes are passing. Pod 2 is in a `Pending` state and, while the liveness probe is passing, the readiness probe is not since the Pod is still starting up. Pod 3 passes the readiness probe but fails the liveness probe, meaning it will likely soon be restarted by kubelet.

Exercise 8.8

Create a Pod spec that uses an init container to create a file and configure the liveness and readiness probes of the app container to expect that the file exists. Create the Pod and then see its behavior. Exec into the Pod to delete the file and see its behavior.

8.2.3   *Application monitoring and alerting*

In addition to status and readiness/liveness, applications typically have vital metrics that can be used to determine their overall health. This is the foundation of operational monitoring and alerting: watch a set of metrics and set off alarms when they deviate from allowable values. But what metrics should be monitored, and what are the permissible values?

Fortunately, there has been a lot of research done on this topic, and it has been well covered in other books and articles. Rob Ewaschuk described the "four golden signals" as the most important metrics to focus on at a high level. This provides a useful framework for thinking about metrics:[9]

- *Latency*—The time it takes to service a request
- *Traffic*—A measure of how much demand is placed on the system
- *Errors*—The rate of requests that are not successful
- *Saturation*—How "full" your service is

---

[9]   https://landing.google.com/sre/sre-book/chapters/monitoring-distributed-systems/.

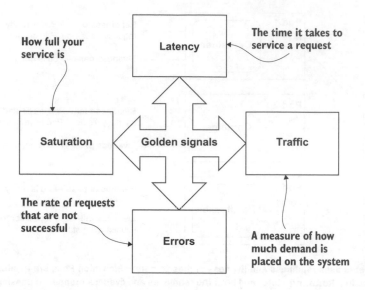

How full your service is

Latency

The time it takes to service a request

Saturation

Golden signals

Traffic

The rate of requests that are not successful

Errors

A measure of how much demand is placed on the system

Figure 8.11   The four "golden signals," latency, traffic, errors, and saturation, are the critical metrics to measure that indicate the system's overall health. Each measures a specific operational aspect of the system. Any given problem in the system is likely to manifest itself by adversely impacting one or more of the "golden signal" metrics.

Brendan Gregg proposed the USE Method for characterizing the performance of system resources (like infrastructure, such as Kubernetes nodes):[10]

- *Utilization*—The average time that the resource was busy servicing work
- *Saturation*—The degree to which the resource has extra work that it can't service, often queued
- *Errors*—The count of error events

For request-driven applications (like microservices), Tom Wilkie defined the RED Method:[11]

- *Rate*—The number of requests per second a service is processing
- *Errors*—The number of failed requests per second
- *Duration*—Distributions of the amount of time each request takes

While a more in-depth discussion of determining application health through metrics is beyond this book's scope, we highly recommend reading the three related footnoted references summarized here.

Once you have identified the metrics to evaluate application health, you need to monitor them and generate alerts when they fall outside of allowable values. In traditional operational environments, this would typically be done by a human operator staring at a dashboard, but perhaps by an automated system. If the monitoring detects an issue, an alert is raised, triggering the on-call engineer to look at the system. The

---

[10] http://www.brendangregg.com/usemethod.html.
[11] http://mng.bz/MX97.

on-call engineer analyzes the system and determines the correct course of action to resolve the alert. This might be to stop the rollout of a new release to the fleet of servers or perhaps even roll back to the previous version.

All this takes time and delays the recovery of the system back to an optimal running state. What if the GitOps system could help improve this situation?

Consider the case where all the Pods come up successfully. All the readiness checks are successful, but once the application begins processing, the length of time required to process each request suddenly increases by two times (the duration of the RED method). It may be that a recent code change introduced a performance bug that is degrading the performance of the application.

Ideally, such a performance issue should be caught while testing in preproduction. If not, might it be possible for the GitOps operator and deployment mechanism to automatically stop or roll back the deployment if particular golden-signal metrics suddenly become degraded and deviate from an established baseline?

This is covered in more detail as part of a discussion of advanced observability use cases in section 8.3.

8.3 GitOps observability

Often administrators will change the system configuration defined in GitOps based on observed application health characteristics. If a Pod is stuck in a `CrashLoopBack-off` state due to an out-of-memory condition, the Pod's manifest may be updated to request more memory for the Pod. If a memory leak causes the out-of-memory condition in the application, perhaps the Pod's image will be updated to one that contains a fix to the memory leak. Maybe the golden signals of the application indicate that it is reaching saturation and cannot handle the load, so the Pod manifest may be updated to request more CPU, or the number of replicas of the Pod is increased to horizontally scale the application.

These are all GitOps operations that would be taken based on the observability of the application. But what about the GitOps process itself? What are the observable characteristics of a GitOps deployment?

8.3.1 GitOps metrics

If the GitOps operator or service is an application, what are its golden signals? Let's consider each area to understand some of the observability characteristics provided by the GitOps operator:

- Latency
  - The time it takes to deploy and make the system's running state match its desired state
- Traffic
  - Frequency of deployments
  - The number of deployments in progress

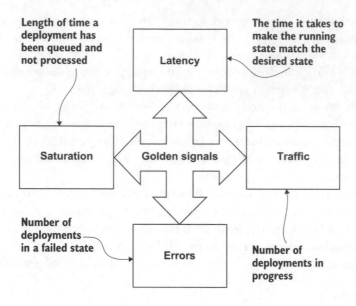

Figure 8.12   The four golden signals for GitOps indicate the health of the GitOps continuous deployment system. Any issue with the GitOps operator/Service will likely manifest itself by adversely impacting one or more of these golden-signal metrics.

- Errors
  - The number of deployments that failed and the current number of deployments in a failed state
  - The number of out-of-sync deployments where the system's running state does not match its desired state

- Saturation
  - Length of time a deployment has been queued and not processed

The implementation of each of these metrics and how they are exposed will be different for each GitOps tool. This will be covered in more detail in part 3 of this book.

8.3.2   *Application sync status*

The most important status the GitOps operator must provide is whether the desired state of the application in the Git repo is the same as the current state of the application (in sync) or not (out of sync). If the application is out of sync, the user should be alerted that a deployment (or redeployment) may be needed.

But what would cause an application to become out of sync? This is part of the regular operation of GitOps; a user commits a change to the desired state of the system. At the moment that change is committed, the current state of the application doesn't match the desired state.

Let's consider how the Basic GitOps operator described in section 2.5.1 of chapter 2 functioned. In that example, a CronJob periodically runs the basic GitOps operator so that the repository is checked out, and the manifests contained in the repo are automatically applied to the running system.

In this basic example of a GitOps operator, the question of application sync status is entirely sidestepped for the sake of simplifying the example. The basic GitOps operator assumed that the application was out of sync at every scheduled execution (or polling interval) and needed to be deployed. This simplistic approach is not suitable for real-world production use because the user has no visibility into whether changes exist that need to be deployed or what those changes are. It might also add unnecessary additional load on the GitOps operation, Git server, and Kubernetes API server.

SAMPLE APPLICATION

Let's run through several different deployment scenarios with our `sample-app` to explore other Application sync status aspects. The `sample-app` is a simple Go application that returns an HTTP response message of "Kubernetes ♡ <input>".

First, log in to GitHub and fork the https://github.com/gitopsbook/sample-app-deployment repository. If you have previously forked this repo, it's recommended to delete the old fork and refork to be sure to start with a clean repository without any changes from previous exercises.

After forking, clone your fork repository using the following command:

```
$ git clone git@github.com:<username>/sample-app-deployment.git
$ cd sample-app-deployment
```

Let's manually deploy the `sample-app` to minikube:

```
$ minikube start
😄  minikube v1.11.0 on Darwin 10.14.6
✨  Automatically selected the hyperkit driver
👍  Starting control plane node minikube in cluster minikube
🔥  Creating hyperkit VM (CPUs=2, Memory=2200MB, Disk=20000MB) ...
🐳  Preparing Kubernetes v1.16.10 on Docker 19.03.8 ...
🔎  Verifying Kubernetes components...
🌟  Enabled addons: default-storageclass, storage-provisioner
🏄  Done! kubectl is now configured to use "minikube"
$ kubectl create ns sample-app
namespace/sample-app created
$ kubectl apply -f . -n sample-app
deployment.apps/sample-app created
service/sample-app created
```

> **NOTE** At the time of this writing, Kubernetes v1.18.3 reports additional differences using the `kubectl diff` command. If you experience this issue while completing the following exercises, you can start minikube with an older version of Kubernetes using the command `minikube start --kubernetes-version=1.16.10`.

DETECTING DIFFERENCES

Now that the `sample-app` has been successfully deployed, let's make some changes to the deployment. Let's increase the number of replicas of the `sample-app` to 3 in the deployment.yaml file. Use the following command to change the replica count of the Deployment resource:

```
$ sed -i '' 's/replicas: .*/replicas: 3/' deployment.yaml
```

Or you could use your favorite text editor to change `replicas: 1` to `replicas: 3` in the deployment.yaml file. Once the change has been made to deployment.yaml, run the following command to see the uncommitted differences in your Git fork repository:

```
$ git diff
diff --git a/deployment.yaml b/deployment.yaml
index 5fc3833..ed2398a 100644
--- a/deployment.yaml
+++ b/deployment.yaml
@@ -3,7 +3,7 @@ kind: Deployment
 metadata:
   name: sample-app
 spec:
-  replicas: 1
+  replicas: 3
   revisionHistoryLimit: 3
   selector:
     matchLabels:
```

Finally, use `git commit` and `git push` to push changes to the remote Git fork repository:

```
$ git commit -am "update replica count"
[master 5a03ca3] update replica count
 1 file changed, 1 insertion(+), 1 deletion(-)
$ git push
Enumerating objects: 5, done.
Counting objects: 100% (5/5), done.
Delta compression using up to 4 threads
Compressing objects: 100% (3/3), done.
Writing objects: 100% (3/3), 353 bytes | 353.00 KiB/s, done.
Total 3 (delta 1), reused 0 (delta 0)
remote: Resolving deltas: 100% (1/1), completed with 1 local object.
To github.com:tekenstam/sample-app-deployment.git
   09d6663..5a03ca3  master -> master
```

Now that you have committed a change to the `sample-app` deployment repo, the `sample-app` GitOps sync status is out of sync because the current state of the deployment still only has three replicas. Let's just confirm that this is the case:

```
$ kubectl get deployment sample-app -n sample-app
NAME         READY    UP-TO-DATE    AVAILABLE    AGE
sample-app   1/1      1             1            3m27s
```

From this command, you see there are `1/1` `READY` replicas for the `sample-app` deployment. But is there a better way to compare the deployment repo, which represents the desired state, against the running application's actual state? Luckily Kubernetes provides tools for detecting differences.

KUBECTL DIFF

Kubernetes provides the `kubectl diff` command, which takes a file or directory as input and displays the differences between the resources defined in those files and the current resources of the same names in the Kubernetes cluster. If we run `kubectl diff` against our existing deployment repo, we see the following:

```
$ kubectl diff -f . -n sample-app
@@ -6,7 +6,7 @@
    creationTimestamp: "2020-06-01T04:17:28Z"
-   generation: 2
+   generation: 3
    name: sample-app
    namespace: sample-app
    resourceVersion: "2291"
@@ -14,7 +14,7 @@
    uid: eda45dca-ff29-444c-a6fc-5134302bcd81
  spec:
    progressDeadlineSeconds: 600
-   replicas: 1
+   replicas: 3
    revisionHistoryLimit: 3
    selector:
      matchLabels:
```

From this output, we can see that `kubectl diff` correctly identified that `replicas` was changed from 1 to 3.

While this is an elementary example to illustrate the point, this same technique can identify more extensive changes across multiple different resources. This gives the GitOps operator or service the ability to determine when the deployment repo containing the desired state in Git is out of sync with the current live state of the Kubernetes cluster. More importantly, the `kubectl diff` output provides a preview of the changes that would be applied to the cluster if the deployment repo is synced. This is a crucial feature of GitOps observability.

Exercise 8.9

Make a fork of the `sample-app` deployment repository. Deploy the `sample-app` to your minikube cluster as described in the `sample-app-deployment` README.md. Now change the `sample-app` service to be of `type: LoadBalancer`. Run the `kubectl diff -f . -n sample-app` command. Do you see any unexpected changes? Why? Apply the changes using `kubectl apply -f . -n sample-app`. Now you should see the `sample-app` web page using the command `minikube service sample-app -n sample-app`.

KUBEDIFF

In the previous sections, we covered how to see the differences between revisions in the Git repository using `git diff` and the differences between the Git repository and the live Kubernetes cluster using `kubectl diff`. In both cases, the diff tools give you a very raw view of the differences, outputting lines before and after the differences for context. And `kubectl diff` may also report differences that are system managed (like `generation`) and not relevant to the GitOps use case. Wouldn't it be cool if there was a tool that gave you a concise report of each resource's specific attributes that are different? As it turns out, the folks at Weaveworks[12] have released an open source tool called `kubediff`[13] that does precisely that.

Here is the output of `kubediff` run against our deployment repo of the `sample-app`:

```
$ kubediff --namespace sample-app .
## sample-app/sample-app (Deployment.v1.apps)

.spec.replicas: '3' != '1'
```

`kubediff` can also output JSON structured output, allowing it to be more easily used programmatically. Here is the same command run with JSON output:

```
$ kubediff --namespace sample-app . --json
{
  "./deployment.yaml": [
    ".spec.replicas: '3' != '1'"
  ]
}
```

Exercise 8.10
Run `kubediff` against the `sample-app-deployment` repository. If not installed already in your environment, you will first need to install Python and `pip` and run `pip install -r requirements.txt` as described in the `kubediff` README.

8.3.3 *Configuration drift*

But how else could an application become out of sync with the desired state defined in the Git repo? Possibly a user modified the running application directly (like by performing a `kubectl edit` on the Deployment resource) instead of committing the desired change to the Git repo. We call this *configuration drift.*

This is usually a big "no-no" when managing a system with GitOps; you should avoid directly modifying the system outside of GitOps. For example, if your Pods are running out of capacity, you might just simply perform a `kubectl edit` to increase the replica count to increase capacity.

This situation sometimes happens. When it does, the GitOps operator will need to "observe" the current state and detect a difference with the desired state and indicate to the user that the application is out of sync. A particularly aggressive GitOps operator might automatically redeploy the last previously deployed configuration, thereby overwriting the manual changes.

Using minikube and the `sample-app-deployment` repository we've been using for the last few sections, run `kubectl apply -f . -n sample-app` to make sure the current contents are deployed to Kubernetes. Now run `kubectl diff -f . -n sample-app`; you should see no differences.

---

[12] https://www.weave.works/.
[13] https://github.com/weaveworks/kubediff.

Now, let's simulate a change being made to the application deployment outside of the GitOps system by running the following command:

```
$ kubectl scale deployment --replicas=4 sample-app -n sample-app
deployment.apps/sample-app scaled
```

Now, if we rerun the `kubectl diff` command, we see that the application is out of sync, and we have experienced configuration drift:

```
$ kubectl diff -f . -n sample-app
@@ -6,7 +6,7 @@
    creationTimestamp: "2020-06-01T04:17:28Z"
-   generation: 6
+   generation: 7
    name: sample-app
    namespace: sample-app
    resourceVersion: "16468"
@@ -14,7 +14,7 @@
    uid: eda45dca-ff29-444c-a6fc-5134302bcd81
 spec:
    progressDeadlineSeconds: 600
-   replicas: 4
+   replicas: 3
    revisionHistoryLimit: 3
    selector:
      matchLabels:
```

Or if you run `kubediff`, you see the following:

```
$ kubediff --namespace sample-app .
## sample-app/sample-app (Deployment.v1.apps)

.spec.replicas: '3' != '4'
```

Configuration drift is very similar to an application being out of sync. In fact, as you see, the effect is the same; the current live state of the configuration is different from the desired configuration as defined in the Git deployment repo. The difference is that typically an application is out of sync when a new version is committed to the Git deployment repo that hasn't been deployed yet. In contrast, configuration drift happens when changes to the configuration have been made outside of the GitOps system.

In general, one of two things must occur when configuration drift is encountered. Some systems would consider the configuration drift an error state and allow a self-healing process to be initiated to sync the system back to the declared state. Other systems may detect this drift and allow the manual change to be integrated back into the declared state saved in Git (such as two-way syncing). However, our view is that two-way syncing is not desirable because it allows and encourages manual changes to the cluster and bypasses the security and review process that GitOps provides as one of its core benefits.

Exercise 8.11
From the `sample-app-deployment`, run the command `kubectl delete -f . -n sample-app`. Oops, you just deleted your application! Run `kubectl diff -f . -n`

sample-app. What differences do you see? How can you restore your application to a running state? Hint: it should be easy.

8.3.4 GitOps change log

Earlier in this chapter, we discussed how event logs are a key aspect of observability. For GitOps, the "event log" of the application deployment is primarily composed of the deployment repository's commit history. Since all changes to the application deployment are made by changing the files representing the application's desired state, by observing the commits, pull request approvals, and merge requests, we can understand what changes have been made in the cluster.

For example, running the `git log` command on the `sample-app-deployment` repository displays all the commits made to this repo since it was created:

```
$ git log --no-merges
commit ce920168912a7f3a6cdd57d47e630ac09aebc4e1 (origin/tekenstam-patch-2)
Author: Todd Ekenstam <tekenstam@gmail.com>
Date:   Mon Nov 9 13:59:25 2020 -0800

    Reduce Replica count back to 1

commit 8613d1b14c75e32ae04f3b4c0470812e1bdec01c (origin/tekenstam-patch-1)
Author: Todd Ekenstam <tekenstam@gmail.com>
Date:   Mon Nov 9 13:58:26 2020 -0800

    Update Replica count to 3

commit 09d6663dcfa0f39b1a47c66a88f0225a1c3380bc
Author: tekenstam <tekenstam@gmail.com>
Date:   Wed Feb 5 22:14:35 2020 -0800

    Update deployment.yaml

commit 461ac41630bfa3eee40a8d01dbcd2a5cd032b8f1
Author: Todd Ekenstam <Todd_Ekenstam@intuit.com>
Date:   Wed Feb 5 21:51:03 2020 -0800

    Update sample-app image to gitopsbook/sample-app:cc52a36

commit 99bb7e779d960f23d5d941d94a7c4c4a6047bb22
Author: Alexander Matyushentsev <amatyushentsev@gmail.com>
Date:   Sun Jan 26 22:01:20 2020 -0800

    Initial commit
```

From this output, we can see Alex authored the first commit to this repo on Jan 26. The most recent commit was authored by Todd, which, according to the commit title, reduces the Replica count back to one. We can look at the actual differences in the commit by running the following command:

```
$ git show ce920168912a7f3a6cdd57d47e630ac09aebc4e1
commit ce920168912a7f3a6cdd57d47e630ac09aebc4e1 (origin/tekenstam-patch-2)
```

```
Author: Todd Ekenstam <tekenstam@gmail.com>
Date:   Mon Nov 9 13:59:25 2020 -0800

    Reduce Replica count back to 1

diff --git a/deployment.yaml b/deployment.yaml
index ed2398a..5fc3833 100644
--- a/deployment.yaml
+++ b/deployment.yaml
@@ -3,7 +3,7 @@ kind: Deployment
 metadata:
   name: sample-app
 spec:
-  replicas: 3
+  replicas: 1
   revisionHistoryLimit: 3
   selector:
     matchLabels:
```

From this we see that the line `replicas: 3` was changed to `replicas: 1`. The same information is available in the GitHub UI.

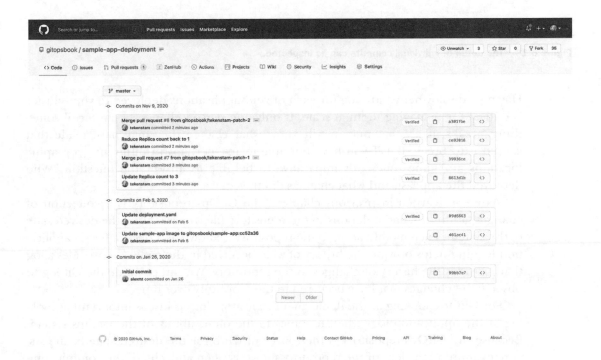

Figure 8.13 Reviewing the GitHub commit history of a deployment repository allows you to see all the changes that have been made to the application deployment over time.

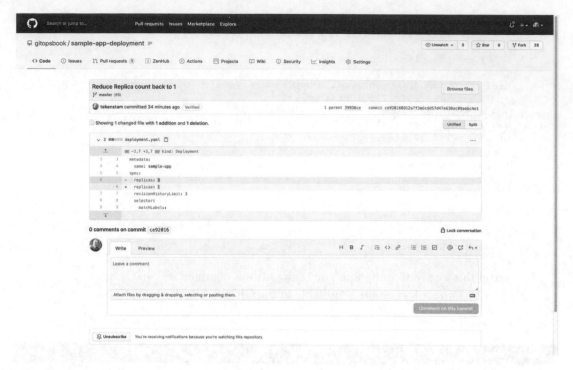

Figure 8.14   The detail of individual commits can be inspected.

Having a deployment audit log for each of your applications deployed to your cluster is critical for managing them at scale. If only one person changes a cluster, if something breaks, likely that person will know what change they may have made that caused it to break. But if you have multiple teams, perhaps in different geographic locations and time zones, it's imperative to be able to answer the question "Who deployed the app last, and what changes did they make?"

As we've learned in previous chapters, the GitOps repository is a collection of changes, additions, and deletions to the repository files representing the desired state of the system. Each modification to the repository is known as a *commit*. Just as application logging helps provide the history of what occurred in the code, Git provides a log that provides the history of changes to the repository. We can examine the Git log to observe the changes that have occurred to the repository over time.

For GitOps, looking at the deployment repository logs is just as important as looking at the application logs when it comes to the observability of the GitOps system. Because the GitOps repository is the source of truth for the desired state of the system, examining the logs of the repository shows us when and why (if the commit comment is descriptive enough) changes were made to the desired state of the system, as well as who made and approved those changes.

This is a critically important aspect of how GitOps provides observability to users. While the GitOps operator or service may also provide application logs detailing its execution, the Git log of the deployment repository usually will give you an excellent understanding of what changes have been going on in the system.

Exercise 8.12

Using the same Git fork of the `sample-app-deployment` repository you've been using throughout this chapter, run the command `git log`. Examine the output. Can you trace your process through the sections of this chapter? Do you see any earlier commits to this repo by the authors?

Summary

- Aspects of observability can be measured by monitoring event logging, metrics, and tracing.
- A data collector such as Logstash, Fluentd, or Scribe can collect the application output (events) in stdout and store the log messages in a centralized data store for later analysis.
- Observe the application output using `kubectl logs`.
- Prometheus collects metrics from both nodes and Pods to provide a snapshot of the performance and operation of all system components.
- Use Jaeger (Open Tracing) to monitor distributed calls to gain system insight such as error and latency.
- Application health: is the application operating correctly? If a new version of the application is deploying using GitOps, is the system "better" than before?
- Use `kubectl describe` to monitor application health.
- Application sync status: is the running state of the application the same as the desired state defined in the deployment Git repo?
- Configuration drift: has the application's configuration been changed outside of the declarative GitOps system (such as either manually or imperatively)?
- Use `kubectl diff` and `kubediff` to detect Application sync status and configuration drift
- GitOps change log: what changes were recently made to the GitOps system? Who made them, and for what reason?

Part 3

Tools

This part goes over several enterprise-grade GitOps tools that simplify and automate your GitOps processes.

Chapter 9 describes the motivation and design for Argo CD. It also discusses how to deploy an application using Argo CD and its enterprise features.

Chapter 10 describes the motivation and design for Jenkins X. It also discusses how to deploy and promote an application to various environments.

Chapter 11 describes the motivation and design for Flux. It also discusses how to deploy an application using Flux and set up for multitenancy.

Argo CD

9

This chapter covers

- What is Argo CD?
- Deploying an application using Argo CD
- Using Argo CD enterprise features

In this chapter, you will learn how to use the Argo CD GitOps operator to deploy a reference example application to Kubernetes. You will also learn how Argo CD addresses enterprise considerations such as single sign-on (SSO) and access control.

We recommend you read chapters 1, 2, 3, and 5 before reading this chapter.

9.1 What is Argo CD?

Argo CD is an open source GitOps operator for Kubernetes.[1] The project is a part of the Argo family, a set of cloud-native tools for running and managing jobs and applications on Kubernetes. Along with Argo Workflows, Rollouts, and Events, Argo CD focuses on application delivery use cases and makes it easier to combine three modes of computing: services, workflows, and event-based processing. In

---

[1] https://argoproj.github.io/projects/argo-cd.

2020, Argo CD was accepted by the Cloud Native Computing Foundation (CNCF) as an incubation-level hosted project.

> **CNCF**   The Cloud Native Computing Foundation is a Linux Foundation project that hosts critical components of the global technology infrastructure.

The company behind Argo CD is Intuit, the creator of TurboTax and QuickBooks. In early 2018, Intuit decided to adopt Kubernetes to speed up cloud migration. At the time, the market already had several successful continuous deployment tools for Kubernetes, but none of them fully satisfied Intuit's needs. So instead of adopting an existing solution, the company decided to invest in a new project and started working on Argo CD. What is so special about Intuit's requirements? The answer to that question explains how Argo CD is different from other Kubernetes CD tools and explains its main project use cases.

9.1.1   *Main use cases*

The importance of a GitOps methodology and benefits of representing infrastructure as code is not questionable. However, the enterprise scale demands additional requirements. Intuit is a cloud-based software-as-a-service company. With around 5,000 developers, the company successfully runs hundreds of microservices on-premises and in the cloud. Given that scale, it was unreasonable to expect that every team would run its own Kubernetes cluster. Instead, it was decided that a centralized platform team would run and maintain a set of multitenant clusters for the whole company. At the same time, end users should have the freedom and necessary tools to manage workloads in those clusters. These considerations have defined the following additional requirements on top of the decision to use GitOps.

AVAILABLE AS A SERVICE

A simple onboarding process is extremely important if you are trying to move hundreds of microservices to Kubernetes. Instead of asking every team to install, configure, and maintain the deployment operator, it should be provided by the centralized team. With several thousands of new users, SSO integration is crucial. The service must integrate with various SSO providers instead of introducing its own user management.

ENABLE MULTITENANCY AND MULTICLUSTER MANAGEMENT

In multitenant environments, users need an effective and flexible access control system. Kubernetes has a great built-in role-based access control system, but that is not enough when you have to deal with hundreds of clusters. The continuous deployment tool should provide access control on top of multiple clusters and seamlessly integrate with existing SSO providers.

ENABLE OBSERVABILITY

Last, but not least, the continuous deployment tool should provide developers insights about the state of managed applications. That assumes a user-friendly interface that quickly answers the following questions:

- Is the application configuration in sync with the configuration defined in Git?
- What exactly is not matching?
- Is the application up and running?
- What exactly is broken?

The company needed the GitOps operator ready for enterprise scale. The team evaluated several GitOps operators, but none of them satisfied all the requirements, so it was decided to implement Argo CD.

Exercise 9.1
Reflect on your organization's needs and compare them to use cases that Argo CD is focused on. Try to decide if Argo CD solves the pain points your team has.

9.1.2 Core concepts

In order to effectively use Argo CD, we should understand two basic concepts: the Application and the Project. Let's have a closer look at the Application first.

APPLICATION

The Application provides a logical grouping of Kubernetes resources and defines a resources manifest's source and destination.

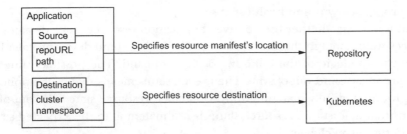

Figure 9.1 The main properties of the Argo CD Application are the source and destination. The source specifies a resource manifest's location in the Git repository. The destination specifies where resources should be created in the Kubernetes cluster.

The Application source includes the repository URL and the directory inside of the repository. Typically repositories include multiple directories, one per application environment such as QA and Prod. The sample directory structure of such a repository is represented here:

```
.
├── prod
│   └── deployment.yaml
└── qa
    └── deployment.yaml
```

Each directory does not necessarily contain plain YAML files. Argo CD does not enforce any configuration management tool and instead provides first-class support for various config management tools. So the directory might as well contain a Helm chart definition as YAML along with Kustomize overlays.

The Application destination defines where resources must be deployed and includes the API server URL of the target Kubernetes cluster, along with the cluster Namespace name. The API server URL identifies the cluster where all application manifests must be deployed. It is impossible to deploy application manifests across several clusters, but different applications might be deployed into different clusters. The Namespace name is used to identify the target Namespace of all Namespace-level application resources.

So the Argo CD Application represents an environment deployed in the Kubernetes cluster and connects it to the desired state stored in the Git repository.

Exercise 9.2

Consider the real service deployed in your organization and come up with a list of Argo CD applications. Define the source repository URL, directory, and target cluster with the Namespace for one of the applications from your list.

9.1.3   *Sync and health statuses*

In addition to the source and destination, the Argo CD application has two more important properties: sync and health statuses.

Sync status answers whether the observed application resources state deviates from the resources state stored in the Git repository. The logic behind deviation calculation is equivalent to the logic of the `kubectl diff` command. The possible values of a sync status are in-sync and out-of-sync. The in-sync status means that each application resource is found and fully matching to the expected resource state. The out-of-sync status means that at least one resource status is not matching to the expected state or not found in the target cluster.

The health status aggregates information about the observed health status of each resource that makes up the application. The health assessment logic is different for each Kubernetes resource type and results in one of the following values:

- *Healthy*—For example, the Kubernetes deployment is considered healthy if the required number of Pods is running and each Pod successfully passes both readiness and liveness probes.
- *Progressing*—Represents a resource that is not healthy yet but is still expected to reach a healthy state. The Deployment is considered progressing if it is not healthy yet but still without a time limit specified by the `progressing-DeadlineSeconds`[2] field.

---

[2] http://mng.bz/aomz.

- *Degraded*—The antipode of a healthy status. The example is a Deployment that could not reach a healthy status within an expected timeout.
- *Missing*—Represents the resource that is stored in Git but not deployed to the target cluster.

The aggregated application status is the worst status of every application resource. The healthy status is the best, descending to progressing, degraded, and missing (the worst). So if all application resources are healthy and only one is degraded, the aggregated status is also degraded.

Exercise 9.3

Consider an application consisting of two Deployments. The following information is known about the resources:

- Deployment 1 has an image that does not match the image stored in the Git repository. All Deployment Pods have failed to start for several hours while Deployment `progressingDeadlineSeconds` is set to 10 minutes.
- Deployment 2 is not fully matching the expected state and has all Pods running.

What are the application sync and health statuses?

The health and sync statuses answer the two most important questions about an application:

- Is my application working?
- Am I running what is expected?

PROJECT

Argo CD applications provide a very flexible way to manage different applications independently of each other. This functionality provides very useful insights to the team about each piece of infrastructure and greatly improves productivity. However, this is not enough to support multiple teams with different access levels:

- The mixed list of applications creates confusion that creates a human error possibility.
- Different teams have different access levels. As has been described in chapter 6, an individual might use the GitOps operator to escalate their own permissions to get full cluster access.

The workaround for these issues is a separate Argo CD instance for each team. This is not a perfect solution since a separate instance means management overhead. In order to avoid management overhead, Argo CD introduces the Project abstraction. Figure 9.2 illustrates the relationship between Applications and Projects.

A Project provides a logical grouping of Applications, isolates teams from each other, and allows for fine-tuning access control in each Project.

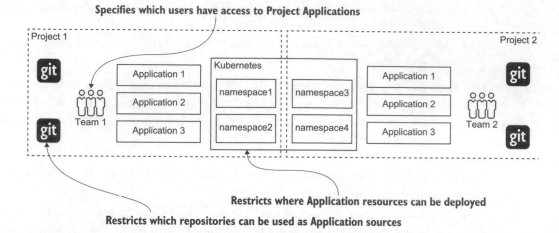

Specifies which users have access to Project Applications

Restricts where Application resources can be deployed

Restricts which repositories can be used as Application sources

Figure 9.2   Demonstrates the relationship between Applications and Projects. A Project provides a logical grouping of Applications, isolating teams from each other and enabling using Argo CD in multitenant environments.

In addition to separating sets of applications, a Project provides the following set of features:

- Restricts which Kubernetes clusters and Git repositories might be used by Project Applications
- Restricts which Kubernetes resources can be deployed by each Application within a Project

Exercise 9.4

Try to come up with a list of projects in your organization. Using Projects, you can restrict what kind of resource users can deploy, source repositories, and destination clusters available within the Project. Which restrictions would you configure for your projects?

9.1.4   *Architecture*

At first glance, the implementation of the GitOps operator does not look too complex. In theory, all you need is to clone the Git repository with manifests and use `kubectl diff` and `kubectl apply` to detect and handle config drifts. This is true until you are trying to automate this process for multiple teams and manage the configuration of dozens of clusters simultaneously. Logically this process is split into three phases, and each phase has its own challenges:

- Retrieve resource manifests.
- Detect and fix the deviations.
- Present the results to end users.

Each phase consumes different resources, and the implementation of each phase has to scale differently. A separate Argo CD component is responsible for each phase.

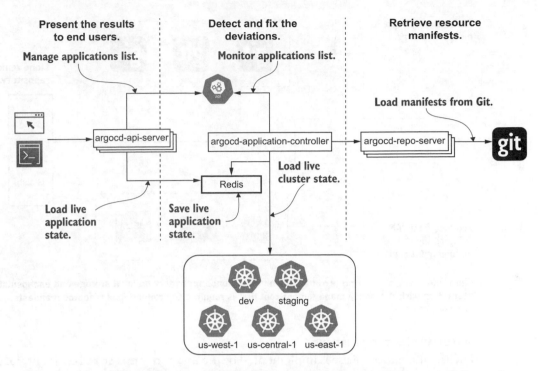

Figure 9.3 Argo CD consists of three main components that implement GitOps reconciliation cycle phases. The `argocd-repo-server` retrieves manifests from Git. The `argocd-application-controller` compares manifests from Git with resources in the Kubernetes cluster. The `argocd-api-server` presents reconciliation results to the user.

Let's go through each phase and the corresponding Argo CD component implementation details.

RETRIEVE RESOURCE MANIFESTS

The manifest generation in Argo CD is implemented by the `argocd-repo-server` component. This phase presents a whole set of challenges.

Manifest generation requires you to download Git repository content and produce ready-to-use manifest YAML. First of all, it is too time consuming to download the whole repository content every time you need to retrieve expected resource manifests. Argo CD solves this by caching the repository content on local disk and using the `git fetch` command to download only recent changes from the remote Git repository. The next challenge is related to memory usage. In real life, resource manifests are rarely stored as plain YAML files. In most cases, developers prefer to use a config management tool such as Helm or Kustomize. Every tool invocation causes a spike in memory usage. To handle the memory usage issues, Argo CD allows the user to limit the number of parallel manifest generations and scale up the number of `argocd-repo-server` instances to improve performance.

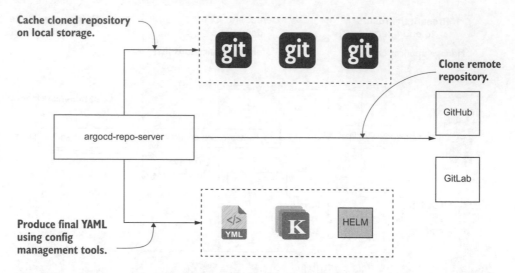

Cache cloned repository on local storage.

Clone remote repository.

argocd-repo-server

Produce final YAML using config management tools.

Figure 9.4 `argocd-repo-server` **caches the cloned repository on local storage and encapsulates interaction with the config management tool that is required to produce final resource manifests.**

DETECT AND FIX THE DEVIATIONS

The reconciliation phase is implemented by the `argocd-application-controller` component. The controller loads the live Kubernetes cluster state, compares it with the expected manifests provided by the `argocd-repo-server`, and patches deviated resources. This phase is probably the most challenging one. In order to correctly detect deviations, the GitOps operator needs to know about each resource in the cluster, and compare and update thousands of resources.

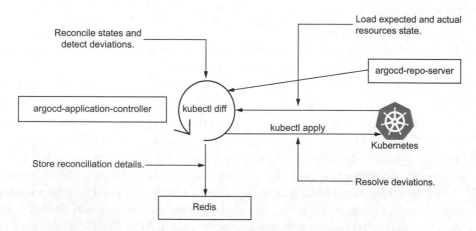

Reconcile states and detect deviations.

Load expected and actual resources state.

argocd-application-controller

argocd-repo-server

kubectl diff

kubectl apply

Kubernetes

Store reconciliation details.

Resolve deviations.

Redis

Figure 9.5 `argocd-application-controller` **performs resource reconciliation. The controller leverages the** `argocd-repo-server` **component to retrieve expected manifests and compare manifests with the lightweight in-memory Kubernetes cluster state cache.**

The controller maintains a lightweight cache of each managed cluster and updates it in the background using the Kubernetes watch API. This allows the controller to perform reconciliation on an application within a fraction of a second and empowers it to scale and manage dozens of clusters simultaneously. After each reconciliation, the controller has exhaustive information about each application resource, including the sync and health status. The controller saves that information into the Redis cluster so it can be presented to the end user later.

PRESENT THE RESULTS TO END USERS

Finally, the reconciliation results must be presented to end users. This task is performed by the `argocd-server` component. While the heavy lifting was already done by the `argocd-repo-server` and `argocd-application-controller`, this last phase has the highest resiliency requirements. The `argocd-server` is a stateless web application that loads the information about reconciliation results and powers the web user interface.

The architecture design allows Argo CD to serve GitOps operations for large enterprises with minimal maintenance overhead.

Exercise 9.5

Which components serve user requests and require multiple replicas for resiliency? Which components might require a lot of memory to scale?

9.2 *Deploy your first application*

While Argo CD is an enterprise-ready, complex distributed system, it is still lightweight and can easily run on minikube. The installation is trivial and includes a few simple steps. Please refer to appendix B for more information on how to install Argo CD, or follow the official Argo CD instructions.[3]

9.2.1 *Deploying the first application*

As soon as Argo CD is running, we are ready to deploy our first application. As it's been mentioned before, to deploy an Argo CD application, we need to specify the Git repository that contains deployment manifests and target the Kubernetes cluster and Namespace. To create the Git repository for this exercise, open the following GitHub repository and create a repository fork:[4]

```
https://github.com/gitopsbook/sample-app-deployment
```

Argo CD can deploy into the external cluster as well as into the same cluster where it is installed. Let's use the second option and deploy our application into the default Namespace of our minikube cluster.

> **RESET YOUR FORK** Have you already forked the deployment repository while working on previous chapters? Please make sure to revert changes for the best experience. The simplest way is to delete the previously forked repository and fork it again.

---

[3] https://argoproj.github.io/argo-cd/getting_started/.
[4] https://help.github.com/en/github/getting-started-with-github/fork-a-repo.

The application might be created using the web user interface, using the CLI, or even programmatically using the REST or gRPC APIs. Since we already have Argo CD CLI installed and configured, let's use it to deploy an application. Go ahead and execute the following command to create an application:

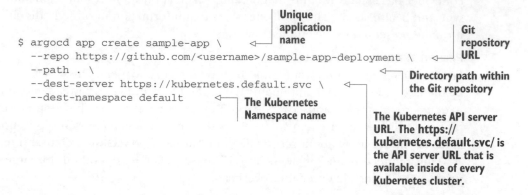

As soon as the application is created, we can use the Argo CD CLI to get the information about the application state. Use the following command to get the information about the `sample-app` application state:

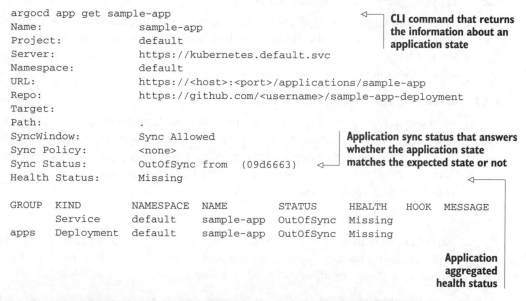

As we can see from the command output, the application is out of sync and not healthy. By default, Argo CD does not push resources defined in the Git repository into the cluster if it detects a deviation. In addition to the high-level summary, we can see the details of every application resource. Argo CD detected that the application is supposed to have a Deployment and a Service, but both resources are missing. To deploy the resources, we need to either configure automated application syncing using the sync policy[5] or trigger syncing manually. To trigger the sync and deploy the resources, use the following command:

```
                                              CLI command that triggers
                                              application sync
$ argocd app sync sample-app        ←┘
TIMESTAMP                    GROUP      KIND       NAMESPACE    NAME       STATUS
    HEALTH       HOOK  MESSAGE                                            ←┐
2020-03-17T23:16:50-07:00   Service    default    sample-app   OutOfSync Missing
2020-03-17T23:16:50-07:00   apps       Deployment default      sample-app
    OutOfSync  Missing
                                                       Initial application state
                                                       before the sync operation
Name:            sample-app
Project:         default
Server:          https://kubernetes.default.svc
Namespace:       default
URL:             https://<host>:<port>/applications/sample-app
Repo:            https://github.com/<username>/sample-app-deployment
Target:
Path:            .
SyncWindow:      Sync Allowed
Sync Policy:     <none>
Sync Status:     OutOfSync from  (09d6663)
Health Status:   Missing

Operation:       Sync
Sync Revision:   09d6663dcfa0f39b1a47c66a88f0225a1c3380bc
Phase:           Succeeded
Start:           2020-03-17 23:17:12 -0700 PDT
Finished:        2020-03-17 23:17:21 -0700 PDT       Final application
Duration:        9s                                  state after the
Message:         successfully synced (all tasks run) sync is completed

GROUP  KIND       NAMESPACE  NAME        STATUS   HEALTH       HOOK  MESSAGE  ←┐
       Service    default    sample-app  Synced   Healthy            service/
    sample-app created
apps   Deployment default    sample-app  Synced   Progressing        deployment
    .apps/sample-app created
```

As soon as the sync is triggered, Argo CD pushes the manifests stored in Git into the Kubernetes cluster and then reevaluates the application state. The final application state is printed to the console when the synchronization completes. The `sample-app` application was successfully synced, and each result matches the expected state.

9.2.2 *Inspect the application using the user interface*

In addition to the CLI and API, Argo CD provides a user-friendly web interface. Using the web interface, you might get the high-level view of all your applications deployed across multiple clusters as well as very detailed information about every application resource. Open the https://<host>:<port> URL to see the applications list in the Argo CD user interface.

---

[5] https://argoproj.github.io/argo-cd/user-guide/auto_sync/.

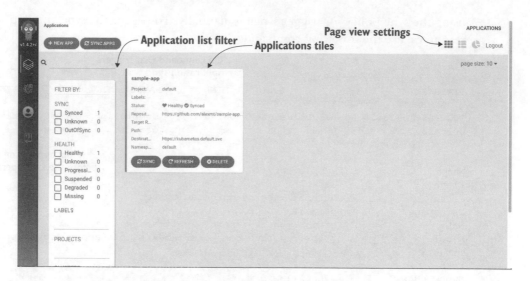

Figure 9.6 Application list page showing available Argo CD applications. The page provides high-level information about each application, such as sync and health status.

The application list page provides high-level information about all deployed applications, including health and synchronization status. Using this page, you can quickly find if any of your applications have degraded or have configuration drift. The user interface is designed for large enterprises and able to handle hundreds of applications. You can use search and various filters to quickly find the desired applications.

Exercise 9.6

Experiment with the filters and page view settings to learn which other features are available in the applications list page.

APPLICATION DETAILS PAGE

The additional information about the application is available on the application details page. Navigate to the application details page by clicking on the "sample app" application tile.

   The application details page visualizes the application resources hierarchy and provides additional details about synchronization and health status. Let's take a closer look at the application resource tree and learn which features it provides.

   The root element of the resource tree is the application itself. The next level consists of managed resources. The managed resources are resources that the manifest defined in Git and are controlled by Argo CD explicitly. As we've learned in chapter 2, Kubernetes controllers often leverage delegation and create child resources to delegate the work. The third and deeper levels represent such resources. That provides complete information about every application element and makes the application details page an extremely powerful Kubernetes dashboard.

   In addition to this information, the user interface allows executing various actions against each resource. It is possible to delete any resource, re-create it by running sync

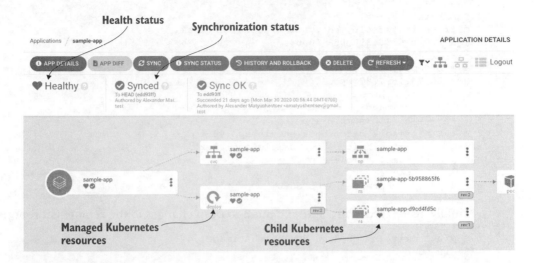

Figure 9.7 The application details page provides information about the application resource hierarchy as well as detailed information about each resource.

actions, update the resource definition using a built-in YAML editor, and even run resource-specific actions such as Deployment restart.

Exercise 9.7

Go ahead, use the application details page to inspect your application. Try to find how to view the resource manifests, locate Pods, and see the live logs.

9.3   *Deep dive into Argo CD features*

So far, we've learned how to deploy new applications using Argo CD and get detailed application information using the CLI and the user interface. Next, let's learn how to deploy a new application version using GitOps and Argo CD.

9.3.1   *GitOps-driven deployment*

In order to perform GitOps deployment, we need to update resource manifests and let the GitOps operator push changes into the Kubernetes cluster. As a first step, clone the Deployment repository using the following command:

```
$ git clone git@github.com:<username>/sample-app-deployment.git
$ cd sample-app-deployment
```

Next, use the following command to change the image version of the Deployment resource:

```
$ sed -i '' 's/sample-app:v.*/sample-app:v0.2/' deployment.yaml
```

Use the `git diff` command to make sure that your Git repository has the expected changes:

```
$ git diff
diff --git a/deployment.yaml b/deployment.yaml
index 5fc3833..397d058 100644
--- a/deployment.yaml
+++ b/deployment.yaml
@@ -16,7 +16,7 @@ spec:
       containers:
       - command:
         - /app/sample-app
-         image: gitopsbook/sample-app:v0.1
+         image: gitopsbook/sample-app:v0.2
         name: sample-app
         ports:
         - containerPort: 8080
```

Finally, use `git commit` and `git push` to push changes to the remote Git repository:

```
$ git commit -am "update deployment image"
$ git push
```

Let's use the Argo CD CLI to make sure that Argo CD correctly detected manifest changes in Git and then triggered a synchronization process to push the changes into the Kubernetes cluster:

```
$ argocd app diff sample-app --refresh
===== apps/Deployment default/sample-app ======
21c21
<           image: gitopsbook/sample-app:v0.1
---
>           image: gitopsbook/sample-app:v0.2
```

Exercise 9.8

Open the Argo CD UI and use the application details page to check the application sync status and inspect the managed resources status.

Use the `argocd sync` command to trigger the synchronization process:

```
$ argocd app sync sample-app
```

Great, you just performed GitOps deployment using Argo CD!

9.3.2   *Resource hooks*

Resource manifest syncing is just the basic use case. In real life, we often need to execute additional steps before and after actual deployment. For example, set the maintenance page, execute database migration before the new version deployment, and finally remove the maintenance page.

Traditionally these deployment steps are scripted in the CI pipeline. However, this again requires production access from the CI server, which involves a security threat. To solve that problem, Argo CD provides a feature called *resource hooks*. These hooks allow running custom scripts, typically packaged into a Pod or a Job, inside of the Kubernetes cluster during the synchronization process.

The hook is a Kubernetes resource manifest stored in the Git repository and annotated with the `argocd.argoproj.io/hook` annotation. The annotation value contains a comma-separated list of phases when the hook is supposed to be executed. The following phases are supported:

- *Pre-sync*—Executes prior to the applying of the manifests
- *Sync*—Executes after all pre-sync hooks completed and were successful, at the same time as the apply of the manifests
- *Skip*—Indicates to Argo CD to skip the apply of the manifest
- *Post-sync*—Executes after all sync hooks completed and were successful, a successful apply, and all resources in a healthy state
- *Sync-fai*—Executes when the sync operation fails

The hooks are executed inside of the cluster, so there is no need to access the cluster from the CI pipeline. The ability to specify the sync phase provides the necessary flexibility and allows a mechanism to solve the majority of real-life deployment use cases.

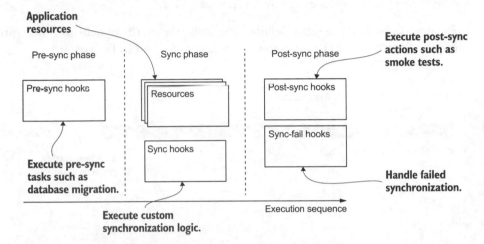

Figure 9.8   The synchronization process includes three main phases. The pre-sync phase is used to execute preparation tasks such as database migration. The sync phase includes the synchronization of application resources. Finally, the post-sync phase runs postprocessing tasks, such as email notifications.

It is time to see the hooks feature in action! Add the hook definition into the sample app deployment repository and push changes to the remote repository:

```
$ git add pre-sync.yaml
$ git commit -am 'Add pre-sync hook'
$ git push
```

Listing 9.1   http://mng.bz/go7l

```
apiVersion: batch/v1
kind: Job
metadata:
```

```
  name: before
  annotations:
    argocd.argoproj.io/hook: PreSync
spec:
  template:
    spec:
      containers:
      - name: sleep
        image: alpine:latest
        command: ["echo", "pre-sync"]
      restartPolicy: Never
  backoffLimit: 0
```

The Argo CD user interface provides much better visualization of a dynamic process than the CLI. Let's use it to better understand how hooks work. Open the Argo CD UI using the following command:

```
$ minikube service argocd-server -n argocd --url
```

Navigate to the sample-app details page and trigger the synchronization process using the Sync button. The syncing process is represented in figure 9.9.

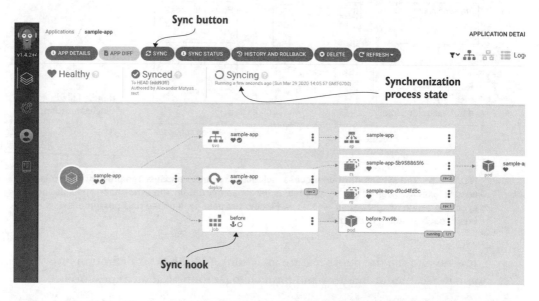

Figure 9.9   The application detail page allows the user to trigger the synchronization as well as view detailed information about the synchronization progress, including synchronization hooks.

As soon as the sync is started, the application details page shows live process status in the top-right corner. The status includes information about operation start time and duration. You can view the syncing status panel with detailed information, including sync hook results, by clicking the Sync Status icon.

The hooks are stored as the regular resource manifests in the Git repository and also visualized as regular resources in the Application resource tree. You can see the real-time status of the "before" job and use the Argo CD user interface to inspect child Pods.

In addition to phases, you might customize the hook deletion policy. The deletion policy allows automating hook resources deletion that will save you a lot of manual work.

Exercise 9.9

Read more details in the Argo CD documentation[6] and change the "before" job deletion policy. Use the Argo CD user interface to observe how various deletion policies affect hook behavior. Synchronize the application and observe how hook resources got created and deleted by Argo CD.

9.3.3 *Postdeployment verification*

Resource hooks allow encapsulating the application synchronization logic, so we don't have to use scripts and continuous integration tools. However, some of such use cases naturally belong to continuous integration processes, and it is still preferable to use tools like Jenkins.

One such use case is postdeployment verification. The challenge here is that GitOps deployment is asynchronous by nature. After the commit is pushed to the Git repository, we still need to make sure that changes are propagated to the Kubernetes cluster. Even after changes are propagated, it is not safe to start running tests. In most cases, the update of a Kubernetes resource is not instant, either. For example, the Deployment resource update triggers the rolling-update process. The rolling update might take several minutes or even fail if the new application version has an issue. So if you start tests too early, you might end up testing the previously deployed application version.

Argo CD makes this issue trivial by providing tools that help to monitor application status. The `argocd app wait` command monitors the application and exits after the application reaches a synced and healthy state. As soon as the command exits, you can assume that all changes are successfully rolled out, and it is safe to start postdeployment verification. The `argocd app wait` command is often used in conjunction with `argocd app sync`. Use the following command to synchronize your application and wait until the change is fully rolled out, and the application is ready for testing:

```
$ argocd app sync sample-app && argocd app wait sample-app
```

9.4 *Enterprise features*

Argo CD is pretty lightweight, and it is really easy to start using it. At the same time, it scales well for a large enterprise and is able to accommodate the needs of multiple teams. The enterprise features can be configured as you go. If you are rolling out an Argo CD for your organization, then the first question is how to configure the end user and effectively manage access control.

---

[6] http://mng.bz/e5Ez.

9.4.1   Single sign-on

Instead of introducing its own user management system, Argo CD provides integration with multiple SSO services. The list includes Okta, Google OAuth, Azure AD, and many more.

> **SSO**   SSO is a session and user authentication service that allows a user to use one set of login credentials to access multiple applications.

The SSO integration is great because it saves you a lot of management overhead, and end users don't have to remember another set of login credentials. There are several open standards for exchanging authentication and authorization data. The most popular ones are SAML, OAuth, and OpenID Connect (OIDC). Of the three, SAML and OIDC satisfy the best requirements of a typical enterprise and can be used to implement SSO. Argo CD decided to go ahead with OIDC because of its power and simplicity.

The number of steps required to configure an OIDC integration depends on your OIDC provider. The Argo CD community already contributed a number of instructions for popular OIDC providers such as Okta and Azure AD. After performing the configuration on the OIDC provider side, you need to add the corresponding configuration to the `argocd-cm` ConfigMap. The following snippet represents the sample Okta configuration:

```
apiVersion: v1
kind: ConfigMap
metadata:
  name: argocd-cm
  namespace: argocd
  labels:
    app.kubernetes.io/name: argocd-cm
    app.kubernetes.io/part-of: argocd
data:
  url: https://<myargocdhost>        ⟵  The externally facing
  oidc.config: |                         base URL Argo CD URL
    name: Okta                        ⟵  OIDC configuration that
    issuer: https://yourorganization.oktapreview.com  includes Okta application
    clientID: <your client id>           client id and secret
    clientSecret: <your client secret>
    requestedScopes: ["openid", "profile", "email", "groups"]
    requestedIDTokenClaims: {"groups": {"essential": true}}
```

What if your organization does not have an OIDC-compatible SSO service? In this case, you can use a federated OIDC provider, Dex,[7] which is bundled into the Argo CD by default. Dex acts as a proxy to other identity providers and allows establishing integration with SAML, LDAP providers, or even services like GitHub and Active Directory.

GitHub often is a very attractive option, especially if it is already used by developers in your organization. Additionally, organizations and teams configured in GitHub nat-

---

[7] https://github.com/dexidp/dex.

urally fit the access control model required to organize cluster access. As you are going to learn soon, it is very easy to model Argo CD access using the GitHub team membership. Let's use GitHub to enhance our Argo CD installation and enable SSO integration.

First of all, we need to create a GitHub OAuth application. Navigate to https://github.com/settings/applications/new and configure the application settings as represented in figure 9.10.

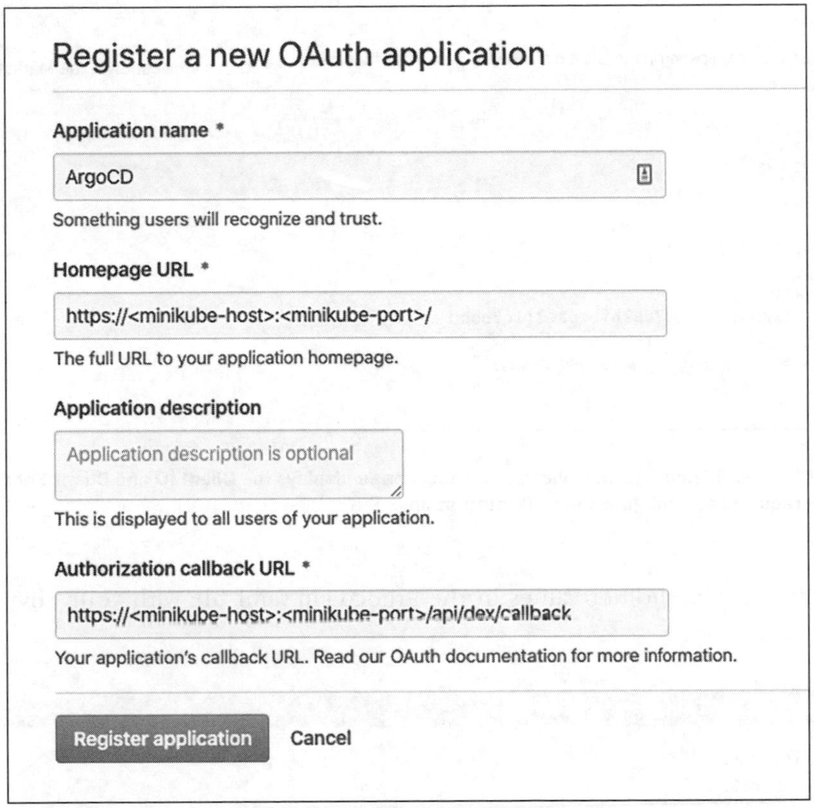

Figure 9.10 New GitHub OAuth application settings include the application name and description, home page URL, and, most importantly, the authorization callback URL.

Specify the application name of your choice and the home page URL that matches the Argo CD web user interface URL. The most important application setting is the callback URL. The callback URL value is the Argo CD web user interface URL plus the /api/dex/callback path. The sample URL with minikube might be http://192.168.64.2:32638/api/dex/callback.

After creating the application, you will be redirected to the OAuth application settings page. Copy the application Client ID and Client Secret. These values will be used to configure the Argo CD settings.

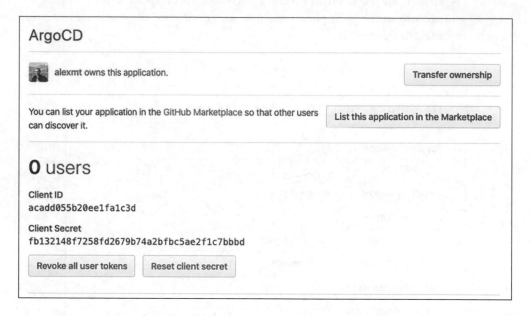

Figure 9.11   The GitHub OAuth application settings page displays the Client ID and Client Secret values, which are required to configure the SSO integration.

Substitute the placeholder values in the argocd-cm.yaml file with your environment values.

Listing 9.2   http://mng.bz/pV1G

```
apiVersion: v1
kind: ConfigMap
metadata:
  name: argocd-cm
  labels:
    app.kubernetes.io/name: argocd-cm
    app.kubernetes.io/part-of: argocd
data:
  url: https://<minikube-host>:<minikube-port>        ⟵  The externally facing
                                                           base URL Argo CD URL
  dex.config: |
    connectors:
    - type: github
      id: github
      name: GitHub
```

```
config:
    clientID: <client-id>           ◁┘  GitHub OAuth
    clientSecret: <client-secret>   ◁┐   application client ID
    loadAllGroups: true               │  GitHub OAuth application
                                         client secret
```

Update the Argo CD ConfigMap using the `kubectl apply` command:

```
$ kubectl apply -f ./argocd-cm.yaml -n argocd
```

You are ready to go! Open the Argo CD user interface in the browser and use the Login Via GitHub button.

9.4.2 Access control

You might notice that after a successful login using GitHub SSO integration, the application list page is empty. If you try creating a new application, you will see a "permission denied" error. This behavior is expected because we have not given any permission to the new SSO user yet. In order to provide the user with appropriate access, we need to update the Argo CD access control settings.

Argo CD provides a flexible role-based access control (RBAC) system whose implementation is based on Casbin,[8] a powerful open source access control library. Casbin provides a very solid foundation and allows configuring various access control rules.

The RBAC Argo CD settings are configured using `argocd-rbac-cm ConfigMap`. To quickly dive into the configuration details, let's update the ConfigMap fields and then go together through each change.

Substitute the `<username>` placeholder with your GitHub account username in the argocd-rbac-cm.yaml file.

> **Listing 9.3 http://mng.bz/OEPn**

```
apiVersion: v1
kind: ConfigMap
metadata:
  name: argocd-rbac-cm
  labels:
    app.kubernetes.io/name: argocd-rbac-cm
    app.kubernetes.io/part-of: argocd
data:
                                            The policy.csv contains
  policy.csv: |                        ◁┘   role-based access rules.
    p, role:developer, applications, *, */*, allow
    g, role:developer, role:readonly

    g, <username>, role:developer        The scopes setting specifies
                                         which JWT claim is used to
  scopes: '[groups, preferred_username]'  ◁┘ infer user groups.
```

---

[8] https://github.com/casbin/casbin.

Apply the RBAC changes using the `kubectl apply` command:

```
$ kubectl apply -f ./argocd-rbac-cm.yaml -n argocd
```

The `policy.csv` field in this configuration defines a role named `role:developer` with full permissions on Argo CD applications and read-only permissions over Argo CD system settings. The role is granted to any user that belongs to a group whose name matches your GitHub account username. As soon as changes are applied, refresh the applications list page and try syncing the `sample-app` application.

We've introduced quite a few new terms. Let's step back and discuss what roles, groups, and claims are and how they work together.

ROLE

The role allows or denies a set of actions on an Argo CD object to a particular subject. The role is defined in the form

```
p, subject, resource, action, object, effect
```

where

- p indicates the RBAC policy line.
- subject is a group.
- resource is one of the Argo CD resource types. Argo CD supports the following resources: `"clusters"`, `"projects"`, `"applications"`, `"repositories"`, `"certificates"`, `"accounts"`.
- action is an action name that might be executed against a resource. All Argo CD resources support the following actions: `"get"`, `"create"`, `"update"`, `"delete"`. The `"*"` value matches any action.
- object is a pattern that identifies a particular resource instance. The `"*"` value matches any instance.
- effect defines whether the role grants or denies the action.

The `role:developer` role from this example allows any action against any Argo CD application:

```
p, role:developer, applications, *, */*, allow
```

GROUP

A group provides the ability to identify a set of users and works in conjunction with OIDC integration. After performing the successful OIDC authentication, the end user receives a JWT token that verifies the user identity as well as provides additional metadata stored in the token claims.

> **JWT TOKEN**   A JWT token is an internet standard for creating JSON-based access tokens that assert some number of claims.[9]

---

[9] https://en.wikipedia.org/wiki/JSON_Web_Token.

The token is supplied with every Argo CD request. The Argo CD extracts the list of groups that a user belongs to from a configured list of token claims and uses it to verify user permissions.

Following is a token claims example generated by Dex:

```
{
  "iss": "https://192.168.64.2:32638/api/dex",
  "sub": "CgY0MjY0MzcSBmdpdGh1Yg",
  "aud": "argo-cd",
  "exp": 1585646367,
  "iat": 1585559967,
  "at_hash": "rAz6dHslBWvU6PiWj_o9g",
  "email": "AMatyushentsev@gmail.com",
  "email_verified": true,
  "groups": [
    "gitopsbook"
  ],
  "name": "Alexander Matyushentsev",
  "preferred_username": "alexmt"
}
```

The token contains two claims that might be useful for authorization:

- `groups` includes a list of GitHub organizations and teams the user belongs to.
- `preferred_username` is the GitHub account username.

By default, Argo CD uses `groups` to retrieve user groups from the JWT token. We've added the `preferred_username` claim using the `scopes` setting to allow identifying GitHub users by name.

Exercise 9.10
Update the `argocd-rbac-cm` ConfigMap to provide admin access to the GitHub user based on their email.

> **NOTE** This chapter covers important foundations of Argo CD and gets you ready for further learning. Explore the Argo CD documentation to learn about diffing logic customization, fine-tuning config management tools, advanced security features such as auth tokens, and much more. The project keeps evolving and getting new features in every release. Check out the Argo CD blog to stay up to date with the changes, and don't hesitate to ask questions in the Argoproj slack channel.

9.4.3 *Declarative management*

As you might've noticed, Argo CD provides a lot of configuration settings. The RBAC policies, SSO settings, Applications, and Projects—all of those are settings that have to be managed by someone. The good news is that you can leverage GitOps and use Argo CD to manage itself!

All Argo CD settings are persisted in Kubernetes resources. The SSO and RBAC settings stored in ConfigMap and Applications and Projects are stored in custom resources, so you can store these resource manifests in a Git repository and configure Argo CD to use it as a source of truth. This technique is very powerful and allows us to manage configuration settings as well as seamlessly upgrade the Argo CD version.

As a first step, let's demonstrate how to convert the SSO and RBAC changes we've just made imperatively into a declarative configuration. To do so we would need to create a Git repository that stores manifest definitions of every Argo CD component. Instead of starting from scratch, you can just use the code listings in the repository at https://github.com/gitopsbook/resources as a starting point. Navigate to the repository GitHub URL and create your personal fork so you can store settings specific to your environment.

The required manifest files are located in the chapter-09 directory, and the first file we should look at is represented in the following listing.

Listing 9.4   http://mng.bz/YqRN

```
apiVersion: kustomize.config.k8s.io/v1beta1          The remote file URL containing
kind: Kustomization                                  default Argo CD manifests
resources:
- https://raw.githubusercontent.com/argoproj/argo-cd/stable/manifests/
     install.yaml

patchesStrategicMerge:      The file path that contains argocd-cm
- argocd-cm.yaml            ConfigMap modifications
- argocd-rbac-cm.yaml
- argocd-server.yaml                 The file path that contains argocd-
                                     rbac-cm ConfigMap modifications

                            The file path that contains argocd-
                            server Service modifications
```

The kustomization.yaml file contains references to the default Argo CD manifests and files with the environment-specific changes.

The next step is to move your environment-specific changes into Git and push them into the remote Git repository. Clone the forked Git repository:

```
$ git clone git@github.com:<USERNAME>/resources.git
```

Repeat the changes to the argocd-cm.yaml and argocd-rbac-cm.yaml files described in sections 9.4.1 and 9.4.2. Add SSO configuration to the ConfigMap manifest in argocd-cm.yaml. Update the RBAC policy in the argocd-rbac-cm.yaml file. Once the files are updated, commit and push the changes back to the remote repository:

```
$ git commit -am  "Update Argo CD configuration"
$ git push
```

The hardest part is done! Argo CD config changes are not version controlled and can be managed using GitOps methodology. The last step is to create an Argo CD application that deploys Kustomize-based manifests from your Git repository into the argocd Namespace:

```
$ argocd app create argocd \
--repo https://github.com/<USERNAME>/resources.git \
--path chapter-09 \
--dest-server https://kubernetes.default.svc \
--dest-namespace argocd \
--sync-policy auto
application 'argocd' created
```

As soon as the application is created, Argo CD should detect already deployed resources and visualize the detected deviations.

So how about managing applications and projects? Both are represented by the Kubernetes custom resource and might be managed using GitOps as well. The manifest in the next listing represents the declarative definition of the `sample-app` Argo CD application that we created manually earlier in the chapter. In order to start managing `sample-app` declaratively, add the sample-app.yaml into the resources section of kustomization.yaml and push the change back to your repository fork.

Listing 9.5   http://mng.bz/Gx9q

```
apiVersion: argoproj.io/v1alpha1
kind: Application
metadata:
  name: sample-app
spec:
  destination:
    namespace: default
    server: https://kubernetes.default.svc
  project: default
  source:
    path: .
    repoURL: https://github.com/<username>/sample-app-deployment
```

As you can see, you don't have to choose between declarative and imperative management styles. Argo CD supports using both simultaneously so that some settings are managed using GitOps and some are managed using imperative commands.

Summary

- Argo CD is designed with enterprises in mind and can be offered as a centralized service to support multitenancy and multiclustering for large enterprises.
- As a continuous deployment tool, Argo CD also provides detail diff among Git, target Kubernetes clusters, and running states for observability.
- Argo CD automates three phases in deployment:
  - Retrieve resource manifests.
  - Detect and fix the deviations.
  - Present the results to end users.
- Argo CD provides CLI for configuring Application deployment and can be incorporated into CI solutions through scripting.

- Argo CD's CLI and web interface can be used to inspect applications' sync and health statuses.
- Argo CD provides resource hooks to enable additional customization of the deployment life cycle.
- Argo CD also provides support to ensure deployment completion and application readiness.
- Argo CD supports both SSO and RBAC integration for enterprise-level SSO and access control.

Jenkins X

This chapter was written with contributions from Viktor Farcic and Oscar Medina.

In this chapter, you will learn how to use Jenkins X to deploy our reference example application to Kubernetes. You will also learn how Prow, Jenkins X pipeline operator, and Tekton work together to build a CI/CD pipeline.

We recommend you read chapters 1, 2, 3, and 5 before reading this chapter.

10.1 What is Jenkins X?

To understand the intricacies and inner workings of Jenkins X, we need to understand Kubernetes. However, we do not need to understand Kubernetes to use Jenkins X. That is one of the main contributions of the project. Jenkins X allows us to harness the power of Kubernetes without spending an eternity learning the ever-growing list of the things Kubernetes does. Jenkins X[1] is an open source tool that simplifies complex processes into concepts that can be adopted quickly and without spending months trying to figure out "the right way to do stuff." It helps by removing and simplifying some of the problems caused by the overall complexity of Kubernetes and its ecosystem. If you are indeed a Kubernetes ninja, you will appreciate all the effort put into Jenkins X. If you're not, you will be able to jump right in and harness the power of Kubernetes without ripping your hair out in frustration caused by Kubernetes complexity. In section 10.2, we will discuss Jenkins X patterns and tools in detail.

> **NOTE** Jenkins X is a free, open source tool with enterprise support offered by CloudBees.[2]

Today, most software vendors arc building their next generation of software to be Kubernetes-native or, at least, to work better inside it. A whole ecosystem is emerging and treating Kubernetes as a blank canvas. As a result, new tools are being added on a daily basis, and it is becoming evident that Kubernetes offers near-limitless possibilities. However, with that comes increased complexity. It is harder than ever to choose which tools to use. How are we going to develop our applications? How are we going to manage different environments? How are we going to package our applications? Which process are we going to apply for application life cycles? And so on and so forth. Assembling a Kubernetes cluster with all the tools and processes takes time, and learning how to use what we assembled feels like a never-ending story. Jenkins X aims to remove those and other obstacles.

Jenkins X is opinionated. It defines many aspects of the software development life cycle, and it makes decisions for us. It tells us what to do and how. It is like a tour guide on your vacation who shows you where to go, what to look at, when to take a photo, and when it's time to take a break. At the same time, it is flexible and allows power users to tweak it to fit their own needs.

The real power behind Jenkins X is the process, the selection of tools, and the glue that wraps everything into one cohesive unit that is easy to learn and use. We (people working in the software industry) tend to reinvent the wheel all the time. We spend countless hours trying to figure out how to develop our applications faster and how to have a local environment that is as close to production as possible. We dedicate time searching for tools that will allow us to package and deploy our applications more efficiently. We design the steps that form a continuous delivery pipeline. We write scripts that automate repetitive tasks. And yet, we cannot escape the feeling that we are likely reinventing things that were already done by others. Jenkins X is designed to help us with those decisions, and it helps us to pick the right tools for a job. It is a collection of the industry's best practices. In some cases, Jenkins X is the one defining those practices, while in others, it helps us in adopting those defined by others.

---

[1] https://jenkins-x.io/.
[2] https://www.cloudbees.com/.

If we are about to start working on a new project, Jenkins X will create the structure and the required files. If we need a Kubernetes cluster with all the tools selected, installed, and configured, Jenkins X will do that. If we need to create Git repositories, set webhooks,[3] and create continuous delivery pipelines, all we need to do is execute a single `jx` command. The list of what Jenkins X does is vast, and it grows every day.

> **JENKINS VS. JENKINS X** If you are familiar with Jenkins, you need to clear your mind of any Jenkins experience you might already have. Sure, Jenkins is there, but it is only a part of the package. Jenkins X is very different from the "traditional Jenkins." The differences are so massive that the only way for you to embrace it is to forget what you know about Jenkins and start from scratch.

10.2 *Exploring Prow, Jenkins X pipeline operator, and Tekton*

The serverless flavor of Jenkins X or, as some call it, Jenkins X Next Generation, is an attempt to redefine how we do continuous delivery and GitOps inside Kubernetes clusters. It does that by combining quite a few tools into a single easy-to-use bundle. As a result, most people will not need to understand the intricacies of how the pieces work independently or how they are all integrated. Instead, many will merely push a change to Git and let the system do the rest. But, there are always those who would like to know what's happening under the hood. To satisfy those craving for insight, we'll explore the processes and components involved in the serverless Jenkins X platform. Understanding the flow of an event initiated by a Git webhook will give us insight into how the solution works and help us later when we go deeper into each of the new components.

Everything starts with a push to a Git repository, which, in turn, sends a webhook request to the cluster. Where things differ from a traditional Jenkins setup is that there is no Jenkins to accept those requests. Instead, we have Prow.[4] It does quite a few things, but, in the context of webhooks, its job is to receive requests and decide what to do next. Those requests are not limited to only push events, but also include slash commands (such as `/approve`) we can specify through pull request comments.

Prow consists of a few distinct components (deck, hook, crier, tide, and more). However, we won't go into the roles of each of them. For now, the vital thing to note is that Prow is the entry point to the cluster. It receives Git requests generated either by Git actions (such as push) or through slash commands in comments.

Prow might do quite a few things upon receiving a request. If the request comes from a command from a Git comment, it might rerun tests, merge a pull request, assign a person, or one of the many other Git-related actions. If a webhook informs it that a new push was made, it will send a request to the Jenkins X pipeline operator

---

[3] https://developer.github.com/webhooks/.
[4] https://github.com/kubernetes/test-infra/tree/master/prow.

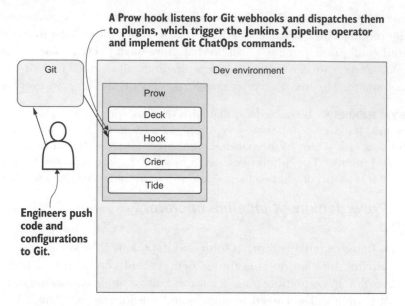

A Prow hook listens for Git webhooks and dispatches them to plugins, which trigger the Jenkins X pipeline operator and implement Git ChatOps commands.

Figure 10.1   Engineers push code and configurations to Git. A Prow hook listens for Git webhooks and dispatches them to plugins.

that will make sure that a build corresponding to a defined pipeline is run. Finally, Prow also reports the status of a build back to Git.

Those features are not the only types of actions Prow might perform but, for now, you've probably got the general gist. Prow is in charge of communication between Git and the processes inside our cluster.

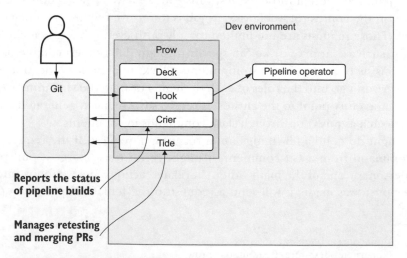

Figure 10.2   When a Prow hook receives a request from a Git webhook, it forwards it to Jenkins X pipeline operator.

The role of the operator is to fetch the jenkins-x.yml file from the repository that initiated the process and to transform it into Tekton tasks and pipelines. They, in turn, define the complete pipeline that should be executed as a result of pushing a change to Git.

TEKTON　Tekton is a Kubernetes-native open source framework CI/CD systems.[5]

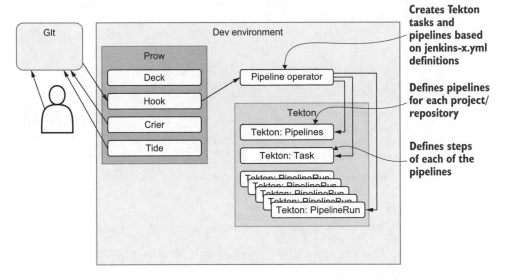

Figure 10.3　The pipeline operator simplifies definitions of our continuous delivery processes, and Tekton does the heavy lifting to define pipelines for each project/repository.

Tekton is a very low-level solution and is not meant to be used directly. Writing Tekton definitions can be quite painful and complicated. The pipeline operator simplifies that through easy-to-learn and -use YAML format for defining pipelines. Listing 10.1 is an example of what the base pipeline will provide.

NOTE　As you will discover in section 10.3, the pipeline file for your project will be called jenkins-x.yml, which includes the single line "`buildPack: go`" to reference the following pipeline file. If you'd like to learn more about how pipelines work, please refer to the Jenkins X documentation.[6]

Listing 10.1　http://mng.bz/zx0a

```
extends:
  import: classic
  file: go/pipeline.yaml
```

[5] https://cloud.google.com/tekton.
[6] https://jenkins-x.io/docs/reference/components/build-packs/.

```
pipelines:
  pullRequest:
    build:
      steps:
      - sh: export VERSION=$PREVIEW_VERSION && skaffold build -f
    skaffold.yaml
        name: container-build
    postBuild:
      steps:
      - sh: jx step post build --image $DOCKER_REGISTRY/$ORG/
    $APP_NAME:$PREVIEW_VERSION
        name: post-build
    promote:
      steps:
      - dir: /home/jenkins/go/src/REPLACE_ME_GIT_PROVIDER/REPLACE_ME_ORG/
    REPLACE_ME_APP_NAME/charts/preview
        steps:
        - sh: make preview
          name: make-preview
        - sh: jx preview --app $APP_NAME --dir ../..
          name: jx-preview

  release:
    build:
      steps:
      - sh: export VERSION=`cat VERSION` && skaffold build -f skaffold.yaml
        name: container-build
      - sh: jx step post build --image $DOCKER_REGISTRY/$ORG/$APP_NAME:\$(cat
    VERSION)
        name: post-build
    promote:
      steps:
      - dir: /home/jenkins/go/src/REPLACE_ME_GIT_PROVIDER/REPLACE_ME_ORG/
    REPLACE_ME_APP_NAME/charts/REPLACE_ME_APP_NAME
        steps:
        - sh: jx step changelog --version v\$(cat ../../VERSION)
          name: changelog
        - comment: release the helm chart
          name: helm-release
          sh: jx step helm release
        - comment: promote through all 'Auto' promotion Environments
          sh: jx promote -b --all-auto --timeout 1h --version \$(cat ../../
    VERSION)
          name: jx-promote
```

Tekton creates a `PipelineRun` for each build initiated by each push to one of the associated branches (master branch, PRs). It performs all the steps we need to validate a push. It runs tests, stores binaries in registries (Docker registry, Nexus, and ChartMuseum), and deploys a release to a temporary (PR) or a permanent Stage or Prod environment.

The complete flow can be seen in figure 10.4.

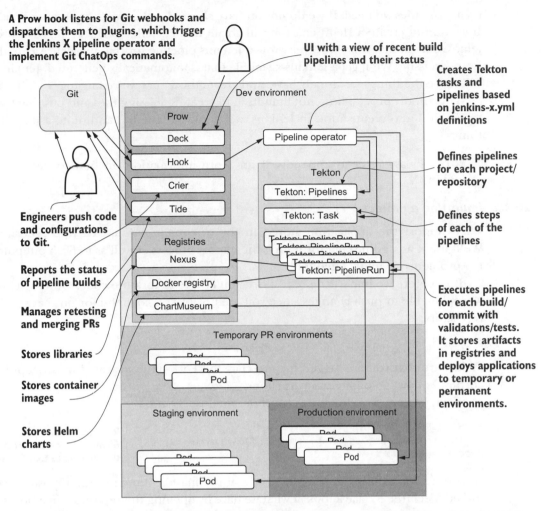

A Prow hook listens for Git webhooks and dispatches them to plugins, which trigger the Jenkins X pipeline operator and implement Git ChatOps commands.

UI with a view of recent build pipelines and their status

Creates Tekton tasks and pipelines based on jenkins-x.yml definitions

Defines pipelines for each project/ repository

Defines steps of each of the pipelines

Engineers push code and configurations to Git.

Reports the status of pipeline builds

Manages retesting and merging PRs

Stores libraries

Stores container images

Stores Helm charts

Executes pipelines for each build/ commit with validations/tests. It stores artifacts in registries and deploys applications to temporary or permanent environments.

Figure 10.4   The complete flow of events starts from PR, webhook in Prow, pipeline operator, to Tekton. Jenkins X will execute pipelines for each build/commit and deploy applications.

Exercise 10.1
Which component will receive the Git webhook request? Which component will orchestrate the deployment?

10.3   *Importing projects into Jenkins X*

You can see how we can fast-track the development and continuous delivery of new applications with Jenkins X quick starts. However, it is likely that your company was not formed yesterday. That means that you already have some apps, and hopefully, you'd like to move them to Jenkins X.

From a Jenkins X perspective, importing an existing project is relatively straightforward. All we have to do is execute jx import, and Jenkins X will do its magic. It will create the files we need. If we do not yet have skaffold.yml, it will be generated for us. If we do not create a Helm chart, it will create that as well. No Dockerfile? No problem. We'll get that as well. Never wrote a Jenkins pipeline for that project? Again, that is not an issue. We'll get a jenkins-x.yml file that is automatically generated. Jenkins X will reuse the things we already have, and create those that we're missing.

The import process does not limit itself to creating missing files and pushing them to Git. It'll also create a job in Jenkins, webhooks in GitHub, and quite a few other things.

> **NOTE**   Please refer to appendix B for more information on how to install Jenkins X.

10.3.1 *Importing a project*

We'll import the application stored in the `gitopsbook/sample-app` repository. We'll use it as a guinea pig for testing the import process as well as to flesh out potential problems we might encounter.

But, before we import the repository, you'll have to fork the code. Otherwise, you won't be able to push changes since you are not (yet) a collaborator on that specific repository:

```
$ open "https://github.com/gitopsbook/sample-app"
```

Make sure that you are logged in, and click the Fork button located in the top-right corner. Follow the onscreen instructions.

Next, you need to clone the repository you just forked:

```
$ GH_USER=[...]
$ git clone https://github.com/$GH_USER/sample-app.git
$ cd sample-app
```

Replace [...] with your GitHub user before executing the commands that follow.

Now you should have the intended code in the master branch of the repository you forked. Feel free to take a look at what we have by opening the repository in a browser. Fortunately, there is a `jx` command that does just that:

```
$ jx repo --batch-mode
```

Let's quickly explore the files of the project, before we import it into Jenkins X:

```
$ ls -1
Dockerfile
Makefile
README.md
main.go
```

As you can see, there's (almost) nothing in that repository but Go[7] code (*.go).

That project is one extreme of the possible spectrum of projects we might want to import to Jenkins X. It only has the code of the application. There is a `Dockerfile`.

---

[7] https://golang.org/.

However, there is no Helm chart or even a script for building a binary, nor is there a mechanism to run tests, and there is definitely no jenkins-x.yml file that defines a continuous delivery pipeline for the application. There's only code, and (almost) nothing else.

Such a situation might not be your case. Maybe you do have scripts for running tests or building the code. Or perhaps you are already a heavy Kubernetes user, and you do have a Helm chart. You might have other files as well. We'll discuss those situations later. For now, we'll work on the case when there is nothing but the code of an application.

Let's see what happens when we try to import that repository into Jenkins X:

```
$ jx import
intuitdep954b9:sample-app byuen$ jx import
WARNING: No username defined for the current Git server!
? github.com username: billyy                          ←——| GitHub
                                                           username
To be able to create a repository on github.com we need an API Token
Please click this URL and generate a token              ←——| Generates a
https://github.com/settings/tokens/new?scopes=repo,        new token
    read:user,read:org,user:email,write:repo_hook,delete_repo


Then COPY the token and enter it below:

? API Token: *****************************************
performing pack detection in folder /Users/byuen/git/sample-app
--> Draft detected Go (48.306595%)
selected pack: /Users/byuen/.jx/draft/packs/github.com/jenkins-x-buildpacks/
    jenkins-x-kubernetes/packs/go
replacing placeholders in directory /Users/byuen/git/sample-app
app name: sample-app, git server: github.com, org: billyy, Docker registry
    org: hazel-charter-283301
skipping directory "/Users/byuen/git/sample-app/.git"     Default "No"
Draft pack go added                                       for preview
? Would you like to define a different preview Namespace? No  ←—— Namespace
Pushed Git repository to https://github.com/billyy/sample-app.git
Creating GitHub webhook for billyy/sample-app for url http://hook-
    jx.34.74.32.142.nip.io/hook
Created pull request: https://github.com/billyy/environment-cluster-1-dev/
    pull/1
Added label updatebot to pull request https://github.com/billyy/environment-
    cluster-1-dev/pull/1
created pull request https://github.com/billyy/environment-cluster-1-dev/
    pull/1 on the development git repository https://github.com/billyy/
    environment-cluster-1-dev.git
regenerated Prow configuration
PipelineActivity for billyy-sample-app-master-1
upserted PipelineResource meta-billyy-sample-app-master-cdxm7 for the git
    repository https://github.com/billyy/sample-app.git
upserted Task meta-billyy-sample-app-master-cdxm7-meta-pipeline-1
upserted Pipeline meta-billyy-sample-app-master-cdxm7-1
created PipelineRun meta-billyy-sample-app-master-cdxm7-1
created PipelineStructure meta-billyy-sample-app-master-cdxm7-1


Watch pipeline activity via:    jx get activity -f sample-app -w
Browse the pipeline log via:    jx get build logs billyy/sample-app/master
```

```
You can list the pipelines via: jx get pipelines
When the pipeline is complete:  jx get applications

For more help on available commands see: https://jenkins-x.io/developing/
    browsing/

Note that your first pipeline may take a few minutes to start while the
    necessary images get downloaded!
```

We can see from the output that Jenkins X detected that the project is 100% written in Go, so it selected the Go build pack. It applied the build pack to the local repository and pushed the changes to GitHub. Furthermore, it created a Jenkins project as well as a GitHub webhook that will trigger builds whenever we push changes to one of the selected branches. Those branches are by default master, develop, PR-.*, and feature.*. We could have changed the pattern by adding the --branches flag. But, for our purposes, and many others, those branches are just what we need.

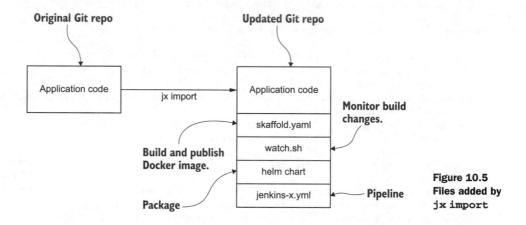

Figure 10.5
Files added by
`jx import`

Now let's take another look at the files in the local copy of the repository:

```
$ ls -1
Dockerfile
Makefile
OWNERS
OWNERS_ALIASES
README.md
charts
jenkins-x.yml
main.go
skaffold.yaml
watch.sh
```

We can see that quite a few new files were added to the project through the import process. We have a Dockerfile that will be used to build container images, and we have a jenkins-x.yml that defines all the steps of our pipeline.

We also got a Makefile that defines targets to build, test, and install the application. There is also the charts directory that contains files in Helm format for packaging, installing, and upgrading our application. We also got watch.sh, which monitors build changes and invokes skaffold.yaml. skaffold.yaml contains the instruction to build and publish the container images. There are a few other new files (ex: OWNERS) added to the mix.

Now that the project is in Jenkins X, we should see it as one of the activities and observe the first build in action. You already know that we can limit the retrieval of Jenkins X activities to a specific project and that we can use `--watch` to watch the progress.

> **NOTE** Wait until the `jx promote` and `PullRequest` complete before proceeding to the rest of the tutorial. If the process takes more than 60 minutes, the pull request will show a "Failed" status. If you check GitHub, the PR will still merge after `jx promote` completes.

```
$ jx get activities --filter sample-app --watch
STEP                                                      STARTED AGO DURATION
    STATUS
billyy/sample-app/master #1                               11h31m0s   1h4m20s
    Succeeded Version: 0.0.1
 meta pipeline                                            1h25m2s      31s
    Succeeded
    Credential Initializer                                1h25m2s       0s
    Succeeded
    Working Dir Initializer                               1h25m2s       1s
    Succeeded
    Place Tools                                           1h25m1s       1s
    Succeeded
    Git Source Meta Billyy Sample App Master R Xnfl4 Vrvtm 1h25m0s      8s
    Succeeded https://github.com/billyy/sample-app.git
    Setup Builder Home                                    1h24m52s      0s
    Succeeded
    Git Merge                                             1h24m52s      1s
    Succeeded
    Merge Pull Refs                                       1h24m51s      1s
    Succeeded
    Create Effective Pipeline                            1h24m50s       7s
    Succeeded
    Create Tekton Crds                                    1h24m43s      12s
    Succeeded
 from build pack                                          1h23m49s  1h13m39s
    Succeeded
    Credential Initializer                                1h23m49s      2s
    Succeeded
    Working Dir Initializer                               1h23m47s      2s
    Succeeded
    Place Tools                                           1h23m45s      4s
    Succeeded
    Git Source Billyy Sample App Master Releas 658x6 Nzdbp 1h23m41s    21s
    Succeeded https://github.com/billyy/sample-app.git
    Setup Builder Home                                    1h23m20s      2s
    Succeeded
```

```
      Git Merge                                          1h23m18s      11s
        Succeeded
      Setup Jx Git Credentials                           1h23m7s       12s
        Succeeded
      Build Make Build                                   1h22m55s      1s
        Succeeded
      Build Container Build                              1h22m54s      11m56s
        Succeeded
      Build Post Build                                   1h10m58s      4s
        Succeeded
      Promote Changelog                                  1h10m54s      6s
        Succeeded
      Promote Helm Release                               1h10m48s      8s
        Succeeded
      Promote Jx Promote                                 1h10m40s      1h0m30s
        Succeeded
    Promote: staging                                     1h10m31s
      Running
      PullRequest                                        1h10m31s  1h0m21s Failed
        PullRequest: https://github.com/billyy/environment-cluster-1-staging/pull/1
```

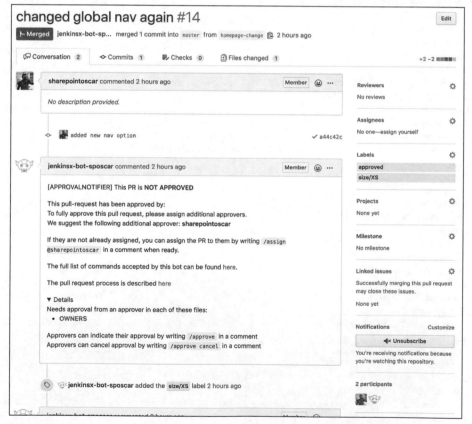

Figure 10.6   Jenkins X will generate a pull request to add a new version of our app. This is GitOps at work!

The pipeline activities give you a lot of detail on the pipeline stages and steps. However, one of the most important details is the PR that gets merged into the staging environment. This tells Jenkins X to add that new version of our app into the env/requirements.yaml file. This is GitOps at work!

So far, Jenkins X created the files it needs, it created a GitHub webhook, it created a pipeline, and it pushed changes to GitHub. As a result, we got our first build, and by the look of it, it was successful. But let's double-check that everything is OK.

Open the PullRequest link on your browser by clicking on the link from the activity output, as shown in Figure 10.5.

So far, so good. The `sample-app` job created a pull request to the environment-cluster-1-staging repository. As a result, the webhook from that repository should have initiated a pipeline activity, and the result should be a new release of the application in the staging environment. We won't go through that part of the process just yet. For now, just note that the application should be running, and we'll check that soon.

The information we need to confirm that the application is indeed running is in the list of the applications running in the staging environment. We'll explore the environments later. For now, just run the command that follows:

```
$ jx get applications
APPLICATION STAGING PODS URL
sample-app  0.0.1        http://sample-app-jx-staging.34.74.32.142.nip.io
```

We can see the address through which our application should be accessible in the URL column. Copy it and use it instead of [...] in the command that follows:

```
$ STAGING_ADDR=[...]                    ◁─┐ Staging
$ curl "$STAGING_ADDR/demo/hello"          │ URL address
Kubernetes ♡ Golang!
```

The output shows Kubernetes ♡ Golang!, thus confirming that the application is up and running and that we can reach it.

Before we proceed, we'll go out of the sample-app directory. We have reached the final stage, at least from the application life cycle point of view.

> **NOTE** For a complete application life cycle reference, please refer to figure 4.6 in chapter 4 (pipelines).

Actually, we skipped creating a pull request, which happens to be one of the most important features of Jenkins X. Nevertheless, we do not have enough space to cover all Jenkins X features, so we'll leave PRs and others for you to discover on your own (PR can be found from output of the `jx get activities` command). For now, we'll focus on the final stage of the application life cycle by exploring promotions to production. We've already covered the following:

1 We saw how to import an existing project and how to create a new one.
2 We saw how to develop build packs that will simplify those processes for the types of applications that are not covered with the existing build packs or for those that deviate from them.

3 Once we added our app to Jenkins X, we explored how it implements GitOps processes through environments (such as staging and production).

4 Then we moved into the application development phase and explored how DevPods help us to set a personal application-specific environment that simplifies the "traditional" setup that forced us to spend countless hours setting it on our laptop and, at the same time, avoids the pitfalls of shared development environments.

5 Once the development of a feature, a change, or a bug fix is finished, we created a pull request, we executed automatic validations, and we deployed the release candidate to a PR-specific preview environment so that we can check it manually as well. Once we were satisfied with the changes we made, we merged it to the master branch, and that resulted in deployment to the environments set to receive automatic promotions (such as staging) as well as in another round of testing. Now that we are comfortable with the changes we did, all that's left is to promote our release to production.

The critical thing to note is that promotion to production is not a technical decision. By the time we reach this last step in the software development life cycle, we should already know that the release is working as expected. We already gathered all the information we need to make a decision to go live. Therefore, the choice is business-related. "When do we want our users to see the new release?" We know that every release that passes all the steps of the pipeline is production-ready, but we do not know when to release it to our users. But, before we discuss when to release something to production, we should decide who does that. The actor will determine when is the right time. Does a person approve a pull request, or is it a machine?

Business, marketing, and management might be decision-makers in charge of promotion to production. In that case, we cannot initiate the process when the code is merged to the master branch (as with the staging environment), and that means that we need a mechanism to start the process manually through a command. If executing a command is too complicated and confusing, it should be trivial to add a button (we'll explore that through the UI later). There can also be the case when no one makes a decision to promote something to production. Instead, we can promote each change to the master branch automatically. In both cases, the command that initiates the promotion is the same. The only difference is in the actor that executes it. Is it us (humans) or Jenkins X (machines)?

At the moment, our production environment is set to receive manual promotions. As such, we are employing continuous delivery that has the whole pipeline fully automated and requires a single manual action to promote a release to production. All that's left is to click a button or, as is our case, to execute a single command. We could have added the step to promote production to `Jenkinsfile`, and in that case, we'd be practicing continuous deployment (not delivery). That would result in a deployment of every merge or push to the master branch. But, we aren't practicing continuous deployment today, and we'll stick with the current setup and jump into the last stage of continuous delivery. We'll promote our latest release to production.

10.3.2 *Promoting a release to the production environment*

Now that we feel that our new release is production-ready, we can promote it to production. But, before we do that, we'll check whether we already have something running in production:

```
$ jx get applications --env production
APPLICATION
sample-app
```

How about staging? We must have the release of our `sample-app` application running there. Let's double-check:

```
$ jx get applications --env staging
APPLICATION STAGING PODS URL
sample-app  0.0.1   1/1  http://sample-app-jx-staging.34.74.32.142.nip.io
```

For what we're trying to do, the important piece of the information is the version displayed in the `STAGING` column.

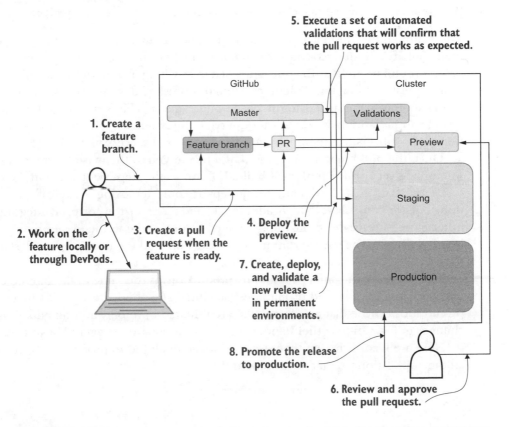

Figure 10.7 The `jx promote` command will create a new branch in the production environment as well as deploy to preview. At the end of the command execution, the new release will be promoted to production.

Now we can promote the specific version of `sample-app` to the production environment:

```
$ VERSION=[...]
$ jx promote sample-app --version $VERSION --env production --batch-mode
```

Before executing the command that follows, make sure to replace [...] with the version from the STAGING column from the output of the previous command.

It'll take a minute or two until the promotion process is finished. You can use the following command again to monitor the status:

```
$ jx get activities
...
Promote: production                                     4m3s    1m36s  Succeeded
    PullRequest                                         4m3s    1m34s  Succeeded
    PullRequest: https://github.com/billyy/environment-cluster-1-production/pull/2
     Merge SHA: 33b48c58b3332d3abc2b0c4dcaba8d7ddc33c4b3
    Update                                              2m29s      2s  Succeeded
    Promoted                                            2m29s      2s  Succeeded
    Application is at: http://sample-app-jx-production.34.74.32.142.nip.io
```

The command we just executed will create a new branch in the production environment (environment-pisco-sour-production). Further on, it'll follow the same practice based on pull requests as the one employed in anything else we did so far. It'll create a pull request and wait until a Jenkins X build is finished and successful. You might see errors stating that it failed to query the pull request. That's normal. The process is asynchronous, and `jx` is periodically querying the system until it receives the information that confirms that the pull request was processed successfully.

Once the pull request is processed, it'll be merged to the master branch, and that will initiate yet another Jenkins X build. It'll run all the steps we defined in the repository's `Jenkinsfile`. By default, those steps are only deploying the release to production, but we could have added additional validations in the form of integration or other types of tests. Once the build initiated by the merge to the master branch is finished, we'll have the release running in production, and the final output will state that merge status checks all passed, so the promotion worked!

The process of manual promotion (production) is the same as the one we experienced through automated promotions (staging). The only difference is who executes promotions. Those that are automated are initiated by application pipelines pushing changes to Git. On the other hand, manual promotions are triggered by us (humans).

Next, we'll confirm that the release is indeed deployed to production by retrieving all the applications in that environment:

```
$ jx get applications --env production
APPLICATION PRODUCTION PODS URL
sample-app  0.0.1                   http://sample-app-jx-production.35.185.219.24.nip.io
```

In our case, the output states that there is only one application (`sample-app`) running in production and that the version is 0.0.1.

To be on the safe side, we'll send a request to the release of our application running in production:

```
$ PROD_ADDR=[...]
$ curl "$PROD_ADDR/demo/hello"
Kubernetes ♡ Golang!
```

◁─┐ **Before executing the commands that follow, make sure to replace [...] with the URL column from the output of the previous command.**

Summary

- Jenkins X defines the process, the selection of tools, and the glue that wraps everything into one cohesive unit that is easy to learn and use.
- Prow provides GitHub automation in the form of policy enforcement and automatic PR merging.
- The pipeline operator is used to orchestrate and simplify definitions of our continuous delivery processes.
- Tekton is a Kubernetes-native open source framework for creating continuous integration and delivery (CI/CD) systems.
- To import projects into Jenkins X, you just need to execute `jx import` which will add all the necessary files to your repo and create the pipelines and environments.
- To promote release into production environments, you can simply execute the `jx promote` command, which will generate PR to add the new release, deploy to preview for testing, and promote (deploy) to production.

11

Flux

In this chapter, you will learn how to use the Flux GitOps operator to deploy our reference example application to Kubernetes. You will also learn how Flux can be used as part of a multitenancy solution.

We recommend you read chapters 1, 2, 3, and 5 before reading this chapter.

11.1 What is Flux?

Flux is an open source project that implements GitOps-driven continuous deployment for Kubernetes. The project was started in 2016 at Weaveworks[1] and joined the CNCF Sandbox three years later.

---

[1] https://www.weave.works/.

284

Notably, Weaveworks is the same company that coined the term *GitOps*. Along with other great open source projects for Kubernetes, the company formulated GitOps best practices and contributed a lot to GitOps evangelizing. The Flux evolution illustrates how the idea of GitOps evolved over time, based on practical experience, into its current form.

The Flux project was created to automate container image delivery to Kubernetes and fill the gap between the continuous integration and continuous deployment processes. The workflow described in the project introduction blog is focused on Docker registry scanning, calculating the latest image version, and promoting it to the production cluster. After several iterations, the Flux team realized all the benefits of a Git-centric approach. Before publishing the v1.0 release, the project architecture was reworked to use Git as the source of truth and formulated the main phases of the GitOps workflow.

11.1.1 What Flux does

Flux is laser focused on automated manifest delivery to the Kubernetes cluster. The project is probably the least opinionated GitOps operation of the operators described in this book. Flux does not introduce any additional layers on top of Kubernetes, such as applications or its own access control system. A single Flux instance manages one Kubernetes cluster and requires the user to maintain one Git repository that represents the cluster state. Instead of introducing user management, SSO integration, and its own access control, Flux typically runs inside of the managed cluster and relies on Kubernetes RBAC. This approach significantly simplifies the Flux configuration and helps flatten the learning curve.

> **RBAC** Kubernetes supports role-based access control (RBAC), which allows containers to be bound to roles that give them permission to operate on various resources.

The simplicity of Flux also makes it virtually maintenance free and simple to integrate into cluster bootstrapping since no new component or admin privilege is required. With the Flux command-line interface, Flux deployment can be easily incorporated into the cluster provisioning scripts to enable automated cluster creation.

Flux is not limited to only cluster bootstrapping. It is successfully used as a continuous deployment tool for applications. In the multitenant environment, each team can install an instance of Flux with limited access and use it to manage a single Namespace. That fully empowers the team to manage resources in the application Namespace and is still 100% secure because Flux access is managed by Kubernetes RBAC.

The simplicity of the project brings advantages and disadvantages that are viewed differently by different teams. One of the most important considerations is that Flux has to be configured and maintained by the Kubernetes end user. That implies that the team gets more power but also has more responsibility. The alternate approach, which is taken by Argo CD, is to provide GitOps functions as a service.

11.1.2 *Docker registry scanning*

In addition to the core functionality of GitOps, the project offers one more notable feature. Flux is able to scan the Docker registry and automatically update images in the deployment repository when new tags get pushed into the registry. Although this functionality is not a core GitOps feature, it simplifies the lives of developers and increases productivity. Let's consider the developer workflow without automated deployment repository updates.

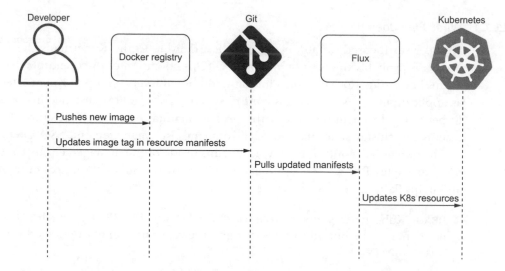

Figure 11.1   A Developer pushes new images manually using continuous integration tools, and then updates the deployment Git repository with a new image's tag. Flux notices the manifest change in Git and propagates it to the Kubernetes cluster.

Developer teams often complain about the second step, because it requires manual work, and they try to automate it. Typically the solution is to automate manifest updates using the CI pipeline. The CI approach solves the problem but requires scripting and might be fragile.

Flux goes one step beyond and automates the deployment repository updates. Instead of using the CI system and scripting, you can configure Flux to automatically update the deployment repository every time a new image is pushed to the Docker registry. The developer's workflow with automated Docker registry scanning is represented in figure 11.2.

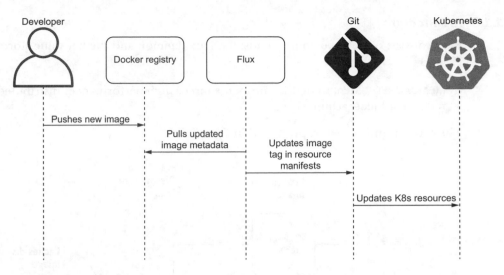

Figure 11.2 When automated repository updates are enabled, Flux takes full control over both the deployment repository and Kubernetes cluster management.

The developer's only responsibility is to make a code change and let the CI system push the updated Docker image into the registry. The automated deployment repository management is especially useful if the image tags follow semantic versioning convention.

SEMANTIC VERSIONING Semantic versioning[2] is a formal convention for specifying compatibility using a three-part version number: major version, minor version, and patch.

Flux allows configuring the image tag filter that leverages the semantic version convention. The typical use case is to automate minor and patch releases that are supposed to be safe and backward compatible and manually deploy major releases.

The obvious benefit of the Docker registry scanning feature, compared to using the continuous integration pipeline, is that you don't have to spend time to implement the repository update step in your pipeline. The convenience, however, comes with more responsibility. Incorporating a deployment repository update into the continuous integration pipeline gives full control and allows us to run more tests after an image is pushed to the Docker registry. If Flux Docker registry scanning is enabled, you have to make sure that the image is well tested before pushing it to the Docker registry to avoid accidentally deploying to production.

Exercise 11.1
Consider the advantages and disadvantages of the Docker registry monitoring feature and try to decide if it is suitable for your team.

---

[2] https://semver.org/.

11.1.3 *Architecture*

Flux consists of only two components: the Flux daemon and the key-value store Memcached.[3]

> **MEMCACHED**   Memcached is an open source, high-performance, distributed memory object-caching system.

The Flux architecture is represented in figure 11.3.

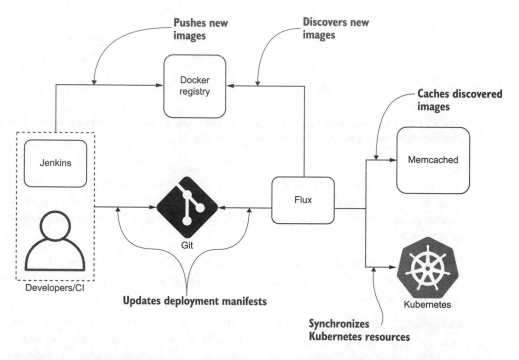

Figure 11.3   The Flux daemon is the main component responsible for the majority of Flux features. It clones the Git repository, generates manifests, propagates changes to the Kubernetes cluster, and scans to the Docker registry.

There must be only one replica of the Flux daemon running at any time. This is not an issue, however, because even if the daemon crashes in the middle of a deployment, it restarts quickly and idempotently resumes the deployment process.

The main purpose of Memcached is to support Docker registry scanning. Flux uses it to store a list of available image versions of each Docker image. The Memcached deployment is an optional component and not required unless you want to use the Docker registry scanning feature. To remove it, just use the `--registry-disable-scanning` flag during the installation step.

---

[3] https://memcached.org/.

Exercise 11.2

Which component logs should you check to troubleshoot deployment issues?

11.2 Simple application deployment

We've learned a lot about Flux already, and now it is time to see it in action. First of all, we need to get it running. The Flux installation consists of two steps: installing the Flux CLI and configuring the demon in your cluster. Use appendix B to learn how to install `fluxctl` and get ready to deploy your first application.

11.2.1 Deploying the first application

The `fluxctl` and `minikube` applications are the only two components required to start managing Kubernetes resources with Flux. The next step is to prepare the Git repository with the Kubernetes manifests. The manifests for our sample application are available at the following link:

https://github.com/gitopsbook/sample-app-deployment

Go ahead and create a repository fork[4] as the first step. Flux requires write permissions to the deployment repository to automatically update image tags in the manifests.

> **RESET YOUR FORK** Have you already forked the deployment repository while working on previous chapters? Make sure to revert changes for the best experience. The simplest way is to delete the previously forked repository and fork it again.

Use `fluxctl` to install and configure the Flux daemon:

```
$ kubectl create ns flux
$ export GHUSER="YOURUSER"
$ fluxctl install \
--git-user=${GHUSER} \
--git-email=${GHUSER}@users.noreply.github.com \
--git-url=git@github.com:${GHUSER}/sample-app-deployment.git \
--git-path=. \
--namespace=flux | kubectl apply -f -
```

This command creates the Flux daemon and configures it to deploy manifests from your Git repository. Make sure the Flux daemon is running using the following command:

```
$ kubectl rollout status deploy flux -n flux
```

As part of this tutorial, we are going to try an automated repository update feature, so we need to give the Flux repository write access. The convenient and secure way to provide write access to the GitHub repository is to use the deploy key.

---

[4] https://help.github.com/en/github/getting-started-with-github/fork-a-repo.

DEPLOY KEY   A deploy key is an SSH key that is stored on your server and grants access to a single GitHub repository.

There is no need to generate the new SSH key manually. Flux generates a key during the first start and uses it to access the deployment repository. Run the following command to get the generated SSH key:

```
$ fluxctl identity --k8s-fwd-ns flux
```

Navigate to https://github.com/<username>/sample-app-deployment/settings/keys /new, and use the output of the `fluxctl` identity command to create a new deployment key. Make sure to check the "Allow write access" check box to provide write access to the repository.

The configuration is done! While you are reading this, Flux should be cloning the repository and deploying manifests. Go ahead and check the Flux daemon logs to confirm that.

Can you see `kubectl apply` in the logs?

```
$ kubectl logs deploy/flux -n flux -f
caller=sync.go:73 component=daemon info="trying to sync git changes to the
    cluster" old=6df71c4af912e2fc6f5fec5d911ac6ad0cd4529a
    new=1c51492fb70d9bdd2381ff2f4f4dc51240dfe118
caller=sync.go:539 method=Sync cmd=apply args= count=2
caller=sync.go:605 method=Sync cmd="kubectl apply -f -" took=1.224619981s
    err=null output="service/sample-app configured\ndeployment.apps/sample-
    app configured"
caller=daemon.go:701 component=daemon event="Sync: 1c51492, default:service/
    sample-app" logupstream=false
```

Great, that means Flux successfully performed the deployment. Next, run the following command to confirm that the sample app deployment resource has been created:

```
$ kubectl get deploy sample-app -n default
```

Congratulations! You successfully deployed your first application using Flux.

11.2.2 *Observing application state*

Reading the logs of the Flux daemon is not the only way to get information about resources managed by Flux. The `fluxctl` CLI provides a set of commands that allow us to get detailed information about cluster resources. The first one we should try is `fluxctl list-workloads`. The command prints information about all Kubernetes resources that manage Pods in the cluster. Run the following command to output information about the `sample-app` deployment:

```
$ fluxctl list-workloads --k8s-fwd-ns flux
WORKLOAD                CONTAINER    IMAGE                         RELEASE
deployment/sample-app   sample-app   gitopsbook/sample-app:v0.1    ready
```

As you can see from the output, Flux is managing one deployment that creates a
`sample-app` container using the `v0.1` version of the `gitopsbook/sample-app`
image.

In addition to the information about the current image, Flux has scanned the
Docker registry and collected all available image tags. Run the following command to
print the list of discovered image tags:

```
$ fluxctl list-images --k8s-fwd-ns flux -w default:deployment/sample-app
WORKLOAD                CONTAINER  IMAGE                  CREATED
deployment/sample-app   sample-app gitopsbook/sample-app
                                          |   v0.2    27 Jan 20 05:46 UTC
                                          '-> v0.1    27 Jan 20 05:35 UTC
```

From the command output, we can see that Flux correctly discovered both available
image versions. In addition, Flux identified `v0.2` as a newer version and is ready to
upgrade our deployment if we configure automated upgrades. Let's go ahead and do so.

11.2.3 Upgrading the deployment image

By default, Flux does not upgrade the resource image version unless the resource has
the `fluxcd.io/automated: 'true'` annotation. This annotation tells Flux that the
resource image is managed automatically, and the image should be upgraded as soon
as a new version is pushed to the Docker registry. The following listing contains the
`sample-app` Deployment manifest with the applied annotation.

Listing 11.1 deployment.yaml

```
apiVersion: apps/v1
kind: Deployment
metadata:
  name: sample-app
  annotations:
    fluxcd.io/automated: 'true'        <- Annotation that enables
spec:                                     automated management
  replicas: 1
  revisionHistoryLimit: 3
  selector:
    matchLabels:
      app: sample-app
  template:
    metadata:
      labels:
        app: sample-app
    spec:
      containers:
      - command:
        - /app/sample-app
        image: gitopsbook/sample-app:v0.1   <- The deployment
        name: sample-app                        image tag
        ports:
        - containerPort: 8080
```

One way to add the annotation is to manually edit the deployment.yaml file and commit it to the deployment repository. During the next reconciliation cycle, Flux should detect the annotation and enable automated management. `fluxctl` provides convenience commands, `automate` and `deautomate`, which can add or remove the annotation for you. Run the following command to automate the `sample-app` deployment management:

```
$ fluxctl automate --k8s-fwd-ns flux -w default:deployment/sample-app
WORKLOAD                           STATUS   UPDATES
default:deployment/sample-app  success
Commit pushed:      <commit-sha>
```

The command updates the manifest and pushes the change into the Git repository. If you check the repository history using GitHub, you will see two commits where the first commit updates the deployment annotation and the second updates the image version.

Finally, let's verify the deployment status using the `fluxctl list-workloads` command:

```
$ fluxctl list-workloads --k8s-fwd-ns flux
WORKLOAD                     CONTAINER    IMAGE                          RELEASE
deployment/sample-app   sample-app   gitopsbook/sample-app:v0.2   ready
```

The deployment image has been successfully updated to use the `v0.2` version of the `gitopsbook/sample-app` image. Don't forget to pull the changes executed by Flux into the local Git repository:

```
$ git pull
```

11.2.4 *Using Kustomize for manifest generation*

Managing plain YAML files in the deployment repository is not a very difficult task but is also not very practical in real life. As we've learned in previous chapters, it is common practice to maintain the base set of manifests for the application and generate environment-specified manifests using tools like Kustomize or Helm. Integration with config management tools solves that problem, and Flux enables that feature using generators. Let's learn what generators are and how to use them.

Instead of providing first-class support for the selected set of config management tools, Flux provides the ability to configure the manifest generation process and integrate with any config management tool. The generator is a command that invokes the config management tool inside the Flux daemon that produces the final YAML. Generators are configured in the file named .flux.yaml stored in the deployment manifest repository.

Let's dive deep into the feature and learn configuration details on a real example. First of all, we need to enable manifest generation in our Flux deployment. This is done using the `--manifest-generation` CLI flag of the Flux daemon. Run the following command to inject the flag into the Flux deployment using the JSON patch:

```
kubectl patch deploy flux --type json -n flux -p \
'[{ "op": "add", "path": "/spec/template/spec/containers/0/args/-", "value":
    "--manifest-generation"}]'
```

JSON PATCH JSON Patch[5] is a format for describing changes to a JSON document. The patch document is a sequential list of operations that are applied to JSON objects, allowing changes such as adding, removing, and replacing.

As soon as the Flux configuration is updated, it is time to introduce Kustomize into our deployment repository and start leveraging it. Add the kustomization.yaml file using the following code.

Listing 11.2 kustomization.yaml

```
apiVersion: kustomize.config.k8s.io/v1beta1
kind: Kustomization

resources:            ◁─┐ List of manifests including
- deployment.yaml       │ resource manifests
- service.yaml

                              Transformer that
images:                   ◁─┐ changes image tag
- name: gitopsbook/sample-app
  newTag: v0.1
```

The next step is to configure a generator that uses Kustomize. Add the following .flux.yaml file to the `sample-app-deployment` repository:

Listing 11.3 flux.yaml

```
version: 1              │ List of
patchUpdated:          ◁─┘ generators       Generator command that leverages
  generators:                            ◁─┘ Kustomize to generate manifests
  - command: kustomize build .       ◁─┘
    patchFile: flux-patch.yaml  ◁─┐ Name of the file that stores manifest
                                   modifications; required for
                                   automated image updates
```

The configuration is done. Go ahead and push the changes to the deployment repository:

```
$ git add -A
$ git commit -am "Introduce kustomize" && git push
```

Let's take a look at .flux.yaml one more time and learn what was configured in detail. The generators section configures Flux to use Kustomize for manifest generation. You can run the exact same command locally to verify that Kustomize is producing the expected YAML manifests.

---

[5] http://jsonpatch.com/.

But what is the `patchFile` property? This is an updater configuration. To demonstrate how it works, lets trigger the Flux release using the following commands:

```
$ kubectl patch deploy sample-app -p '[{ "op": "add", "path": "/spec/
    template/spec/containers/0/image", "value": "gitopsbook/sample-
    app:v0.1"}]' --type json -n default

$ fluxctl sync --k8s-fwd-ns flux
```

We've downgraded the `sample-app` deployment back to the `v0.1` version and asked Flux to fix it. The `sync` command starts the reconciliation loop, which, once completed, should update the image tag and push changes back to the Git repository. Since manifests are now generated using Kustomize, Flux no longer knows which file to update. The `patchFile` property specifies the file path within the deployment repository where image tag updates must be stored. The file contains the JSON merge patch that is automatically applied to the generator output.

> **JSON MERGE PATCH**   The JSON merge patch is a JSON document that describes changes to be made to a target JSON and contains the nodes of the target document, which should be different after the patch is applied.

The generated merge patch includes managed resource image changes. During the synchronization process, Flux generates and pushes the file with a merge patch to the Git repository and applies it on the fly to the generated YAML manifests.

Don't forget to pull the changes executed by Flux into the local Git repository:

```
$ git pull
```

11.2.5 *Securing deployment using GPG*

Flux is a very practical tool and focuses on real-life use cases. The deployment changes verification is one such case. As we've learned in chapter 6, commits in the deployment repository should be signed and validated using a GPG key to ensure the author identity of the commit, preventing unauthorized changes being pushed to the cluster.

The typical approach is to incorporate the GPG validation into the continuous integration pipeline. Flux provides this integration out of the box, which saves time and provides a more robust implementation. The best way to learn how that feature operates is to try it.

First of all, we need a valid GPG key that can be used to sign and verify Git commits. If you've completed the chapter 6 tutorials, then you already have a GPG key and can sign commits. Otherwise, use the steps described in appendix C to create the GPC key. After configuring the GPG key, we need to make it available to Flux and enable commit verification.

To verify the commit, Flux needs to have access to which GPG key we trust. The key can be configured using a ConfigMap. Use the following command to create the ConfigMap and store your public key in it:

```
$ kubectl create configmap flux-gpg-public-keys -n flux --from-
    literal=author.asc="$(gpg --export --armor <ID>)"
```

The next step is to update the Flux deployment to enable commit verification. Update the username in the flux-deployment-patch.yaml file represented in the following listing.

Listing 11.4   flux-deployment-patch.yaml

```
spec:
  template:
    spec:
      volumes:
      - name: gpg-public-keys                    Kubernetes Volume that uses
        configMap:                               ConfigMap as a data source
          name: flux-gpg-public-keys
          defaultMode: 0400
      containers:
      - name: flux                         Volume mount that stores ConfigMap
        volumeMounts:                      keys in /root/gpg-public-keys directory
        - name: gpg-public-keys
          mountPath: /root/gpg-public-keys
          readOnly: true
        args:
        - --memcached-service=
        - --ssh-keygen-dir=/var/fluxd/keygen
        - --git-url=git@github.com:<USERNAME>/sample-app-deployment.git
        - --git-branch=master
        - --git-path=.
        - --git-label=flux
        - --git-email=<USERNAME>@users.noreply.github.com
        - --manifest-generation=true
        - --listen-metrics=:3031
        - --git-gpg-key-import=/root/gpg-public-keys    The --git-verify-signatures arg
        - --git-verify-signatures                       enables commit verification.
        - --git-verify-signatures-mode=first-parent     The --git-verify-signatures
                                                        -modes=first-parent arg
  The --git-gpg-key-import                              allows having unsigned
  arg specifies the location of                         commits in repo history.
  trusted GPG keys.
```

Apply the Flux deployment modifications using the following command:

```
$ kubectl patch deploy flux -n flux -p "$(cat ./flux-deployment-patch.yaml)"
```

Commit verification is now enabled. To prove it is working, try triggering sync using the `fluxctl sync` command:

```
$ fluxctl sync --k8s-fwd-ns flux
Synchronizing with ssh://git@github.com/<USERNAME>/sample-app-deployment.git
Failed to complete sync job
Error: verifying tag flux: no signature found, full output:
 error: no signature found

Run 'fluxctl sync --help' for usage.
```

The command fails as expected, since the most recent commit in the deployment repository is not signed. Let's go ahead and fix it. First create an empty signed Git commit using this command, and sync again:

```
$ git commit --allow-empty -S -m "verified commit"
$ git push
```

The next step is to sign the sync tag maintained by Flux:

```
$ git tag --force --local-user=<GPG-KEY_ID> -a -m "Sync pointer" flux HEAD
$ git push --tags --force
```

The repository is successfully synced. Finally, use the `fluxctl sync` command to confirm that verification is configured correctly:

```
fluxctl sync --k8s-fwd-ns flux
Synchronizing with ssh://git@github.com/<USERNAME>/sample-app-deployment.git
Revision of master to apply is f20ac6e
Waiting for f20ac6e to be applied ...
Done.
```

11.3   *Multitenancy with Flux*

Flux is a powerful and flexible tool but does not have features that are built specifically for multitenancy. So the question is, can we use it in a large organization with multiple teams? The answer is definitely yes. Flux embraces the "Git PUSH all" philosophy and relies on GitOps to manage multiple Flux instances deployed in a multitenant cluster.

With a multitenant cluster, cluster users have only limited Namespace access and cannot create new Namespaces or any other cluster-level resources. Each team owns their own Namespace resources and performs operations on them independently of each other. In this case, it does not make sense to force everyone to use a single Git repository and rely on the infrastructure team to review every configuration change. On the other hand, the infrastructure team is responsible for overall cluster health and needs tools to manage cluster services. The application teams can still rely on Flux to manage the Application resource. The infrastructure team uses Flux to provision Namespaces as well as multiple Flux instances configured with the proper Namespace-level access. Figure 11.4 demonstrates the idea.

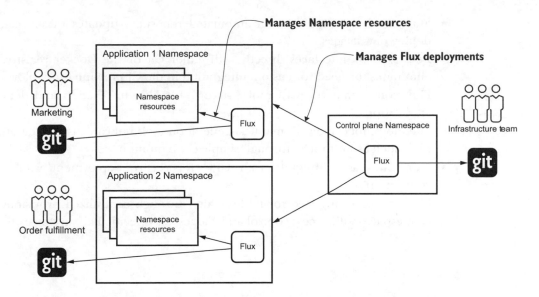

Figure 11.4 The cluster has one "control plane" Namespace and a centralized cluster Git repository managed by the infrastructure team. The centralized repository contains manifests that represent centralized Flux deployment and team-specific Namespaces and Flux configurations.

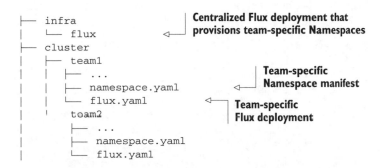

The application team can onboard themselves by creating the pull request to the centralized repository and adding the Namespace and Flux manifests. As soon as the pull request is merged, the central Flux creates the Namespace and provision-team-specific Flux, ensuring the correct RBAC settings.

The team-specific Flux instance is configured to pull manifests from the separate Git repository that is managed by the application team. That means the application team is fully independent and doesn't have to involve the infrastructure team to update resources within their Namespace.

Summary

- Flux is simple to install and maintain because Flux does not require new components and uses Kubernetes RBAC for access control.

- Flux can be configured with automated repository updates to automatically deploy new images.
- Because Flux interfaces directly with either Git or the Docker registry, Flux eliminates the need for custom integration in the CI pipeline for deployment.
- Flux comes with the CLI tool `fluxctl` for Flux installation and deploying applications.
- Flux does not come with manifest-generation tools but can easily integrate with tools such as Kustomize through simple configuration.
- Flux can easily integrate with GPG for secure deployment with simple configuration.
- Flux can be configured for multitenancy through centralized provisioning of Namespaces with access control and Namespace-specific Flux instances.

appendix A
Setting up a test
Kubernetes cluster

A full production-capable Kubernetes cluster is a very complex system consisting of multiple components that must be installed and configured based on your particular needs. How to deploy and maintain Kubernetes in production goes way beyond the focus of this book and is covered elsewhere.

Luckily for us, there are several projects that handle the configuration complexity and allow running Kubernetes locally with a single CLI command. Running Kubernetes locally on your laptop is useful to get your hands dirty with Kubernetes and prepare you for completing the exercises in this book. To the extent possible, all the exercises will utilize a cluster running on your laptop using an application called minikube. However, if you prefer to use your own cluster running on a cloud provider (or even on premises), the exercises will work there as well.

> **MINIKUBE** Minikube is an official tool maintained by the Kubernetes community to create a single-node Kubernetes cluster inside a VM on your laptop. It supports macOS, Linux, and Windows. In addition to actually running the cluster, minikube provides features that simplify accessing services inside Kubernetes, volume management, and much more.

Other projects you can consider using are

- *Docker for desktop*—If you are using Docker on your laptop, you might already have Kubernetes installed! Starting with version 18.6.0, both Windows and Docker Desktop for Mac come with bundled Kubernetes binaries and developer productivity features.
- *K3s*—As the name implies, K3s is a lightweight Kubernetes deployment. According to its authors, K3s is five less than eight, so K8s minus five is K3s.

Besides the funny name, K3s is indeed extremely lightweight, fast, and a great choice if you need to run Kubernetes as part of a CI job or on hardware with limited resources. Installation instructions are available at https://k3s.io.

- *Kind*—Another tool developed by the Kubernetes community, kind was developed by maintainers for Kubernetes v1.11+ conformance testing. Installation instructions are available at https://kind.sigs.k8s.io/.

While these tools simplify Kubernetes deployment to a single CLI command and provide great experience, minikube is still the safest choice to get started with Kubernetes. With all-platforms support, thanks to virtualization, and a great set of developer productivity features, this is a great tool for both beginners and experts. All exercises and samples in this book rely on minikube.

A.1   Prerequisites for working with Kubernetes

The following tools and utilities are needed to work with Kubernetes.

In addition to Kubernetes itself, you need to install kubectl. Kubectl is a command-line utility that allows interacting with the Kubernetes control plane and doing virtually anything with Kubernetes.

A.1.1   Configure kubectl

To get started, go ahead and install minikube as described at https://kubernetes.io/docs/tasks/tools/install-kubectl/. If you are a macOS or Linux user, you can complete the installation process in one step using the Homebrew package manager along with the following command:

```
$ brew install kubectl
```

> **HOMEBREW**   Homebrew is a free and open source software package management system that simplifies the installation of software on Apple's macOS operating system and Linux. More information is available at https://brew.sh/.

A.2   Installing minikube and creating a cluster

Minikube is an application that allows you to run a single-node Kubernetes cluster on your desktop or laptop machine. Installation instructions are available at https://kubernetes.io/docs/tasks/tools/install-minikube/.

Most (but not all) exercises in this book can be completed using a local minikube cluster.

A.2.1   Configuring minikube

The next step is to install and start the minikube cluster. The installation process is described at https://minikube.sigs.k8s.io/docs/start/. The minikube package is also available via Homebrew:

```
$ brew install minikube
```

If everything goes smoothly so far, we are ready to start minikube and configure our first deployment:

```
$ minikube start
minikube/default)
😊   minikube v1.1.1 on darwin (amd64)
🔥   Creating virtualbox VM (CPUs=2, Memory=2048MB, Disk=20000MB) ...
📦   Configuring environment for Kubernetes v1.14.3 on Docker 18.09.6
🐳   Pulling images ...
🚀   Launching Kubernetes ...
⌛   Verifying: apiserver proxy etcd scheduler controller dns
🏄   Done! kubectl is now configured to use "minikube"
```

A.3   Creating a GKE cluster in GCP

The Google Cloud Platform (GCP) offers the Google Kubernetes Engine (GKE) as part of its free tier:

https://cloud.google.com/free/

You can create a Kubernetes GKE cluster to run the exercises in this book:

https://cloud.google.com/kubernetes-engine/

Keep in mind that while GKE itself is free, you may be charged for other GCP resources that are created by Kubernetes. It is recommended that you delete your test cluster after completing each exercise in order to avoid unexpected costs.

A.4   Creating an EKS cluster in AWS

Amazon Web Services (AWS) offers a managed Kubernetes service called Elastic Kubernetes Service (EKS). You can create a free AWS account and create an EKS cluster to run the exercises in this book. However, while relatively inexpensive, EKS is not a free service (it costs $0.20/hour at the time of this writing) and you may also be charged for other resources created by Kubernetes. It is recommended that you delete your test cluster after completing each exercise in order to avoid unexpected costs.

There is a tool called `eksctl` by Weaveworks that allows you to easily create an EKS Kubernetes cluster in your AWS account:

https://github.com/weaveworks/eksctl/blob/master/README.md

appendix B
Setting up GitOps tools

This appendix will go over step-by-step instructions to set up the tools required for the tutorials in part 3.

B.1 Installing Argo CD

Argo CD supports several installation methods. You might use the official Kustomize-based installation, the community-maintained Helm chart,[1] or even the Argo CD operator[2] to manage your Argo CD deployments. The simplest possible installation method requires using only a single YAML file. Go ahead and use the following commands to install Argo CD into your minikube cluster:

```
$ kubectl create namespace argocd
$ kubectl apply -n argocd -f https://raw.githubusercontent.com/argoproj/
    argo-cd/stable/manifests/install.yaml
```

This command installs all Argo CD components with the default settings that work for most users out of the box. For security reasons, the Argo CD UI and API are not exposed outside of the cluster by default. It is totally safe to open full access on minikube.

Enable load balancer access[3] in your minikube cluster by running the following command in a separate terminal:

```
$ minikube tunnel
```

Use the following command to open access to the `argocd-server` service and get the access URL:

```
$ kubectl patch svc argocd-server -n argocd -p '{"spec": {"type":
    "LoadBalancer"}}'
```

---

[1] https://github.com/argoproj/argo-helm/tree/master/charts/argo-cd.
[2] https://github.com/argoproj-labs/argocd-operator.
[3] https://minikube.sigs.k8s.io/docs/handbook/accessing/#loadbalancer-access.

Argo CD provides both a web-based user interface and a command-line interface (CLI). To simplify the instructions, we are going to use the CLI tool in this tutorial. Let's go ahead and install the CLI tool. You might use the following command to install Argo CD CLI on Mac or follow the official getting-started instructions[4] to install the CLI on your platform:

```
$ brew tap argoproj/tap
$ brew install argoproj/tap/argocd
```

As soon as Argo CD is installed, it has a preconfigured admin user. The initial admin password is autogenerated to be the Pod name of the Argo CD API server that can be retrieved using this command:

```
$ kubectl get pods -n argocd -l app.kubernetes.io/name=argocd-server -o name |
    cut -d'/' -f 2
```

Use the following command to get the Argo CD server URL and update the generated password using the Argo CD CLI:

```
$ argocd login <ARGOCD_SERVER-HOSTNAME>:<PORT>
$ argocd account update-password
```

The <ARGOCD_SERVER-HOSTNAME>:<PORT> is a minikube API and service port that should be obtained from the Argo CD URL. The URL might be retrieved using the following command:

```
minikube service argocd-server -n argocd --url
```

The command returns the HTTP service URL. Make sure to remove http:// and use only the hostname and the port to log in using the Argo CD CLI.

Finally, log in to the Argo CD user interface. Please open the Argo CD URL in the browser and log in using the admin username and your password. You are ready to go!

B.2 Installing Jenkins X

The Jenkins X CLI depends on kubectl[5] and Helm[6] and will do its best to install those tools. However, the number of possible permutations of what we have on our laptops is close to infinite, so you're better off installing those tools yourself.

> **NOTE** At the time of this writing, February 2021, Jenkins X does not yet support Helm v3+. Make sure that you're using Helm CLI v2+.

---

[4] https://argoproj.github.io/argo-cd/cli_installation/#download-with-curl.
[5] https://kubernetes.io/docs/tasks/tools/install-kubectl/.
[6] https://docs.helm.sh/using_helm/#installing-helm.

B.2.1   *Prerequisites*

You can use (almost) any Kubernetes cluster, but it needs to be publicly accessible. The main reason for that lies in GitHub triggers. Jenkins X relies heavily on GitOps principles. Most of the events will be triggered by GitHub webhooks. If your cluster cannot be accessed from GitHub, you won't be able to trigger those events, and you will have difficulty following the examples.

Now, that poses two significant issues. You might prefer to practice locally using minikube or Docker for Desktop, but neither of the two is accessible from outside your laptop. You might have a corporate cluster that is inaccessible from the outside world. In those cases, we suggest you use a service from AWS, GCP, or somewhere else. Finally, we'll perform some GitHub operations using the command hub. Install it if you don't have it already.

> **NOTE** Please refer to appendix A for more information on configuring AWS or a GCP Kubernetes cluster.

For your convenience, the list of all the tools we'll use is as follows:

- Git
- kubectl
- Helm[7]
- AWS CLI
- eksctl[8] (if using AWS EKS)
- gcloud (if using Google GKE)
- hub[9]

Now let's install the Jenkins X CLI:

```
$ brew tap jenkins-x/jx
$ brew install jx
```

B.2.2   *Installing Jenkins X in a Kubernetes cluster*

How can we install Jenkins X in a better way than how we're used to installing software? Jenkins X configuration should be defined as code and reside in a Git repository, and that's what the community created for us. It maintains a GitHub repository that contains the structure of the definition of the Jenkins X platform, together with a pipeline that will install it, as well as a requirements file that we can use to tweak it to our specific needs.

> **NOTE** You can also refer to the Jenkins X site[10] for setting up Jenkins X in your Kubernetes cluster.

---

[7] https://docs.helm.sh/using_helm/#installing-helm.
[8] https://github.com/weaveworks/eksctl.
[9] https://hub.github.com/.
[10] https://jenkins-x.io/docs/.

Let's take a look at the repository:

```
$ open "https://github.com/jenkins-x/jenkins-x-boot-config.git"
```

Once you see the repo in your browser, you will first create a fork under your GitHub account. We'll explore the files in the repo a bit later.

Next, we'll define a variable `CLUSTER_NAME` that will, as you can guess, hold the name of the cluster we created a short while ago. In the commands that follow, please replace the first occurrence of [. . .] with the name of the cluster and the second with your GitHub user:

```
$ export CLUSTER_NAME=[...]
$ export GH_USER=[...]
```

After we fork the boot repo and we know how our cluster is called, we can clone the repository with a proper name that will reflect the naming scheme of our soon-to-be-installed Jenkins X:

```
$ git clone \
    https://github.com/$GH_USER/jenkins-x-boot-config.git \
    environment-$CLUSTER_NAME-dev
```

The key file that contains (almost) all the parameters that can be used to customize the setup is jx-requirements.yml. Let's take a look at it:

```
$ cd environment-$CLUSTER_NAME-dev
$ cat jx-requirements.yml
cluster:
  clusterName: ""
  environmentGitOwner: ""
  project: ""
  provider: gke
  zone: ""
gitops: true
environments:
- key: dev
- key: staging
- key: production
ingress:
  domain: ""
  externalDNS: false
  tls:
    email: ""
    enabled: false
    production: false
kaniko: true
secretStorage: local
storage:
  logs:
    enabled: false
    url: ""
  reports:
    enabled: false
```

```
    url: ""
  repository:
    enabled: false
    url: ""
versionStream:
  ref: "master"
  url: https://github.com/jenkins-x/jenkins-x-versions.git
webhook: prow
```

As you can see, that file contains values in a format that resembles the requirements.yaml file used with Helm charts. It is split into a few sections.

First, there is a group of values that define our cluster. You should be able to figure out what it represents by looking at the variables inside it. It probably won't take you more than a few moments to see that we have to change at least some of those values, so that's what we'll do next.

Open jx-requirements.yml in your favorite editor and change the following values:

- Set `cluster.clusterName` to the name of your cluster. It should be the same as the name of the environment variable `CLUSTER_NAME`. If you already forgot it, execute `echo $CLUSTER_NAME`.
- Set `cluster.environmentGitOwner` to your GitHub user. It should be the same as the one we previously declared as the environment variable `$GH_USER`.
- Set `cluster.project` to the name of your GKE project, only if that's where your Kubernetes cluster is running. Otherwise, leave that value intact (empty).
- Set `cluster.provider` to `gke` or to `eks` or to any other provider if you decided that you are brave and want to try currently unsupported platforms. Or things may have changed since the writing of this chapter, and your provider is indeed supported now.
- Set `cluster.zone` to whichever zone your cluster is running in. If you're running a regional cluster (as you should), then the value should be the region, not the zone. If, for example, you used our Gist to create a GKE cluster, the value should be `us-east1-b`. Similarly, the one for EKS is `us-east-1`.

We're finished with the `cluster` section, and the next in line is the `gitops` value. It instructs the system how to treat the boot process. It doesn't make sense to change it to false, so we'll leave it as is (true).

The next section contains the list of the environments that we're already familiar with. The keys are the suffixes, and the final names will be a combination of `environment-` with the name of the cluster followed by the key. We'll leave them intact.

The `ingress` section defines the parameters related to external access to the cluster (domain, TLS, and so on).

The `kaniko` value should be self-explanatory. When set to `true`, the system will build container images using `kaniko` instead of, let's say, Docker. That is a much better choice since Docker cannot run in a container and, as such, poses a significant security risk (mounted sockets are evil), and it messes with the Kubernetes scheduler given that it bypasses its API. In any case, `kaniko` is the only supported way to build container images when using Tekton, so we'll leave it as is (true).

Next, we have `secretStorage` currently set to `local`. The whole platform will be defined in this repository, except for Secrets (such as passwords). Pushing them to Git would be childish, so Jenkins X can store the Secrets in different locations. If you changed it to `local`, that location is your laptop. While that is better than a Git repository, you can probably imagine why that is not the right solution. Keeping Secrets locally complicates cooperation (they exist only on your laptop), is volatile, and is only slightly more secure than Git. A much better place for Secrets is HashiCorp Vault. It is the most commonly used solution for Secret management in Kubernetes (and beyond), and Jenkins X supports it out of the box. If you have a vault setup, you can set the value of `secretStorage` to `vault`. Otherwise, you can leave the default value `local`.

Below the `secretStorage` value is the whole section that defines storage for logs, reports, and repositories. If enabled, those artifacts will be stored on a network drive. As you already know, containers and nodes are short lived, and if we want to preserve any of those, we need to store them elsewhere. That does not necessarily mean that network drives are the best place, but rather that's what comes out of the box. Later on, you might choose to change that and, let's say, ship logs to a central database like Elasticsearch, Papertrail, Cloudwatch, Stackdriver, and so on.

For now, we'll keep it simple and enable network storage for all three types of artifacts:

- Set the value of `storage.logs.enabled` to `true`.
- Set the value of `storage.reports.enabled` to `true`.
- Set the value of `storage.repository.enabled` to `true`.

The `versionStream` section defines the repository that contains versions of all the packages (charts) used by Jenkins X. You might choose to fork that repository and control versions yourself. Before you jump into doing just that, please note that Jenkins X versioning is quite complex, given that many packages are involved. Leave it be unless you have a very good reason to take over control of the Jenkins X versioning and you're ready to maintain it.

As you already know, Prow only supports GitHub. If that's not your Git provider, Prow is a no-go. As an alternative, you could set it up in Jenkins, but that's not the right solution either. Jenkins (without X) is not going to be supported for long, given that the future is in Tekton. It was used in the first generation of Jenkins X only because it was a good starting point and because it supports almost anything we can imagine. But the community has embraced Tekton as the only pipeline engine, and that means that static Jenkins is fading away and that it is used mostly as a transition solution for those accustomed to the "traditional" Jenkins.

So, what can you do if Prow is not a choice if you do not use GitHub, and Jenkins' days are numbered? To make things more complicated, even Prow will be deprecated sometime in the future (or past, depending when you read this). It will be replaced with Lighthouse, which, at least at the beginning, will provide similar functionality as

Prow. Its primary advantage when compared with Prow is that Lighthouse will (or already does) support all major Git providers (such as GitHub, GitHub Enterprise, Bitbucket Server, Bitbucket Cloud, GitLab, and so on). At some moment, the default value of webhook will be `lighthouse`. But, at the time of this writing (February 2021), that's not the case since Lighthouse is not yet stable and production ready. It will be soon. In any case, we'll keep Prow as our webhook (for now).

Only execute the following commands if you are using EKS. They will add additional information related to Vault, namely, the IAM user that has sufficient permissions to interact with it. Make sure to replace `[...]` with your IAM user that has sufficient permissions (being admin always works):

```
$ export IAM_USER=[...] # such as jx-boot
echo "vault:
  aws:
    autoCreate: true
    iamUserName: \"$IAM_USER\"" \
    | tee -a jx-requirements.yml
```

Only execute the following commands if you are using EKS. The jx-requirements.yaml file contains a zone entry, and for AWS we need a region. This command will replace one with the other:

```
$ cat jx-requirements.yml \
    | sed -e \
    's@zone@region@g' \
    | tee jx-requirements.yml
```

Let's take a peek at how jx-requirements.yml looks now:

```
$ cat jx-requirements.yml
cluster:
  clusterName: "jx-boot"
  environmentGitOwner: "vfarcic"
  project: "devops-26"
  provider: gke
  zone: "us-east1"
gitops: true
environments:
- key: dev
- key: staging
- key: production
ingress:
  domain: ""
  externalDNS: false
  tls:
    email: ""
  enabled: false
    production: false
kaniko: true
secretStorage: vault
storage:
  logs:
```

```
      enabled: true
      url: ""
  reports:
      enabled: true
      url: ""
  repository:
      enabled: true
      url: ""
versionStream:
  ref: "master"
  url: https://github.com/jenkins-x/jenkins-x-versions.git
webhook: prow
```

Now, you might be worried that we missed some of the values. For example, we did not specify a domain. Does that mean that our cluster will not be accessible from outside? We also did not specify the URL for storage. Will Jenkins X ignore it in that case?

The truth is that we specified only the things we know. For example, if you created a cluster using our Gist, there is no Ingress, so there is no external load balancer that it was supposed to create. As a result, we do not yet know the IP through which we can access the cluster, and we cannot generate a .nip.io domain. Similarly, we did not create storage. If we did, we could have entered addresses into URL fields.

Those are only a few examples of the unknowns. We specified what we know, and we'll let Jenkins X boot figure out the unknowns. Or, to be more precise, we'll let boot create the resources that are missing and thus convert the unknowns into knowns.

Let's install Jenkins X:

```
$ jx boot
```

Now we need to answer quite a few questions. In the past, we tried to avoid answering questions by specifying all answers as arguments to commands we were executing. That way, we had a documented method for doing things that do not end up in a Git repository. Someone else could reproduce what we did by running the same commands. This time, however, there is no need to avoid questions since everything we'll do will be stored in a Git repository.

The first input is asking for a comma-separated list of Git provider usernames of approvers for the Development environment repository. That will create the list of users who can approve pull requests to the Development repository managed by Jenkins X boot. For now, type your GitHub user and hit the Enter key.

We can see that, after a while, we are presented with two warnings stating that TLS is not enabled for Vault and webhooks. If we specified a "real" domain, boot would install Let's Encrypt and generate certificates. But, since we couldn't be sure that you have a domain at hand, we did not specify it, and, as a result, we will not get certificates. While that would be unacceptable in production, it is quite OK as an exercise.

As a result of those warnings, boot is asking us whether we wish to continue. Type y and press the Enter key to continue.

Given that Jenkins X creates multiple releases a day, the chances are that you do not have the latest version of jx. If that's the case, boot will ask if you would like to upgrade to the jx version. Press the Enter key to use the default answer, Y. As a result, boot will upgrade the CLI, but that will abort the pipeline. That's OK. No harm done. All we have to do is repeat the process but, this time, with the latest version of jx:

```
$ jx boot
```

The process starts again. We'll skip commenting on the first few questions from jx boot and continue without TLS. The answers are the same as before (y in both cases).

The next set of questions is related to long-term storage for logs, reports, and repositories. Press the Enter key for all three questions, and boot will create buckets with autogenerated unique names.

From now on, the process will create the Secrets and install CRDs (CustomResourceDefinitions) that provide custom resources specific to Jenkins X. Then, it'll install the NGINX Ingress Controller (unless your cluster already has one) and set the domain to .nip.io since we did not specify one. Further on, it will install cert-manager, which will provide Let's Encrypt certificates. Or, to be more precise, it will provide the certificates if we specified a domain. Nevertheless, it's installed just in case we change our minds and choose to update the platform by changing the domain and enabling TLS later on.

The next in line is Vault. boot will install it and attempt to populate it with Secrets. But, since it does not know them just yet, the process will ask us another round of questions. The first one in this group is the admin username. Feel free to press the Enter key to accept the default value, admin. After that comes the admin password. Type whatever you'd like to use (we won't need it today).

The process will need to know how to access our GitHub repositories, so it asks us for the Git username, email address, and token. You can use your GitHub username and email for the first two questions. As for the token,[11] you'll need to create a new one in GitHub and grant full repo access. Finally, the next question related to Secrets is HMAC token. Feel free to press the Enter key, and the process will create it for you.

Finally comes the last question. Do you want to configure an external Docker registry? Press the Enter key to use the default answer (N), and boot will create it inside the cluster or, as in case of most cloud providers, use the registry provided as a service. In the case of GKE, that would be GCR; for EKS, that's ECR. In any case, by not configuring an external Docker registry, boot will use whatever makes the most sense for a given provider:

```
? Jenkins X Admin Username admin
? Jenkins X Admin Password [? for help] ********
? The Git user that will perform git operations inside a pipeline. It should
    be a user within the Git organisation/own? Pipeline bot Git username
    vfarcic
? Pipeline bot Git email address vfarcic@gmail.com
? A token for the Git user that will perform git operations inside a pipeline.
    This includes environment repository creation, and so this token should
    have full repository permissions. To create a token go to https://
    github.com/settings/tokens/new?scopes=repo,read:user,read:org,
```

---

[11] https://docs.github.com/en/github/authenticating-to-github/creating-a-personal-access-token.

```
        user:email,write:repo_hook,delete_repo then enter a name, click Generate
            token, and copy and paste the token into this prompt.
? Pipeline bot Git token ******************************************
Generated token bb65edc3f137e598c55a17f90bac549b80fefbcaf, to use it press
        enter.
This is the only time you will be shown it so remember to save it
? HMAC token, used to validate incoming webhooks. Press enter to use the
        generated token [? for help]
? Do you want to configure non default Docker Registry? No
```

The rest of the process will install and configure all the components of the platform. We won't go into all of them since they are the same as those we used before. What matters is that the system will be fully operational a while later.

The last step will verify the installation. You might see a few warnings during this last step of the process. Don't be alarmed. boot is most likely impatient. Over time, you'll see the number of running Pods increasing and those that are pending decreasing, until all the Pods are running.

That's it. Jenkins X is now up and running. We have the whole definition of the platform with complete configuration (except for Secrets) stored in a Git repository:

```
verifying the Jenkins X installation in namespace jx
verifying pods
Checking pod statuses
POD                                           STATUS
jenkins-x-chartmuseum-774f8b95b-bdxfh         Running
jenkins-x-controllerbuild-66cbf7b74-twkbp     Running
jenkins-x-controllerrole-7d76b8f449-5f5xx     Running
jenkins-x-gcactivities-1594872000-w6gns       Succeeded
jenkins-x-gcpods-1594872000-m7kgq             Succeeded
jenkins-x-heapster-679ff46bf4-94w5f           Running
jenkins-x-nexus-555999cf9c-s8hnn              Running
lighthouse-foghorn-599b6c9c87-bvpct           Running
lighthouse-gc-jobs-1594872000-wllsp           Succeeded
lighthouse-keeper-7c47467555-c87bz            Running
lighthouse-webhooks-679cc6bbbd-fxw7z          Running
lighthouse-webhooks-679cc6bbbd-zl4bw          Running
tekton-pipelines-controller-5c4d79bb75-75hvj Running
Verifying the git config
Verifying username billyy at git server github at https://github.com
Found 2 organisations in git server https://github.com: IntuitDeveloper,
        intuit
Validated pipeline user billyy on git server https://github.com
Git tokens seem to be setup correctly
Installation is currently looking: GOOD
Using namespace 'jx' from context named 'gke_hazel-charter-283301_us-east1-
        b_cluster-1' on server 'https://34.73.66.41'.
```

B.3   Installing Flux

Flux consists of a CLI client and daemon that run inside of the managed Kubernetes cluster. This section explains how to install the Flux CLI only. The daemon installation requires you to specify the Git repository with access credentials and is covered in chapter 11.

B.3.1   *Installing CLI client*

The Flux distribution includes the CLI client named `fluxctl`. `fluxctl` automates the Flux daemon installation and allows you to get information about Kubernetes resources controlled by the Flux daemon.

Use one of following commands to install the fluxctl in Mac, Linux, and Windows. macOS:

```
brew install fluxctl
```

Linux:

```
sudo snap install fluxctl
```

Windows:

```
choco install fluxctl
```

Find more information about `fluxctl` installation details in the official installation instructions: https://docs.fluxcd.io/en/latest/references/fluxctl/.

appendix C
Configuring GPG key

GPG, or GNU Privacy Guard, is a public key cryptography implementation. GPG allows for the secure transmission of information between parties and can be used to verify that the origin of a message is genuine. Following are the steps to set up a GPG key:

1. First of all, we need to install the GPG command-line tool. Regardless of your operating system, the process might take a while. macOS users might use the `brew` package manager to install GPC with the following command:

   ```
   brew install gpg
   ```

2. The next step is generating a GPG key that will be used to sign and verify commits. Use the following command to generate a key. At the prompt, press Enter to accept default key settings. While entering the user identity information, make sure to use the verified email of your GitHub account:

   ```
   gpg --full-generate-key
   ```

3. Find the ID of the generated key, and use the ID to access the GPG key body:

   ```
   gpg --list-secret-keys --keyid-format LONG
   gpg --armor --export <ID>
   ```

   In this example, the GPG key ID is 3AA5C34371567BD2:

   ```
   gpg --list-secret-keys --keyid-format LONG
   /Users/hubot/.gnupg/secring.gpg
   ------------------------------------
   sec   4096R/3AA5C34371567BD2 2016-03-10 [expires: 2017-03-10]
   uid                          Hubot
   ssb   4096R/42B317FD4BA89E7A 2016-03-10
   ```

4   Use the output of gpg --export and follow the steps described at http://
    mng.bz/0mlx to add the key to your GitHub account.

5   Configure Git to use the generated GPG key:

```
git config --global user.signingkey <ID>
```

index